ACADEMIC COMPETENCE

Theory and Classroom Practice:
Preparing ESL Students for Content Courses

H. D. Adamson
University of Arizona

Longman
New York & London

**Academic Competence: Theory and
Classroom Practice: Preparing ESL
Students for Content Courses**

Longman, 10 Bank Street, White Plains, N.Y. 10606

Associated companies:
Longman Group Ltd., London
Longman Cheshire Pty., Melbourne
Longman Paul Pty., Auckland
Copp Clark Pitman, Toronto

Senior acquisitions editor: Laura McKenna
Sponsoring editor: Naomi Silverman
Development editor: Susan Alkana
Production editor: Linda Moser
Cover design: Anne M. Pompeo
Text art: Pompeo Design
Production supervisor: Anne Armeny

Library of Congress Cataloging-in-Publication Data

Adamson, H. D. (Hugh Douglas)
    Academic competence: theory and classroom practice: preparing ESL students
    for content courses / by H. D. Adamson.
        p.   cm.
    Includes index.
    ISBN 0-8013-0602-7
    1. English language—Study and teaching (Secondary)—Foreign
speakers.   2. English language—Study and teaching (Secondary)—
United States.   3. High school students—United States.   I. Title.
PE1128.A2A23   1993
428′.0071′2—dc20   92-8257
                                                            CIP

1 2 3 4 5 6 7 8 9 10-AL-9695949392

Contents

FIGURES

Preface

INTRODUCTION

Many ESL teachers lead sheltered lives. The goal of those who teach in public schools, colleges, and universities is to prepare students to take mainstream content courses such as history, science, and math, yet the teachers themselves may know very little about what is expected of students in these courses. One reason for this ignorance is that ESL teachers often have little chance to talk to teachers of content subjects. At colleges and universities, ESL instructors often teach at an English Language Institute, where their status and duties are different from those of other faculty members. In public schools, ESL teachers may be part of an isolated intensive ESL program, or they may be itinerant teachers moving from school to school. Such teachers have little time to find out what happens to their students when they join the academic mainstream.

When I was an ESL teacher in several very isolated programs, I often wondered how well my students did after they moved on to content courses with native English speakers. I could not imagine that they did very well, in spite of their high motivation. How could they read and understand a whole chapter in a psychology textbook in one night when they could not understand even a paragraph from such a textbook when it was read in class? How could they talk about the causes of the American Civil War when they were reluctant to talk about what they did on a field trip to the Museum of American History? When I became a trainer of ESL teachers, I began to research how graduates of ESL programs survived in content courses at the intermediate school, high school, and college levels. My graduate students and I tutored over one hundred ESL students in content courses, helping them write papers, study for tests, complete workbook exercises, read textbooks, and do all the other required tasks. We tape-recorded the tutoring sessions, observed the students in their classes, and interviewed their content course teachers. Then we wrote case histories of the students' experiences. As the case studies came in, a fascinating and diverse picture of how ESL students got along in content courses emerged.

The case studies research made it clear that the best way for ESL teachers to prepare their students to succeed in a content course was to teach them effective academic skills and appropriate background knowledge of the content material. The approach to ESL instruction that seemed most compatible with this goal was the language through content approach. As explained in chapter 6, there are several different models for teaching language through content, and the case studies suggested that the most effective was the adjunct model. In adjunct courses, ESL students are enrolled in a content course with native English speakers and are tutored by their ESL teachers in the academic skills and background knowledge necessary to succeed in the course.

In order to set up such a course at my university, I contacted Professor Phyllis Duryee, who was director of the English Language Institute. We immediately ran into problems. The first problem was that because of financial considerations the only way we could offer an adjunct course was for the ESL students to enroll in the content part of the course for credit. Unfortunately, the ESL students at the Institute were not advanced enough to do this. To solve this problem, we developed a new type of language through content course, which we call a *precourse,* in which the ESL students sit in on a regular credit course for several weeks. Before and during their regular credit course attendance, ESL instructors help the students develop appropriate study skills and learn the background information necessary for understanding the content material. The precourse was a great success, and that success inspired the writing of this book.

The aim of this text is to share the insights provided by the case studies research, to place these insights within a theoretical perspective, and to suggest teaching techniques for preparing ESL students for the academic mainstream. The book is intended for researchers in applied linguistics, ESL teachers, and students in a graduate course in the theory and practice of ESL.

HOW THE BOOK IS ORGANIZED

Chapter 1 introduces the notion of academic competence and presents a case study of a seventh-grade ESL student enrolled in a course in earth science. The chapter also summarizes the numerous studies of achievement test scores that show that learning content material is very difficult for ESL students and that it requires a great deal more knowledge than general proficiency in English. Chapter 2 discusses theories of language proficiency, showing how these theories are rooted in the disciplines of linguistics, psychology, and testing theory, and how the notion of proficiency has expanded to include knowledge other than that of linguistic patterns. The controversial claim that proficiency in an academic variety of language is associated with "higher-level" cognitive abilities is also discussed. Chapter 3 presents more of the theoretical background for a theory of academic competence. I discuss four types of knowledge available to ESL students in content courses: "basic-level knowledge," as proposed in the philosophy of experiential realism; Grice's Cooperative Principle; background knowledge of a particular academic subject; and general language proficiency. Some of the material in chapters 2 and 3 assumes that the reader has had an introductory course in linguistics, but even readers without this background should be able to follow the basic argument.

Chapter 4 presents the results of the case studies research of ESL students enrolled in content courses, focusing on the academic strategies that the students employed to complete their assignments. This chapter also contains a description of the precourse mentioned earlier.

In chapter 5, I attempt to draw together the strands of theory and case studies research into an account of academic competence. I propose that this competence includes possessing a critical mass of general language proficiency, background knowledge of the particular content material, and strategies for enhancing and utilizing this knowledge to complete academic tasks. I also suggest that students must be able to vary their strategies, depending on how well they understand the material. Chapter 6 discusses four types of language through content courses, and chapter 7 suggests activities for teaching academic strategies and content material to ESL students.

THE THEME OF THIS BOOK

Many ESL students have great difficulty in content courses, a fact documented by the case studies and by studies of ESL students' achievement test scores. It follows that many ESL programs do not adequately prepare students for mainstream courses. I suggest that the main reason for this failure is that ESL programs are usually isolated from mainstream programs. For example, many ESL programs attempt to prepare students for mainstream courses by using "theme-based" textbooks, which contain selected readings, lectures, and exercises from high school or college textbooks. These texts devote one or two chapters to a variety of subjects such as psychology, U.S. history, and literature. Thus, the ESL students study bits and pieces of "canned" academic material, only some of which is relevant to their academic goals, while real academic material, including textbooks, lectures, and assignments, is available in the school all around them. I suggest that before students leave the ESL program, they should have some access to this real academic environment while they still have the support of their ESL teachers and peers. In other words, I suggest that the walls surrounding the ESL program need to be broken down.

ACKNOWLEDGMENTS

I would like to thank my co-authors Mieko Koike, Dianna Poodiack, and Elizabeth Schepps for writing the case studies presented in chapters 1 and 4. I would also like to thank the writers of the thirty additional case studies on which this book is based: Mofid Abdullah, Margaret Ahmad, Zulgarnain Abu Bakar, Judy Baskin, Merry Cho, Constance Chubb, Carolyn Epps, Yitna Firdyiwek, Melissa Fitzgerald, Judith Getrich, Kari Hannibal, Yukiko Henninger, Monica Hirschler, Arleen Jerezinsky, SooJung Kim, George Kirkland, Carol Koons, Mimi Kramer, Hannah Lefton, Ellen McCarthy, Debra Magner, Suzanne Mehrnama, Rebecca Moscosso, Elizabeth Prisley, Fatima Samad, Denise Smith, Maryann Stoll, Pat Stollhans, Leslie Weaver, and Charlene Weeks.

I am grateful to the following reviewers for their insightful comments during the writing process: Richard P. Durán, University of California, Santa Barbara; Judith Lessow-Hurley, San Jose State University; Teresa Pica, University of Pennsylvania; and Karen Schuster Webb, Howard University.

Thanks to my colleagues Phyllis Duryee, Melissa Allen, and Natalie Hess for putting up with my wild ideas, only some of which worked, and for a most enjoyable collaboration.

Thanks to Donna Johnson, Duane Roen, Muriel Saville-Troike, and Rudolph Troike, who commented insightfully on the manuscript and who are not responsible for its shortcomings.

Thanks to Naomi Silverman, my former editor at Longman.

Special thanks to Ginger Collier for support, both academic and moral.

Thanks to my wife, Alice, and children, Katie and Marie, to whom I dedicate this book.

CHAPTER 1

Introduction: ESL Students in Content Courses

ESL STUDENTS IN U.S. SCHOOLS[1]

The goal of most ESL programs is not only to teach English, but also to prepare students to take mainstream classes. As Saville-Troike (1984) reminds us, "Too often we in ESL have forgotten that teaching English is only a means to an end: the critical outcome . . . is how well (students) succeed in school" (p. 217). For a long time it has been clear that on the whole ESL students are not succeeding. The report of Coleman et al. (1966) showed that Asian Americans, Mexican Americans, and Puerto Ricans lagged behind national norms on twelfth-grade achievement tests. The National Assessment of Educational Progress (1977) found that Hispanic American students performed below the national average in reading, science, mathematics, social studies, and career development. Justenias and Duarte (1982) found that the high school drop-out rate for Mexican-American and mainland Puerto Rican students is between 40 and 50 percent compared to 14 percent for Anglos and 25 percent for African Americans.

Collier (1987) found that ESL students from predominantly Asian and Hispanic backgrounds in a middle-class suburb of Washington, D.C., scored significantly lower than native English speakers on all parts of the SRA achievement test except mathematics. Even worse, as the ESL students progressed through the grades their scores did not get closer to the native speakers' scores, but fell further behind. For example, one group who entered the United States at age twelve was placed in seventh-grade ESL courses. In the eighth grade, these students were mainstreamed and at the end of the eighth grade they took the SRA test. On the reading section of the test, the group received an average score of 45 NCE (approximately the forty-fifth percentile) while the native English-speaking (NES) students received an average score of 68 NCE. Three years later, the NES students maintained their average score of 68 NCE, but the ESL students' average score fell to 35 NCE. Thus, even after three years of mainstreaming, the gap between the ESL students and the NES students on the reading test had widened, as it had on all sections of the test

1

including math. Studies such as these have prompted second language (L2) researchers to ask what kinds of schooling best prepare ESL students for academic success.

Collier (1989) reviewed recent studies of achievement test scores in order to find out how long it takes L2 learners to achieve native speaker norms in content areas. She reached five general conclusions:

1. Students are able to achieve grammatical proficiency in a second language (as measured by a "language arts" test of spelling, punctuation, and simple grammar) after about two years of schooling in the target language country. However, it takes from five to ten years (depending on the students' academic background and the instructional program) to reach national norms in content areas.

2. The students who achieved the greatest academic success were enrolled in bilingual programs that provided solid cognitive academic instruction in both the first and the second language. These programs included Canadian immersion programs in which speakers of a majority language (English) are schooled in English and French (Genesee, 1987) and U.S. programs in which speakers of a minority language (Spanish) are schooled in Spanish and English (Medina & Valenzuela de la Garza, 1987). Students in such programs require from four to seven years to reach national norms on tests of reading, social studies, and science. In programs where students receive cognitive academic language instruction in both languages, social class background does not seem to make a significant difference in academic achievement.

3. The students who take the longest time to reach national norms in content areas are those who arrive at a young age with little or no academic preparation in their first language and who receive no bilingual instruction. These students may require from seven to ten years of schooling in the second language (L2) before they reach native speaker norms, if indeed they ever do.

4. Immigrants who arrive at ages eight to twelve with at least two years of schooling in their first language (L1) and who have no bilingual instruction require from five to seven years to reach national norms in content areas, but as little as two years in mathematics and language arts. There is evidence of transfer of mathematical knowledge from L1 to L2.

5. Adolescent arrivals who have had no L2 exposure in their home countries and who are not able to continue academic work in their L1 do not have enough time left in school to achieve national norms in content areas. This is true for those who have a good academic background in their L1 as well as for those whose schooling has been interrupted.

Perhaps the most important of Collier's conclusions is that bilingual education is the most effective way to prepare ESL students for mainstream courses. Unfortunately, however, bilingual education is not available for many students. Cummins (1989) makes a convincing case that the main reason for the lack of bilingual education in the United States is political, quoting Ronald Reagan's remark that bilingual programs dedicated to preserving students' native languages are "absolutely wrong and against American concepts'' (p. 109). However, it is also true that good bilingual education is sometimes difficult to provide because there are too few students from the same language background to justify hiring a bilingual teacher, or because there is an inadequate supply of teachers or materials for a particular language. Therefore, it often falls to the ESL teacher to prepare nonnative speakers for mainstream content courses without the help of bilingual instruction. The goal of this book is to suggest ways to accomplish this formidable task, but it should be kept in mind that the ESL programs and teaching techniques discussed here are not intended as alternatives to bilingual education, which research clearly shows to be the best route to academic competence. I will argue in chapter 5, however, that content-based ESL instruction at the advanced level is highly desirable for preparing ESL students for mainstream courses, even if they have had bilingual instruction.

Collier's (1989) research review suggests that ESL students' academic success does not depend on their grammatical proficiency in English (as had been widely believed), but rather on their background knowledge of academic material and their academic skills. Collier supports Cummins's (1984a) finding that in general students can acquire surface fluency in English within two years of their arrival in the United States, but that it takes much longer to learn the required background knowledge and academic skills. The most difficult situation in which to learn such knowledge and skills is when a student's education is interrupted, either because the student is out of school for several years or because he or she sits for two years in mainstream classes without understanding what is going on. It should also be noted that all immigrant ESL students, even those with content knowledge and academic skills developed in their native countries, undergo a kind of interruption in their education because their culture (and hence much of their background knowledge) is different from that of their American peers. In addition, their academic skills may not be appropriate for an American school setting. Therefore, all ESL programs must teach the appropriate knowledge and skills if they are to prepare students for mainstream courses.

Collier's review provides a good overall picture of how well ESL students are doing in the public schools. However, it is a picture taken from a distance. It does not show us what goes on in individual content classrooms, where students struggle to complete assignments based on materials they partly understand using academic skills developed (if at all) in very different educational settings.

In the remainder of this chapter, we move in for a closer look at how ESL students survive in content courses. First, we review Saville-Troike's (1984) study of nineteen elementary students in content courses and then consider a case study of a single seventh-grade student in an earth science course.

SAVILLE-TROIKE'S STUDY

One of the first researchers to call attention to the fact that ESL students need more than fluency in English to learn content material was Saville-Troike (1984), who observed nineteen ESL students, ages six to twelve, for one academic year, videotaping the students in their classes and on the playground. All of these students had very little or no prior exposure to English, and all came from middle-class, professional families who valued academic success. Saville-Troike chose to study this group because she assumed that they would be successful and that her research would document how they achieved success.

At the end of the school year, the subjects took three tests of English proficiency and the Comprehensive Test of Basic Skills, an achievement test that covers the areas of reading, language, social studies, science, and math. To her surprise, Saville-Troike found that there were large differences in the achievement test scores: some students did well, but others did very poorly. She also found that the students' scores on the tests of content subjects did not correlate with their scores on the English proficiency tests. This finding supports Cummins's (1984a) and Collier's (1989) claims that proficiency in English is not the most important factor in school success and suggests that specific school-related knowledge and skills are more important.

Saville-Troike also found that the students' abilities in their native languages had an influence on their test scores. For example, students who could infer the meanings of words from context when reading in their first language could transfer this ability to reading in English.

The subjects of the study included four Japanese students, and Koda (1982) attempted to correlate these students' scores on the achievement tests with their attitudes toward school. She found that one of the students was the highest achiever in the entire group of seventeen, one was above average, one was below average, and one was the lowest in the group. Saville-Troike (1984) noted that the successful Japanese students "shared active and competitive coping styles at school and had a confident attitude at the beginning of the year that they would succeed. . . . The high achievers also initiated independent learning activities" (p. 215).

Saville-Troike also examined whether the amount of time the students spent interacting in English correlated with their achievement test scores. As might be expected from Cummins's and Collier's findings regarding English proficiency and achievement test scores, there was no correlation. This fact suggests that effective social interaction, valued in many communicative approaches to ESL teaching, is not so important for academic achievement. Saville-Troike (1984) observed, "We need to recognize that there is a qualitative difference between the communicative tactics and skills that children find effective for meeting their social needs and goals and those that are necessary for academic achievement in the classroom" (p. 216).

Saville-Troike's conclusions about what ESL students need to succeed in content courses are different from what many ESL teachers had imagined. We had thought that the most important factors in academic success were general language proficiency and sociolinguistic competence (knowledge of how to interact in socially appropriate ways). But Saville-Troike (1984) showed that specifically academic factors are necessary as well, and she introduced the term *academic competence* to include these factors. She did not attempt to define academic competence but gave the following guidelines for preparing ESL students for content courses:

1. Vocabulary knowledge in English is the most important aspect of oral English proficiency for academic achievement. Vocabulary taught in ESL should therefore be related as closely as possible to students' learning needs in their subject matter classes.

2. Spoken practice in English may not be necessary for development of English proficiency and may retard it in some instances. Emphasis on interpersonal communication may even inhibit academic achievement.
3. The portions of ESL lessons which focus on structural patterns, especially on English morphology, appear to make little contribution toward meeting students' immediate academic needs. Most beginning students do not use grammatical inflections when they are concerned with communicating real information. Mastery of English grammatical structure is more closely related to native language background than to the ability to use English for academic purposes.
4. Most children do not have to be taught to communicate with one another; they will do that even without a common language. While social interaction between students is certainly to be encouraged, we cannot depend on that alone for developing English language skills.
5. *Most of the children who achieved best in content areas, as measured by tests in English, were those who had the opportunity to discuss the concepts they were learning in their native language* with other children or adults. Even in linguistically heterogeneous classrooms such as those in this study, at least some degree of bilingual education is proving to be feasible and clearly provides the best context for conceptual development—and for learning English [emphasis in original]. (p. 216)

In conclusion, Saville-Troike introduced a new direction in the schooling of ESL students by coining the term *academic competence* and suggesting some of the things this competence includes. In the following chapters, I will attempt to describe academic competence and discuss its relationship to language proficiency and to understanding. First, in order to get a close look at academic competence, we consider a case study of an ESL student who was successful in her content course. The case study was made by Mieko Koike, a Japanese graduate student in an American university (for a description of the research methods employed in the case studies, see chapter 4).

CASE STUDY 1—CEYONG: TUTORING A KOREAN STUDENT THROUGH HER SCIENCE PROJECT, BY MIEKO KOIKE

Ceyong was a seventh-grade Korean student in Jackson Intermediate School. She was taking three hours of ESL classes (grammar, reading, and writing) at the advanced-intermediate levels, an ESL social science class, and mainstream classes in mathematics and science. I decided to tutor her because she was lively and eager to talk to me, because her experience in American schools was in some ways like my own, and because she was having trouble with her science project.

Ceyong had come to America with her family in May of the previous academic year because of her father's job as a diplomat. She had lived in Japan for seven years. She had spoken Japanese in the Japanese school and Korean at home. She had gotten high grades in elementary school. She did not have a chance to learn English in Korea. After she came to America, she went to a public elementary school for a while. She told me she didn't understand English at all and did not remember what she did during this period. From my own experience, I could imagine that her culture shock was strong and that she was engrossed in getting used to a new life in America. Last summer she studied ESL in summer school. Her mother asked her to finish reading one easy English book every day, such as *Mother Goose* for preschool children. Also, her mother tape-recorded her reading and let her listen to the tape when she was home. After her father came home, he would ask her some questions about the book she was reading in English. She even memorized a whole book called *Why It's a Holiday* by Ann McGovern. Even though she did not know the meaning of all the words, Ceyong told me that the memorization helped her a lot because she could capture a sense of English and learn about American customs.

Seven months ago she started at Jackson. At that time, she was in the beginning ESL class and did not speak much English, but she felt the class was too easy. While she was in the class she kept reading one book every day. I was impressed by Ceyong's high motivation and by her parents' eagerness that she learn English. She studied for at least three hours a day. After I started tutoring her, she was always eager to study. She wanted to improve her English very much because good English would help her get good grades in school, pass the entrance examination of the Korean colleges, and finally get a good job in Korea, like her father.

There were only two ESL students in the science class, Ceyong and a Japanese girl. They sat together at the same table. Ceyong was quiet in the class and did not ask any questions. Throughout the class, Ceyong spoke in Japanese with her friend, so that she could understand what was going on and finish the work. She didn't talk to American students at all. She was very shy in the class, very different from the way she was in her ESL class, where she participated enthusiastically and often. She wrote in her dialogue journal that one day she was laughed at by an American when she had said something in English. She had felt very insulted. She wrote that she would never laugh at a person when she spoke English better. I could understand her feeling because I had the same kind of experience, and like most Asian students, I was very afraid to commit mistakes. Ceyong didn't have any American friends, although she had many friends in the ESL class. The ESL teacher was the only native speaker who she spoke English to. She liked this teacher very much and said she felt comfortable in the ESL class.

Ceyong was discouraged about her science project. The teacher had provided a list of topics, and Ceyong's father had chosen one for her: minerals. He chose this topic because Ceyong seemed to know more about it than any other topic. Before writing the paper, Ceyong had to complete an information sheet which asked for definitions of various terms relating to minerals. Ceyong checked some books out of the library and attempted to understand the terms, but the books were too difficult, so she just copied the definitions out of the dictionary. The teacher probably realized this because she suggested that Ceyong write only on quartz and feldspar. Ceyong did not know what these terms meant; she simply knew very little about minerals, even in Korean. When I read the assignment sheet the teacher had handed out, I realized that Ceyong not only had to write a paper, she also had to give an oral report accompanied by a display of graphs, charts, and exhibits. When I told her about the oral presentation, she was very surprised and started worrying about it.

After I found out her problems, I planned how I could help her. First, she needed to get more information about minerals, so I decided to go to the Naturalist Center in the Natural History Museum, which had a library and some experts working there. I thought it might be a good exercise for her to ask questions to the experts. I also expected to get an easy science book for her there. The experiments available there would help her to get information about minerals. Second, I wanted her to call the gemologist whom the science teacher had recommended. It might be a good opportunity to speak with a native speaker. We went to the Naturalist Center the following weekend, although she was not so enthusiastic about going there. I found the easiest book of minerals in the library, but it was still difficult for her. I have italicized some of the words in the book that she didn't understand. From the book *Rocks and Minerals*:

> *Igneous* rocks are formed by the cooling and hardening of magma, a complex *molten* material that originates within the earth. Some important types of igneous rocks are shown in the illustration on the facing page. The major mineral *constituents* and basic rocks shown provide the basis for the *classifications* given on page 9. (p. 6)

There were so many words she didn't know. Even after she knew the dictionary meaning of the words, she couldn't capture the true meaning because of her lack of knowledge about minerals. Therefore, at first she was too discouraged to read the book. I explained roughly what the book told about and asked an expert to show us some stones and how to use the experimenting tools available at the center. We started to check some samples for color and hardness by using a knife, coin, and steel. We checked for specific gravity by using the scale, water, and stones. When the expert explained how to get the specific gravity, Ceyong asked me to take notes because she couldn't do that, and also she needed to concentrate her attention on listening. She told me she never took notes in class. Even in the ESL social studies class, she just listened to what the teacher said. She did not have enough time for taking notes. While we were experimenting with the tools, I tried to get Ceyong to ask questions to the expert. In the beginning, she wanted me to make sure that her sentences were correct. Gradually, she started to ask questions to the expert by herself because she was getting interested in the experiments. We spent almost three hours there. Later, at lunch, she couldn't stop asking me questions. We then discussed about how to organize her paper. The entire session at the center lasted six hours. By that time, she was really interested in the project. After we finished doing the experiments, I asked her to read from the book again. She said she could capture most of the meaning through the personal experience of doing the experiments.

When her project was near completion, Ceyong was spending two to three hours on it every day. She showed me her final charts. I felt she was getting used to the science words in the book. She told me she had finally called the gemologist, and asked about the stones which the gemologist had given her before. I was very glad that she could talk to the gemologist because she had hesitated to do that. Thus, she might have more confidence in her oral report. We planned how she would do the report the following week.

On the day after the oral report, I went to Ceyong's house. She looked very happy and told me the report had gone well. Although she had practiced it with her father many times, she had been very nervous. Nevertheless, she got ninety-eight points, perhaps the highest grade in the class. She was very proud of herself and expressed her thanks to me. I asked her to write about the science project for ten minutes. The following is what she wrote:

> Before I began my science project, I thought that were easy but it wasn't. It was the most difficult that I had never had before. But, I really learned a lot about minerals. In my science class, I think I understand what my teacher says. Sometimes, I didn't understand

when he says difficult things. But I like my science class. I sometimes have to answer or read something in front of people. If I make mistake, they don't laugh. and kind to me. I really like my science class.

I was glad that Ceyong expressed good feelings about the American students in the class. Before she started the science project, she told me she was not comfortable in the class. Later, she called me because she had gotten her report card. She got A's except in science. It was a B + . She told me she was disappointed not to get an A, but she knew the reason was because she didn't get good grades on the short tests before the tutoring began. I think it was very helpful for us to go to the Naturalist Center because she could become interested in the project by using the experiments and become familiar with the scientific vocabulary. After that, she had the confidence to finish the project, and finally did achieve a good grade.

COMMENTS ON THE CASE STUDY OF CEYONG

This case study is one of the thirty-four case studies of ESL students in content courses that are summarized in chapter 4, and it illustrates several common themes. First, Ceyong's major language difficulty was not English syntax or phonology but a lack of background knowledge about mineralogy. Furthermore, this problem could not be solved simply by learning some new vocabulary words. Koike notes, "Even after she knew the dictionary meaning of the words, she couldn't capture the true meaning because of her lack of knowledge about minerals." In order to understand the meaning of individual terms, Ceyong had to acquire a whole network of concepts related to rocks and minerals. The importance of background knowledge is discussed in detail in chapter 3. Meanwhile, a good summary statement is provided by Hirsch (1987) in his bestselling book *Cultural Literacy*. Hirsch observes that language comprehension is not a passive process whereby readers absorb information from a text. Rather:

> The reader's mind is constantly inferring meanings that are not directly stated by the words of a text but are nonetheless part of its essential content. The explicit meanings of a piece of writing are the tip of the iceberg of meaning; the larger part lies below the surface of the text and is composed of the reader's own relevant knowledge. . . . Such background knowledge is a far more important ingredient in the reading process than [has been] supposed. (p. 33)

Because Ceyong "simply knew very little about minerals, even in Korean," it was necessary for her to acquire the background knowledge before she could understand the full meaning of her textbooks and lectures.

A second point to emerge from the case study is that Ceyong lacked many of the study skills necessary for learning in an American school. For example, she did not know how to take notes and had to ask Koike to do it for her. She also lacked "strategic competence," the ability to communicate with limited linguistic resources. At first, she thought that her questions to the mineralogist had to be grammatically correct, but with Koike's help she discovered that correctness was not required and that she was able to communicate by herself. A third point is that Ceyong found it helpful to discuss the content material in a language other than English. In class she carried on a constant dialogue with her friend in Japanese, and later she reviewed the material with Koike in Korean. A final point is that when Ceyong had to complete an information sheet covering material that she could not understand, she did not simply give up but attempted to do the assignment in a mechanical and meaningless way by copying definitions out of the dictionary. In chapter 4 we will examine the use of such *coping strategies*.

Ceyong's amazing success in earth science was due to her own hard work, her parents' support, and to Koike's effective teaching, which exemplifies three principles of how to teach content material to ESL students. First, content instruction should be experiential rather than expository. In other words, hands-on activities are better than lectures and discussions. Ceyong quickly understood specific gravity because she measured it herself with the scales, water, and stones. Second, content instruction should be interactive: the information should flow from the student to the teacher as well as in the other direction. As we have seen, once Ceyong began to understand the subject, she couldn't stop asking questions, which led to an even deeper understanding. Third, content instruction should be interesting. As we will see in chapter 4, the case studies illustrate the truism that when students are interested in what they are learning, they learn it better.

CONCLUSIONS

Recently ESL professionals have realized that general proficiency in English is not all that ESL students need to succeed in mainstream courses. Saville-Troike (1984) introduced the term *academic competence* to refer to the knowledge and abilities students do need. The research reviewed in this chapter suggests that, in addition to general English proficiency, two important components of academic competence are background knowledge of the content material and effective study skills. In the next chapter, we examine the notion of language proficiency and related theoretical issues more closely.

NOTE

1. Several labels have been used to refer to students in U.S. schools who do not speak English natively, including "limited English proficient" (LEP) students and "language minority students." Here I use the term "ESL student," also used by Cummins (1984a). This term refers to nonnative English speakers who are taking ESL or mainstream classes.

CHAPTER **2**

Theories of Language and Language Proficiency

INTRODUCTION

In the next two chapters we consider what it means to know a language. The approach will be historical, tracing the development of linguistic theories and the effects these theories have had on ideas about language proficiency, language testing, and language teaching. We will see that earlier theories equated language proficiency with knowledge of grammatical structures, but that more recent theories have included other kinds of knowledge. One reason for this change is that the discipline of linguistics has expanded to include the study of language phenemona other than grammatical patterns. A second reason is that language acquisition scholars have found that academic success requires more than just knowledge of these patterns, as we saw in chapter 1.

STRUCTURALISM

The reigning linguistic theory of the twentieth century is structuralism, so named because its goal is to analyze linguistic structures such as sounds, words, and sentences. We first briefly review two schools of structuralist linguistics: those of Saussure and the American descriptivists.

Saussure

The father of structuralism was the Swiss linguist Ferdinand de Saussure, who developed his ideas at the University of Geneva during the first decade of the twentieth century. Faced with the task of finding a basic system in the enormous complexity of language, Saussure concentrated on the aspect of language that seemed most amenable to scientific description, namely phonology. At that time, the field of phonology was well developed, and it was understood that each language had a limited set of phonemes that could be combined in a limited number of ways. It seemed to Saussure that the rules for combining phonemes constituted a system to which all speakers of a language had to adhere in order to be understood, but that there were no comparable rules for combining words, which could be strung together in endlessly diverse ways, allowing much more freedom to the individual speaker. Therefore, Saussure believed that syntax and semantics were less systematic than phonology. He theorized that phonology comprised a communal and systematic aspect of language, which he called *langue,* whereas syntax and semantics comprised an individualistic and unsystematic aspect of language, which he called *parole,* and that only *langue* was the proper object of linguistic study. We will see that the strategy of limiting the study of language to an area that is amenable to analysis has been continued by structuralists down to the present time, and that this strategy has influenced ideas about language proficiency.

A second important aspect of Saussure's theory of language was his notion of the *language faculty.* Saussure claimed that linguistic knowledge was fundamentally different from other kinds of knowledge and was localized in Broca's area of the brain. He noted (1966), "There exists a . . . general faculty which governs signs and which would be the linguistic faculty proper" (p. 11). The claim that linguistic knowledge is learned and processed differently from other kinds of knowledge remains an important part of modern linguistic theory.

The American Descriptivists

During the 1920s and 1930s, the structuralist approach to language was established in the United States, principally by Franz Boas and Leonard Bloomfield, who founded the descriptivist school of linguistics. The descriptivists were so named because they believed that linguistics was a taxonomic science, like botany, the goal of which should be to describe and classify linguistic patterns. The descriptivists extended the scope of linguistics to include the study of syntax, adding inventories of grammatical categories and syntactic patterns to Saussure's inventories of phonemes and phonemic patterns. For example, Charles Fries, the most prominent American linguist of the 1940s, claimed that words could be assigned to one of of four grammatical categories (roughly these were noun, verb, adjective, and adverb, although Fries avoided these traditional terms), which could be combined in three basic syntactic patterns: statement, question, and command. Like Saussure, the descriptivists excluded the study of semantics from linguistics because they thought that meaning could not be studied scientifically, at least given the state of knowledge at the time. Bloomfield (1933) consigned the study of semantics to psychology, noting, "In order to give a scientifically accurate definition of meaning we should have to have a scientifically accurate knowledge of everything in the speaker's world" (p. 134). The descriptivists' theory of language, then, was broader than Saussure's but was still very limited because it included only phonology and syntax.

This view of language influenced the descriptivists' views about language learning, which they thought consisted mainly of learning phonological and syntactic patterns. Fries (1945) emphasized this point: "A person has 'learned' a language when he has . . . *within a limited vocabulary* mastered the sound system . . . and the structural devices" [Fries's emphasis] (p. 3).

Another tenet of descriptivism, one that represented a major break with Saussure's theory, involved the question of which of the social sciences linguistics was a part. Saussure placed linguistics within the field of sociology since he believed that the rules for combining phonemes were a matter of social custom, like the rules for courtship or divorce. The descriptivists, on the other hand, placed linguistics within psychology, claiming that because language use is a form of behavior, it should come under the purview of behaviorism, the dominant school of psychology at the time. The alignment of structural linguistics with behaviorist psychology had important consequences for language teaching and testing.

Behaviorists rejected the idea that psychology should be the study of the mind, as the cognitive psychologist Wundt (1911, 1912) had proposed, because the workings of the mind could not be observed. What could be observed was an animal's or human being's behavior (actions) and the environment in which that behavior occurred. Behaviorists attempted to draw connections between particular aspects of the behavior and the environment. For example, a person might be more likely to utter the word *red* in the presence of a red object. Most behaviorists assumed that the mind was like a black box that took in stimuli from the environment and issued commands to the body that resulted in physical responses. The "black box" school of behaviorism did not deny that human beings had minds (as was sometimes claimed by its critics), but did deny that minds could be studied.

According to behaviorism, language learning is a matter of habit formation. If a response to a particular stimulus is rewarded, that response will be likely to follow that stimulus in the future, and gradually a habit will be formed. This theory appeared to fit well with descriptive linguistics because the phonological and syntactic patterns that descriptivists had discovered could be thought of in psychological terms as a set of habits. Thus, learners of English formed the habit of putting adjectives before nouns, whereas learners of Spanish formed the habit of putting adjectives after nouns. All learning, including learning by lower animals such as rats and pigeons, was thought to be of this nature.

The Separate Abilities Theory of Language Proficiency

The behaviorist learning theory implied that being proficient in a language meant possessing a large set of well-learned habits. This hypothesis gave rise to the audio-lingual method of language teaching, which was predominant in the United States during the 1960s and early 1970s. The theory suggested that a good way to learn linguistic patterns was to isolate them from natural discourse and repeat them over and over, and that in such exercises the meaning of the patterns was not important, since the students' attention should be focused on the structure. Therefore, pattern practice exercises were seldom contextualized, and some writers even suggested that nonsense words could be used in the exercises. An audio-lingual exercise for forming the habit of placing adjectives before nouns might go as follows:

TEACHER: I need a red pen. REPEAT.
STUDENT: I need a red pen.
TEACHER: Green.
STUDENT: I need a green pen.

TEACHER: New.

STUDENT: I need a new pen.

TEACHER: Slithy.

STUDENT: I need a slithy pen.

The theory that language proficiency is a set of habits also suggested a method of language testing. Just as pattern drills should teach isolated structures, each corresponding to a habit, proficiency tests should test such separate structures. This reasoning led to the *separate abilities theory* of language proficiency, which claimed that proficiency can be broken down into a large number of discrete abilities. Tests based on this theory are called *discrete point* tests. Harris's (1969) model of language proficiency claimed that these discrete abilities could be grouped into sixteen skills that made up language proficiency, as shown in Figure 2.1. This model implies that the ability to use a linguistic form, for example, the past tense of *sting,* does not generalize to different skills. That is, the ability to write *stung* correctly does not imply the ability to say it correctly.

In practice, many of the questions on discrete point tests did not isolate individual linguistic structures. This is so because language is redundant, providing multiple cues to meaning. For example, the time sequences in a story might be signaled by verb tenses, adverbial expressions, and the nature of the events. Thus, the answers to questions on reading or listening comprehension tests can often be found in several different ways; therefore, the tests measure various kinds of knowledge. To that extent these tests are not discrete point but *integrative* tests.

An important feature of standardized tests based on the separate abilities theory, such as the Comprehensive English Language Test (CELT) or the Test of English as a Foreign Language (TOEFL), is that they do not assume knowledge of a specific content area. The words on the vocabulary section of the CELT, for example, are chosen from a list of the most frequently used English words. The content of the reading and listening comprehension passages assumes a general academic background but not knowledge of a specific academic curriculum. Thus, we should not expect these tests to predict success for students in academic programs that assume knowledge of specific subject matter, as

FIGURE 2.1 Harris's Separate Abilities Model of Language Proficiency.

Components	Language Skills			
	Listening	Speaking	Reading	Writing
Phonology/Ortho-graphy				
Grammar				
Vocabulary				
Rate and General Fluency				

American high school programs assume knowledge of U.S. history, American customs, English and American literature, and so on. Nor do standardized proficiency tests directly measure the ability to use language in socially appropriate and effective ways.

According to language testing theory, the model of proficiency in Figure 2.1 makes a verifiable claim. If proficiency really consists of sixteen skills and a language proficiency test measures six of them, then it should be possible for a student to receive high scores on some sections of the test but low scores on other sections. However, this did not turn out to be the case. Scores on the different sections of the test correlated fairly well, suggesting that the sections do not measure completely separate abilities but rather a general underlying ability (perhaps similar to Saussure's language faculty) that is, to some extent, required on all the sections.

The correlation of scores on the different sections of standardized tests was not the only problem with the separate abilities theory of language proficiency. As we have seen, the theory was based on descriptive linguistics and behaviorism, and during the late 1950s and 1960s, the assumptions and claims of these fields were effectively challenged by Noam Chomsky's theory of generative grammar, which we examine next.

Generative Grammar

In 1957, Chomsky introduced a new paradigm for studying language in his book *Syntactic Structures*. Chomsky is a structuralist, a successor to Saussure, Bloomfield, and Fries, and although he has been an outspoken critic of the descriptivists, his theory integrates and expands the ideas of his predecessors. Chomsky differed from Saussure in his opinion of what kind of science linguistics ought to be. Saussure had thought that linguistic patterns were a type of social custom and, therefore, that linguistics was a branch of sociology. The descriptivists thought that linguistic patterns arose from habits located in the brains of individuals and, therefore, that linguistics was a branch of psychology. Chomsky placed linguistics with psychology, but he denied that linguistic patterns arise from habits. Rather, he adopted the position of cognitive psychology, which is that linguistic patterns arise from knowledge contained in individual minds.

Chomsky's (1959, 1984) concept of mind can be understood by making an analogy with a computer. A computer is a machine that can store and organize information and make decisions based on this information. A computer program is a set of instructions telling the computer how to do these things. What a computer does is best understood in terms of the set of instructions, not in terms of the mechanical operations of the machine itself. This is so because the same program could be run on many different machines, which would perform very different mechanical operations when executing the program. But the logic behind the operations would be the same, and that logic is contained in the program. Like a computer, the brain can store and process information and make decisions. According to the computational view of cognition, the mind can be thought of as the program, or set of instructions, that controls this information processing. Therefore, according to this analogy, the mind is to the brain as a program is to a computer.

A computer program is written in a programming language, which is a *formal system*, a set of mathematical symbols (numbers) and rules that are explicitly defined, like the set of symbols and rules involved in doing addition. Chomsky (1957, 1965) proposed to study the workings of the mind (at least those related to language) by means of a formal system of symbols and rules for describing the linguistic knowledge in the minds of speakers. In this system, linguistic patterns can be modeled as rewrite rules. An example is shown in Rule (1), which states that the symbol NP (which stands for noun phrase) can be rewritten as the symbol det (which stands for determiner) followed by the symbol N (which stands for noun). In other words, a noun phrase such as "the dog" can consist of a noun preceded by a determiner.

1. NP→(det) + N

The grammar of English has no rule permitting a determiner to follow a noun, although some languages do.

Chomsky's goal was to construct a simple and consistent rule system that would specify all and only the grammatical sentences of a language. To accomplish this goal, he employed certain ideas used in mathematics. First, he noted that a language contains an infinite number of grammatical sentences. Saussure had despaired at this great diversity: How can something infinite be described? It was because he could think of no way to do this that Saussure consigned syntax to *parole*, the unsystematic aspect of language. But Chomsky knew that it is possible to describe an infinite number of combinations by using finite means and that in fact such a task is common in mathematics. For example, it is possible to describe the infinite set of even integers by means of Equation (2):

2. $X = 2Y$

where X is an even integer and Y is any integer. Equation (2) is said to *generate* the set of even integers. This does not mean that the equation produces them in a physical sense, the way a turbine produces electricity. Rather *generate* is used in the mathematical sense of "defining" or "specifying" the set of even integers.

Chomskian linguists attempt to write grammars that will, in this technical sense, generate the possible sentences of a language. A brief fragment of such a *generative grammar* appears in Figure 2.2. This grammar will generate sentences (3) and (4).

3. The man bit the dog.
4. The dog bit the man.

The grammar will not generate sentence (5).

FIGURE 2.2 Generative Rules for the Sentences, "The Man Bit the Dog" and "The Dog Bit the Man."

Phrase Structure Rules	Lexical Rules
1. S ⟶ NP VP	4. det ⟶ the
2. NP ⟶ (det) N	5. N ⟶ man, dog
3. VP ⟶ V (NP)	6. V ⟶ bit

   5. *man the dog the bit.

Just as Equation (2) defines a set of numbers, the rules in Figure 2.2 define a set of sentences.

Of course, rules like those in Figure 2.2 generate only written, not spoken, sentences, so they characterize only the syntactic, not the phonological, patterns of the language. A complete grammar would contain a phonological component with similar rules for generating these patterns as well. Thus, a generative grammar generates all and only the sentences of a language and in doing so explicitly characterizes its syntactic and phonological patterns.

Generative grammar is not a model of how a human mind or a computer might produce plans for sentences. Rather, it is a formal system that specifies the possible sentences in a language and the internal structure of these sentences. Thus, generative grammar is a theory of *competence*, not a real-time processing model, which would be a theory of *performance*. A competence theory describes in very abstract terms the information that must somehow be processed by a mind or a computer, but it does not suggest how this processing actually takes place. In terms of the above computer analogy, if the brain is like a computer and the mind is like a program, then a generative grammar is like the logic of the program expressed in purely mathematical terms. Such a mathematical account of what the computer is supposed to do could be translated into different programming languages. According to Chomsky, it is the job of psychology, not linguistics, to find out the nature of the mental program the brain uses, but linguistics can help in this endeavor by specifying, at a very abstract level, what information the program must somehow contain.

Universal Grammar. Chomsky (1965, 1986) endorsed Saussure's notion of the language faculty and his claim that learning a language is different from general learning. According to Chomsky, human beings can access innate knowledge about language stored in a separate "mental organ" of the mind. We will first consider Chomsky's theory in regard to L1 acquisition and then see if it can be extended to L2 acquisition. If so, the theory may help to explain why Collier's (1987) school-age subjects acquired linguistic competence before academic competence because it claims that language learning is "natural," and therefore easier than general learning.

Chomsky (1981, 1986) claims that children possess innate knowledge about language in the form of a "Universal Grammar" (UG). The UG contains principles that provide a kind of blueprint for learning any human language. An example is the principle of hierarchical structure, which can be seen in Figure 2.2, where S is made up of NP and VP, and NP is made up of an optional det and N, and so on. Some UG principles specify the ways in which languages can differ from each other. An example is word order, which varies in different languages, but does not vary without limit. Rule 3 in Figure 2.2 says that in English the most important element (or *head*) of a VP, namely the V, comes at the beginning of its phrase. This order of elements is also correct for prepositional phrases such as "on the table," in which the head (the preposition *on*) comes at the beginning, and for adjective phrases such as "likely to succeed," in which the adjective *likely* comes

---

* Hereafter, an asterisk preceding a sentence indicates that the sentence is ungrammatical.

at the beginning of its phrase. The head-first order is basically correct for NPs as well. If the NP contains a prepositional phrase, as in "the man on the boat," or a relative clause, as in "the man whom you met," the head noun comes before the prepositional phrase or the relative clause. The basic rule for English word order, then, is that a head comes at the beginning of its phrase. This regularity can be expressed by Rule (6), in which X can stand for any of the four major syntactic categories—noun, verb, adjective, or preposition:

6. XP→XY

If X stands for preposition, the rule states that in a prepositional phrase the preposition comes first, followed by the rest of the phrase, and so on.

Of course, not all languages have the head-first order. In Japanese the head comes at the end of its phrase, so a rule for Japanese word order would look like Rule (7), which says that the head (X) of any phrase comes at the end:

7. XP→YX

The point is that for a particular language, all types of phrases generally have the same word order (head first or head last). Chomsky claims that children know this fact innately, so they do not have to learn the pattern for each type of phrase separately. Having learned the head position for one kind of phrase, they will know the basic order for all types. Thus, in regard to word order, the UG provides the learner with only two possibilities or *parameters*. The learner's job is to choose the correct parameter setting on the basis of input from the target language.

The theory of parameter setting helps to explain the "logical problem of language acquisition," namely how children can acquire a very complex symbolic system in just a few years, a task made doubly difficult by the fact that apparently children must learn to produce many grammatical constructions to which they have not been exposed. White (1990) observes, "The input *underdetermines* linguistic competence. Children acquire properties of language which are not immediately obvious and . . . which go far beyond the actual sentences that [they] may happen to have been exposed to" (p. 28). Part of the generative linguist's explanation of this phenomenon is that children need only set the parameters of certain innately specified patterns, rather than learn everything from scratch.

There is considerable debate about whether innate knowledge of UG can be accessed by adults acquiring a second language. The issue involves the question of whether there is a "critical period" for language acquisition (analogous to the critical period during which young birds must learn their species' calls), after which the UG is no longer accessible and language must be learned by means of more general cognitive mechanisms. There is some evidence that UG is accessible, at least to some extent, in L2 acquisition after childhood. One piece of evidence is the fact that given the proper environment, adolescents of fifteen and sixteen years of age can learn a second language as well as, in fact faster than, children can learn a first language (Bley-Vroman, 1988). According to Lenneberg (1967), such learners are well past the critical period, which ends at the onset of puberty. Furthermore, many adults learn to speak a second language very well, in fact some cannot be distinguished from native speakers, and their success, no less than the success of children, requires an answer to the logical problem of language acquisition.

A number of experiments also suggest that UG is available to L2 learners. Bley-Vroman, Felix, and Ioup (1988) investigated whether Korean speakers had acquired the UG principle of *subjacency*. This principle governs the formation of wh questions, among other things. In general, languages can form wh questions in three ways. The first way is to use a questioning word or morpheme in the position where the word or morpheme would go in an indicative sentence. English forms wh questions in this way as in (8).

8. Mary saw *who*?

Korean allows only wh questions of this type.

A second way of forming wh questions is to move the questioned constituent to the front of its clause, as in (9), where the *gap* left by the fronted wh constituent is marked with ∅.

9. Who did Mary see ∅

The Russian language allows only wh questions of these two types. A third way, also allowed by English, is to move the wh constituent into a preceding clause, as in (10), where the final clause boundaries are marked with labeled brackets.

10. Who did Mary say [c that John had seen ∅]

Although English allows questioned constituents to move more freely than Korean or Russian, it still imposes constraints on this movement. For example, wh constituents cannot move into a previous clause over a NP, as shown in (11).

11. *Who did Mary make [NP the claim [c that John had seen ∅]]

Notice that if *who* is not moved, the sentence is grammatical: Mary made the claim that John saw *who*? Like the head principle discussed earlier, the subjacency principle comes with parameters that must be set for individual languages. In English, these parameters specify that a questioned constituent cannot be moved past certain kinds of subordinating conjunctions, such as *whether* as in (12).

12. *Who did Mary wonder [c whether John had seen ∅]]

Again, if *who* is not moved, the sentence is grammatical: Mary wondered whether John had seen *who*? Notice, however, that wh words can be moved across the subordinating conjunction *that*, as in (10).

The subjacency principle, then, says that wh movement is not unlimited; it can occur only over certain kinds of structures. The parameters associated with this principle specify what kinds of structures act as barriers to wh movement. According to UG theory, when children are exposed to a language that allows wh movement, they innately know that it will be constrained by certain abstract syntactic structures. English-speaking children must set the parameters so that the abstract structures that contain *whether,* as in (12), and NPs, as in (11), do not allow wh movement, but that the structure that contains *that,* as in (10), does allow movement.

In order to test whether their adult Korean subjects, who spoke English well, had accessed the subjacency principle and had set its parameters correctly, Bley-Vroman, Felix, and Ioup (1988) asked the subjects to judge the grammaticality of English sentences involving subjacency. The test contained both grammatical sentences that obeyed subjacency restrictions and ungrammatical sentences that violated the restrictions. Although the ninety-two subjects had studied ESL for an average of eight years, the researchers made the safe assumption that the subtle differences between the two kinds of test sentences, such as the difference between (10) and (12), had not been explicitly taught. Therefore, if the subjects were able to make accurate judgements of grammaticality, it could only be because they had some access to UG. Bley-Vroman, Felix, and Ioup (1988) found that although the subjects judged the sentences much less accurately than native speakers, they were "clearly not merely guessing at random; something was causing UG effects" (p. 26). They concluded that "it is extremely difficult to maintain the hypothesis that Universal Grammar is inaccessible to adult learners . . ." (p. 26).

At present, this claim is controversial because a number of other studies, for example those of Clahsen and Muysken (1989) and Schacter (1989), have suggested that adult learners have no access to UG. However, most researchers agree that even if UG is available to adult language learners, L1 acquisition and L2 acquisition are not exactly the same, since only L2 learners already possess a language. White (1990) suggests that what L2 learners must do is to reset many of the parameters from their L1 settings. But this resetting, of course, requires that the learner have access to the knowledge of parameters that is contained in the Language Acquisition Device (LAD). As Cook (1988) observes, "[Innate knowledge] plays a central and vital part in L2 learning, but there are many other parts" (p. 189).

Pedagogical Interpretations of Generative Grammar.   With the emergence of generative grammar in the 1960s, the paradigm of descriptive linguistics and behaviorism, and with it the audio-lingual method and the separate abilities theory of language proficiency, came under a cloud. But it was unclear which testing and teaching methods, if any, the new paradigm implied. An early attempt to apply generative grammar to language teaching was the cognitive code method (Carroll, 1965), embodied in Rutherford's (1968) ESL text *Modern English.* The theory behind the cognitive code method was that generative rules model actual mental operations in the minds of speakers and that consciously knowing these rules will facilitate the mental operations. This mistaken notion resulted from confusing a competence theory with a performance or processing theory.

In practice, the main innovation of the cognitive code method was that teachers were encouraged to teach grammar explicitly, a practice forbidden in the audio-lingual method. However, the principal teaching technique in *Modern English* was still the pattern drill. Rutherford's drills differed from Fries's and Lado's drills mainly in that they were designed to teach the subtle structural patterns that generative linguists had discovered.

For example, an audio-lingual textbook might teach the indirect object form of the dative ("John gave Marsha the book") and the prepositional form of the dative ("John gave the book to Marsha") in different lessons. But Rutherford taught the two structures together, pointing out that some verbs (for example *explain*) do not allow both types of dative. Nevertheless, as in the audio-lingual method, meaning remained less important than structure, and many of Rutherford's drills consisted of unrelated sentences whose meanings did not have to be fully understood. In sum, Rutherford's pedagogical application of generative grammar might be characterized as old wine in new bottles.

Other scholars, including Diller (1978) and Krashen (1981, 1982), provided a more widely accepted assessment of the teaching implications of generative grammar. Rather than focusing on linguistic analysis, these scholars emphasized the psychological implications of Chomsky's theory. As we have seen, Chomsky claimed that language learning is different from other kinds of learning. One piece of evidence supporting this claim is that virtually all human beings learn to speak their native language perfectly without formal instruction. According to generative linguists, such learning can be possible only if much linguistic knowledge is genetically stored in the LAD. For the LAD to do its work, no explicit instruction is needed; language acquisition is automatic for children exposed to language in a natural way.

Diller claimed that the LAD worked, at least partially, in adult L2 acquisition as well, and therefore that the best way to teach a second language was to replicate, to some extent, the natural language-learning environment that children are exposed to. He believed that the audio-lingual method had failed because it presented language in artificial situations and emphasized structure at the expense of meaning. Diller (1978) advocated active, contextualized interaction in the target language: "Being in the presence of the target language is of little help unless we are as active as a child in learning the language, and unless we ask the same questions" (p. 32). As an example of a contextualized, meaning-based method, Diller recommended the direct method of Berlitz, which, in the early lessons, stresses meaningful communication based on the manipulation of physical objects such as pens, books, knives, and forks.

Krashen (1981, 1982) proposed that linguistic knowledge is internalized in two entirely different ways. The first way is through the LAD, which he claimed works in adults in essentially the same way that it works in children. The second way is to consciously learn grammar rules. According to Krashen, these two processes lead to two separate kinds of knowledge that do not interact. Exposure to meaningful input from the target language results in "acquisition" by the LAD—tacit knowledge of linguistic patterns. Conscious memorization of grammar rules, on the other hand, results in "learning" by a separate cognitive component called the "Monitor." Of the two kinds of knowledge, acquired knowledge is by far the most important. Krashen holds that learned knowledge cannot enhance acquired knowledge and can be accessed only when the learner has the time and motivation to summon up a consciously known rule, as on a multiple-choice test.

The monitor model can be considered an extension of Diller's theory of second language acquisition. Like Diller, Krashen claimed that the LAD works in adults more or less as it works in children: both will acquire language naturally if exposed to meaningful input to the target language under affectively appropriate conditons. Krashen went beyond Diller in proposing the Monitor, which was intended to account for the fact that adults can benefit, to a limited extent, from a focus on particular grammatical patterns.

The teaching implications of the monitor model were similar to the teaching implications of Diller's interpretation of Chomsky: the best method is to provide students with meaningful input from the target language under optimal affective conditions. Thus, during the 1970s and 1980s a number of language teaching methods based on meaning and communication emerged, including Total Physical Response (Asher, 1969), community language learning (Stevick, 1980), and the Natural Method (Krashen & Terrell, 1983). These methods did not become popular just because they were compatible with Diller's and Krashen's theories, but because practitioners discovered that meaningful interaction in the target language is effective.

The evidence that Krashen produced in support of the monitor model has been severely criticized, for example, by McLaughlin (1987), and it is now generally accepted that Krashen has not convincingly proved his case (see Larsen-Freeman & Long 1991, p. 225). But while the studies that Krashen cites may be flawed methodologically, a number of other studies, including those done in the UG framework, support the claim that the LAD (in its new incarnation as UG) is accessible to adults as well as to children. If this is so, we are still faced with the question confronted by Diller and Krashen: what are the implications of the human language faculty for L2 teaching? The answers to this question are still speculative, but they are reminiscent of the discussions during the 1970s of the cognitive code method and communicative methods.

Cook (1988) suggests that language teaching syllabi should be grammatical, constructed with the theory of parameter setting in mind, but he does not say exactly how this should be done. He suggests that an emphasis on communication and social interaction (as in a notional-functional syllabus) is not the most effective means of promoting L2 acquisition, and he implies that a focus on particular syntactic structures such as the head-first order of English phrases would be more effective. A teaching method compatible with UG "would emphasize the provision of appropriate evidence rather than communicative interaction or grammatical explanation" (p. 172). But it is not clear that communicative interaction is not the best way to provide appropriate evidence, as Diller and Krashen claimed. Birdsong (1990) asks,

> What's wrong with E-language [i.e., general language] input? After all, it is the vehicle of "appropriate evidence" . . . that learners require for triggering experiences. Quite in keeping with Chomskyan premises, exposure to E-language does not just yield E-language knowledge; rather, it is necessary for the accumulation of [linguistic competence] as well. (p. 334)

In sum, the pedagogical implications of UG theory are unclear at present; however, it is clear that experiments involving the effectiveness of instruction that focuses on parameter setting will comprise a major research agenda for L2 scholarship in the coming years.

COMMON FACTOR THEORIES OF LANGUAGE PROFICIENCY

The emergence of generative linguistics (Chomsky, 1957, 1965) had a strong influence on the field of language testing and on associated theories of language proficiency. After the fall of behaviorism, language testing scholars needed to assess the implications of generative grammar on their field. To the extent that the separate abilities theory was associated with behaviorism, it was challenged by Chomsky's theory of competence and language acquisition. In addition, testing scholars had their own reasons to be unhappy with the separate abilities theory. Research by Holtzman (1967), Spolsky (1968), and Oller (1976) had shown that students' scores on the different sections of language proficiency tests (which supposedly measured separate abilities) correlated highly. As mentioned, this finding suggested that the separate tests were really measuring some single underlying ability. If there really was such an ability, what was needed was a theoretical construct with which to identify this common factor.

Spolsky's Theory

Bernard Spolsky (1968, 1973) suggested that the needed theoretical construct was Chomsky's linguistic competence. He observed:

> The grammar of a language . . . is a description of competence; it . . . necessarily under-
> lies any performance. . . . A moment's thought makes clear that linguistic performance
> may be either active or passive. . . . The implication of this for language learning is
> extremely important, for it suggests that one may learn a language just as well by
> listening as by speaking. The implication for testing is . . . that we can find out about
> "knowledge of a language," which is the same as underlying linguistic competence,
> equally well when we test passive and active skills. (1973, p. 174)

Spolsky claimed that the construct of linguistic competence was "validated," (shown to be measurable) by his analysis of language proficiency tests. Thus, his hypothesis brought together findings in theoretical linguistics and language testing theory.

Spolsky did not claim that linguistic competence is all that is needed to succeed on the different sections of a proficiency test. Obviously, literacy skills are also necessary on the reading and writing sections of the test, and they are not part of linguistic competence. Rather Spolsky's claim was that the abilities to speak, comprehend, read, and write depend *in part* on a knowledge of linguistic patterns, and therefore that all sections of a proficiency test measure linguistic competence to some extent, although they measure other knowledge and skills as well.

Oller's Unitary Competence Hypothesis

Spolsky's theory was extended by Oller (1976, 1979), who proposed the *unitary compe-*
tence hypothesis. Oller no longer holds the strong version of this theory but still endorses
a weak version, which is similar to Spolsky's notion of general proficiency, described
later in this chapter. It is instructive to examine the strong version of the unitary competence hypothesis because it is an important part of the history of language proficiency
theories. Oller's (1976) research replicated Holtzman's (1967) and Spolsky's (1968)
finding that students' scores on the different sections of language proficiency tests correlate. But Oller found a much higher correlation than Spolsky. According to testing theory,
such a correlation suggests that a single factor, which corresponds to an indivisible mental
ability, is responsible for success on the different kinds of tests. In this theory, tests are

considered to be a proving ground for mentalistic theories. Even if a construct such as "linguistic competence," or "decoding skills" is useful from a theoretical or practical perspective, it is not considered psychologically real if it cannot be measured separately from other constructs on some kind of test. Thus, Oller (1979) proposed that "there is a basic grammatical system underlying all uses of language" (p. 67).

Like Spolsky, Oller identified the common underlying ability as "competence," but he did not use this term in Chomsky's sense. Instead he redefined *competence*, as well as *grammar*, to fit his own theory of language use. Oller's (1979) grammar included not only knowledge of phonology, syntax, and lexicon, but also all the other kinds of knowledge and skills necessary to do well on a language proficiency test, including literacy skills and knowledge of the world. He explained,

> It may be objected that what we are referring to here as *grammatical* involves more than what is traditionally subsumed under the heading *grammar*. However, we are not concerned here with grammar in the traditional sense. . . . Rather, we are concerned with the psychological realities of linguistic knowledge as it is internalized in whatever ways by real human beings. By this definition of grammar, the language user's knowledge of how to map utterances . . . onto contexts outside of language . . . must be incorporated into the grammatical system. (p. 24)

A second way in which Oller's mental grammar differed from Chomsky's was that Oller spelled out how the grammar was supposed to operate in sentence comprehension. Thus, despite its name, Oller's theory was a performance theory, not a competence theory.

Oller's model of language comprehension, the *expectancy grammar*, emphasized the fact that language is redundant. Once listeners have heard part of a discourse, they can use their knowledge of linguistic patterns and their knowledge of the world to predict the remaining part. For example, in English a consonant following the sequence /sp/ can only be /r/ or /l/, as in *spring* or *splurge*. Thus, the listener does not actually have to hear every segment of the speech stream; much of it is predictable, or partially predictable, from context. The same principle works in syntax. A word following *the* is likely to be an adjective or a noun, and it cannot be a verb. Similarly, listeners can use their knowledge of the world to predict certain things about discourse. One knows that in a Superman story, Superman will defeat the villain, but will not (really) marry Lois Lane.

Oller's definition of grammar was comprehensive; it encompassed all the knowledge and skills related to using language in oral or written form. In fact, Oller claimed that the expectancy grammar (and thus language proficiency) was closely related to general intelligence, and that a student who can use the expectancy grammar effectively will do well on any kind of test involving language. Thus, Oller's theory of language proficiency was different from earlier theories in two respects. First, it did not equate language proficiency principally with knowledge of linguistic structure. Despite its name, the expectancy grammar required knowledge of the world. Second, Oller drew a connection between language proficiency and mental ability. We shall see these claims repeated in the theories of Bernstein (1972) and Cummins (1984a, 1984b), reviewed later.

The unitary competence hypothesis can be seen as a psychologist's reaction to Chomsky's highly abstract competence theory. Like other psychologists, Oller was not content with a formal theory of linguistic knowledge. He wanted to know how this knowledge is used in the on-line processing of speech and writing. The unitary competence hypothesis was an attempt to explain this process, and as discussed in the next chapter, the expectancy mechanism Oller described is important in language comprehension (although it is not the only mechanism).

Oller has abandoned the strong version of the unitary competence hypothesis. This move was motivated by a reconsideration of some of the assumptions of testing theory previously mentioned. Gould (1981) pointed out that different statistical measures, all of which might reasonably be used to analyze the correlation between different kinds of tests, may find different numbers of "common factors," and he is critical of reifying these factors by claiming that they correspond to some mental ability.

Finally, Vollmer (1983) urges that the results of psychological tests not be considered as proof of theories of mental abilities, but rather as one source of information used to construct such theories. He stresses that the notion of language proficiency should be informed by an understanding of how language in all its forms is learned and processed, and not just constructed to explain the results of standardized tests. Factor analyses of language proficiency tests are helpful, but if the analyses show that theoretically useful constructs such as sociolinguistic competence and linguistic competence correlate highly, that is not a sufficient reason to abandon these constructs. Vollmer (1983) advocates moving "away from . . . mathematical data reduction procedures to a psychologically more informed and better motivated . . . view of language performance" (pp. 3–4).

SUMMARY

Since Saussure, the scope of structural linguistics has broadened considerably, and there has been a concomitant broadening of the notion of language proficiency. All the structuralists, including Chomsky, desired to limit linguistics to some manageable area of study. Saussure included only phonology. The descriptivists added syntax. Chomsky added semantics, although the semantic component associated with Chomsky's (1965) model did not attempt to characterize all knowledge of the world (cf. Katz & Postal, 1964). Oller reacted to Chomsky's theory, emphasizing psychological (processing) concerns, defining *grammar* to include complete knowledge of the world, and drawing a connection between language proficiency and intelligence. Thus, the unitary competence hypothesis represented a major break with the structuralist tradition. This movement toward a more inclusive concept of language proficiency was continued by the theory we examine next: the theory of communicative competence.

COMMUNICATIVE COMPETENCE

The theory of communicative competence claims that language proficiency consists of separate but related abilities that are much broader than those measured by traditional language proficiency tests.

Speech Acts and the Cooperative Principle

Generative grammar was intended to account for all possible sentences in a language, but not for how human beings used those sentences. This narrow conception of language was challenged by the anthropologist Dell Hymes who observed that using a language appropriately and effectively requires knowing much more than its structural patterns. Hymes (1971) noted that a complete theory of language must "account for the fact that a normal child acquires knowledge of sentences not only as grammatical but also as appropriate" (p. 5). For example, children must learn to use sentences effectively for such human purposes as greeting, requesting, apologizing, stating, denying, and so on. These uses or *functions* of language were studied by the British philosophers Austin and Grice. Austin (1962) noticed that language could be used to accomplish certain acts. For example, if a judge utters the words "I now pronounce you man and wife" in the appropriate circumstances, he accomplishes the act of marrying two people. After these words are spoken, an entire set of legal and social privileges and responsibilities comes into effect, including the privilege of having children with society's approval and the responsibility of supporting them.

For mere words to cause such an important change in the state of the world, a rigid set of conditions must be met. The appropriate words must be uttered by a designated authority, not just by anybody. Neither partner can already be married. In some religious ceremonies, the participants must even have the appropriate thoughts and feelings. If one person does not really desire to marry the other but is doing so for social reasons, the marriage may later be annulled.

Austin called acts that are committed by means of words "speech acts." Speech acts with important social consequences are often highly formalized, with the appropriateness conditions written into law. However, Austin noticed that not all speech acts are formal and legally prescribed. There are also everyday speech acts, such as promising, requesting, ordering, apologizing, and many others. Like formal speech acts, everyday speech acts have appropriateness conditions regarding who can commit them and under what circumstances. For example, it is not appropriate to apologize when one has done nothing to offend. Sometimes the appropriateness conditions for committing a particular act are different in different cultures. In Ethiopia it is not appropriate for students to question teachers too closely, even if they do not understand what the teacher has said.

Grice (1975) pointed out that much of the meaning and structure of discourse is not conveyed directly by linguistic devices like tenses, connectors, and negators, but indirectly by inferences about a speaker's intentions. Such inferences are possible because human beings follow a behavioral dictum that Grice called the "Cooperative Principle": "Make your conversational contribution, such as is required, at the stage at which it occurs, by the accepted purpose or direction of the talk exchange in which you are engaged" (p. 45).

Widdowson (1978) provides the following example of how the Cooperative Principle works:

A: That's the telephone.
B: I'm in the bath.
A: O.K. (p. 29)

Although no syntactic devices connect these sentences, the text is coherent because each speaker assumes that the other is following the Cooperative Principle and therefore looks for connections. B knows that A's first statement is a request because there would be no reason to mention the fact that the telephone was ringing if A intended to answer it. Because it is assumed that ringing telephones should be answered, the only reason for bringing up the matter would be to request that B answer the phone. A knows that B's statement is a negative reply to the request because A assumes that B's statement is in some way relevant to the request. The fact that B is in the bath implies that B is unable to answer the phone; therefore, the request is denied. A's second statement is an acknowledgment of B's reply.

Grice suggests that the Cooperative Principle and its corollaries (which Grice calls *maxims*) are universal since they emerge from the very nature of rational behavior. This suggestion[1] was challenged by Keenan (1976), who claimed that Malagasy speakers regularly withhold information from their conversational partners. For example, if asked where her mother was, a speaker might reply, "Either at home or at the market." Such a reply would violate Grice's (1975) first maxim of quantity, which states, "Make your contribution as informative as is required (for the current purposes of the exchange)" (p. 45). But Green (1989) points out that in the Malagasy culture, being the sole possessor of information confers prestige on an individual. Therefore, withholding information involves either "opting out of the first maxim of quantity, to preserve one's status, or flouting the maxim, to flaunt it. Either way, the existence of the maxim of quantity among the Malagasy is entailed; it could not be exploited if it did not exist" (p. 96). Green (1989) endorses the idea that the Cooperative Principle is universal: "It is clear that the value of the Cooperative Principle and the maxims in explaining linguistics is much greater if they are universal (and hence potentially a consequence of some property of human nature or human society) than if they are not" (pp. 95–96). In chapter 3 we will encounter evidence that supports this claim, showing how even students who do not share a language can communicate effectively by exploiting the Cooperative Principle.

The theory of communicative competence expanded the domain of linguistic inquiry. Generative theory claimed that speakers tacitly know a system of constitutive rules that tell them whether an utterance is grammatical. The theory of communicative competence claimed that speakers also tacitly know a system of constitutive rules that tell them whether an utterance is appropriate and that linguistics ought to include the study of both systems. Whereas Chomsky's linguistic competence is knowledge of possible linguistic forms, communicative competence is broader: it includes not only knowledge of linguistic forms but also knowledge of how to use these forms appropriately and effectively.

Canale's and Swain's Theory of Communicative Competence

Canale and Swain (1980) adapted Hymes's notion of communicative competence to language teaching concerns. They proposed that communicative competence has four components: grammatical competence, sociolinguistic competence, strategic competence, and discourse competence.[2] Grammatical competence is knowledge of correct syntactic and phonological forms and general vocabulary. Sociolinguistic competence includes knowledge of how to use speech acts and formal and informal speaking styles appropriately. Strategic competence is the ability to communicate with limited linguistic resources—to get the meaning across even though one is not fluent in the language. Discourse competence includes the ability to comprehend and produce text that is *cohesive* and *coherent*. Cohesion, according to Halliday and Hassan (1976), involves the use of certain syntactic devices to signal the relationship of referents and ideas within a text. These devices include anaphoric reference (*I* saw *them* over *there*); ellipsis (John washed the floor and Mary the dishes); and conjunction, which involves the use of particular connectors such as *although, and, however,* and so forth. Knowledge of these structures is obviously a special kind of syntactic knowledge, and Canale and Swain (1980) observe, "It is not altogether clear to us that rules of discourse will differ substantially from grammatical rules (with respect to cohesion)" (p. 30).

Coherence in a text (written or spoken) can be achieved without cohesive devices by using the Cooperative Principle, as illustrated in the bath episode in the previous section. Coherence also requires making use of appropriate background information. For example, in order to grasp the coherence of the bath episode, the reader must know that many homes have both telephones and bathtubs. In parts of the world where telephones are found only in the local telecommunications office and bathtubs only in the local hotel, the bath episode text might make no sense at all.

Pedagogical Interpretations of Communicative Competence

Although Canale and Swain's (1980; Canale, 1983) model of communicative competence included four separate competencies, most teaching applications of this approach emphasized sociolinguistic competence. This emphasis was perhaps a reaction to the audio-lingual method's overemphasis of grammatical competence. An example of a language teaching program that was based on the theory of communicative competence, but that stressed sociolinguistic competence, was Savignon's (1983) experimental program for teaching French to American college students. The aims of the program were "(1) To give learners the opportunity to use French in practical settings . . . and (2) to free learners of the impression that communication is measured solely in terms of linguistic accuracy" (p. 71). Savignon's lessons included role-plays in both French and English of situations such as two new students meeting in a university residence hall, two students and long-time friends meeting after summer vacation, and a student talking with a professor after class.

These lessons emphasized appropriateness and effectiveness and downplayed accuracy. As Savignon (1983) noted, "the students were . . . encouraged to act French in their own exchanges by adopting the nonverbal aspects of French communication. . . . The focus [was] not *French* but *how to do things in French*" (p. 72). Some other examples of lessons that stressed appropriate communication included asking for help in posting a letter, inquiring about the best way to go from Lyon to Paris, and telling a French student at what time meals are served.

At the end of the term, Savignon tested the overall communications skills of three groups of students: those who had taken the experimental lessons, a control group who had followed an audio-lingual curriculum, and a control group who had attended lectures on French culture given in English. The tests included an informal discussion with a French speaker who was instructed to be friendly and helpful, a formal interview with a French speaker who was instructed not to help the student, an oral report on an assigned topic such as "your winter vacation," and an oral description of the ongoing activities of an actor. The group of students who had received the communicative lessons scored significantly higher on these tests than did the control groups.

THE CHANGING FOCUS OF ESL INSTRUCTION IN THE UNITED STATES

In tracing the development of theories of language proficiency, teaching, and testing, we have only briefly considered an important factor: the nature of the ESL student population on whom scholars and materials developers focused. The language acquisition scholars whose work appeared from the 1950s to the mid-1970s (Fries, Lado, Rutherford, Diller, Spolsky, and Oller) were all college professors, and their theories and methods were developed largely in connection with research on university ESL students. In general, these students had been well educated in their native countries and had considerable background knowledge of academic subjects as well as academic skills. This fact may have influenced theories of language proficiency. For example, standardized tests that measure mainly linguistic and discourse competence, but not sociolinguistic or strategic competence, are useful for placing college students in appropriate mainstream courses because it can usually be assumed that these students have the appropriate background knowledge in science, mathematics, and the humanities as well as at least some academic skills such as taking notes and writing papers. Furthermore, knowledge of particularly American subjects is not critical for success in many college majors, especially those in the sciences.

However, during the 1970s, ESL professionals began to focus on a different group of students. Immigrants from Southeast Asia, Central America, Africa, and other underdeveloped areas of the world were arriving in the United States in large numbers and enrolling in schools, especially adult schools and community colleges. The new immigrants usually did not have academic backgrounds, nor were they necessarily seeking a higher education. Instead, they needed to learn the communicative skills necessary for living and working permanently in the United States. ESL teachers in adult schools and job training programs found that the teaching materials and tests developed for use with academically oriented students were not appropriate for these students, who needed survival skills and strategies for making themselves understood, even in imperfect English. In short, they needed strategic and sociolinguistic competence perhaps more than linguistic competence, and the theory developed by Canale and Swain (1980; Canale, 1983) and the associated methodology described by Savignon (1983) were useful for meeting these needs.

In the 1980s, ESL students in the public schools came to the attention of language researchers. These students included the children of immigrants who had arrived during the 1970s, as well as newly arrived children. They faced the formidable task of catching up to their NES peers in English proficiency, knowledge of content subjects, and academic skills as quickly as possible, and they did not have the knowledge of English structure and content material or the academic skills required to accomplish this task. Therefore, a model of language proficiency, as well as associated pedagogy, that would meet the needs of these students (in short, a model of academic competence) was required.

Cummins's (1979, 1984a, 1984b; Cummins & Swain, 1983) theory of cognitive/academic language proficiency was a response to this need. We will discuss Cummins's important proposals after reviewing some related theories that formed the background to his work.

ACADEMIC LANGUAGE PROFICIENCY

Some investigators have suggested that success in school is related to proficiency in the academic language used in textbooks and lectures. At first glance this hypothesis seems to fit within the structuralist tradition because it focuses on a particular variety of language. But in fact some versions of the hypothesis violate a structuralist axiom by claiming that language proficiency consists of more than just mastery of linguistic forms; it includes reasoning ability as well. This departure from structuralist orthodoxy may be due to the fact that the investigators considered in this section are not primarily linguists but educational researchers, and that their theories were not inspired by developments in theoretical linguistics but by empirical studies of the academic success of students of English as a second language or standard English as a second dialect. We begin by considering what structural linguists mean by the term *language variety*.

Language Varieties

All languages show differences in phonology, syntax, and vocabulary according to the geographical area and social class of speakers. It is difficult to tell when these differences add up to a different variety of the language (or indeed a different language), but there are clear cases. Londoners speak a different variety of English than New Yorkers; working-class New Yorkers speak a different variety than upper-class New Yorkers. Within a particular language variety there are formal and informal styles. Labov (1972) found that in a casual conversation, both working-class and upper-class New Yorkers were likely to delete postvocalic [r], so that *forth floor* is pronounced [fɔəə flɔə]. But in formal speech (as in a job interview) these speakers are more likely to produce the [r]. This phenomenon is called *style shifting*. Labov also found that the percentage of [r] in a middle-class speaker's formal style may be higher than the percentage in an upper-class speaker's informal style. This finding shows that with respect to certain features, language varieties form a continuum, not a series of distinct dialects.

Style shifting also affects syntactic forms. A speaker of a western U.S. variety might say to a friend, "That's all the hotter it gets around here," but if the same speaker were giving a lecture on meteorology, she would more likely say, "It doesn't get any hotter than that around here." Style shifting can also affect the choice of vocabulary. In formal styles one is more likely to hear "however" instead of "but," "residual" instead of "profit," and "Professor Sanford" instead of "Jim."

Linguists insist that such differences are merely formal and that no mature variety of a language has greater expressive power or requires more cognitive ability than another. As discussed in chapter 3, it is true that the grammar of some languages is especially efficient for making certain semantic distinctions; for example, Spanish has the full use of two voices, the indicative and subjunctive, whereas English has the full use of only the indicative. However, the nuances conveyed in Spanish by the subjunctive voice can be conveyed in English by other means, such as conditional tenses and adverbial clauses. Because all language varieties have a large repertoire of lexical, syntactic, and semantic devices for expressing meaning, it is an axiom of structural linguistics that they are equally capable of expressing the full range of a speaker's thoughts.

Restricted Code and Elaborated Code

Bernstein (1964, 1972) claimed that there is a distinct variety of formal language that is commonly used in schools and is very different from the informal language of everyday interaction. He called the formal variety *elaborated code* and the informal variety *restricted code*. Unlike linguists, Bernstein was not primarily interested in investigating the structural properties of these two varieties, but rather in investigating what he believed to be their expressive possibilities. Bernstein claimed that the restricted code was more limited in its range of lexical and syntactic options than the elaborated code: "Whereas there is flexibility in the use of alternatives in an elaborated code, in the case of a restricted code the syntactic organization is marked by rigidity" (1972, p. 474).

A second difference between restricted and elaborated code, according to Bernstein, was that the restricted code relied more on shared background knowledge than the elaborated code. For example, after seeing a movie a woman might remark to her husband, "Perfect," and thereby convey a world of information. But if the woman wanted to convey the same information to a stranger, she would have to provide a framework of background information about her tastes in movies. Bernstein also claimed that restricted code uses the context of the speaking situation, gestures, and facial expressions to express meaning. In elaborated code, on the other hand, information is conveyed primarily by verbal means.

Does Bernstein's theory imply that the elaborated code is a better tool for logical thinking than the restricted code? This is an important question, for if the answer is yes, the theory claims that, in general, working-class speakers are in some sense not as capable of such thinking as middle-class speakers. Gumperz and Hymes (1972) say that the answer is no: "It should . . . be stressed that it is orientation and use of communicative codes that is in question, not fundamental capacity for logical analysis and conceptual thought" (p. 468). Nevertheless, some of Bernstein's claims do seem to suggest that if one controls the elaborated code, one's capacity for reasoning is greater. For example, Bernstein (1972) states

> An elaborated code . . . points up the possibilities which inhere in a complex conceptual hierarchy for the organization and expression of inner experience. This is much less the case where experience is regulated by the restricted code, for this code orients its speakers to a less complex conceptual hierarchy, and so to a low order of casuality. . . . [Working class] children's low performance on verbal IQ tests, their difficulty with abstract concepts, and their failures, within the language area, their general inability to profit from school all may result from the limitations of a restricted code. (p. 480)

It appears, then, that the answer to the question, "Is elaborated code a better tool for reasoning than restricted code?" is not the unequivocal no that Gumperz and Hymes suggest. Therefore, Bernstein's theory can be characterized as a *deficit theory* that claims that one reason working-class children do not succeed in school as well as middle-class children is that they cannot reason as well.

In a strongly critical article, Labov (1972), a structural linguist, observed that in Bernstein's writing, "middle class language is seen as superior [to working-class language] in every respect" (p. 204). Labov then went on to show that a nonstandard variety can serve as a tool of logical analysis and abstract reasoning. In a number of conversations with young black boys about religious questions, Labov elicited some excellent examples of logical analysis expressed in the black vernacular—what Bernstein would call a "restricted code":

INTERVIEWER: . . . Jus' suppose there is a God, would he be black or white?

LARRY: . . . He'd be white, man.

INTERVIEWER: Why?

LARRY: Why? I'll tell you why. 'Cause the average whitcy out here got everything, you dig? And the nigger ain't got shit, y'know? Y'understan'? so—um—for—in order for *that* to happen, you know it ain't no black God that's doin' that bullshit. (p. 217)

Labov contrasts Larry's direct and effective argument with that of a speaker of what Bernstein would call elaborated code, Charles M., who is a college-educated black adult.

INTERVIEWER: Do you know of anything that someone can do, to have someone who has passed on visit him in a dream?

CHARLES M.: Well, I even heard my parents say that there is such a thing as something in dreams, some things like that, and sometimes dreams do come true. I've personally never had a dream come true. I've never dreamt that somebody was dying and they actually died, (Mhn) or that I was going to have ten dollars the next day and somehow I got ten dollars in my pocket. . . . I do feel that in certain cultures there is such a thing as witchcraft, or some sort of *science* of witchcraft; I don't think that it's just a matter of believing hard enough that there is such a thing as witchcraft. I do believe that there is such a thing that a person can put himself in a state of *mind* (Mhn), or that—er—something could be given them to intoxicate them in a certain—to a certain frame of mind—that—that could actually be considered witchcraft. (p. 218)

According to Labov (1972), "Without the extra verbiage and the OK words like *science, culture,* and *intoxicate,* Charles M. appears as something less than a first-class thinker" (p. 220). Labov observes that Charles M.'s variety of speaking is suited to academic discourse only because it identifies him as an educated person. But clear reasoning can be expressed in the nonstandard, and confused, vascillating reasoning can be expressed in the standard.

Labov demonstrated that proficiency in an academic language variety is not necessary for effective reasoning. However, it is true that casual and academic varieties are somewhat different in their vocabulary and structure, that for social reasons proficiency in the academic variety is important for school success, and that middle-class children acquire this proficiency more easily than working-class children because their spoken variety is similar to the academic variety. Thus, the question of how academic language differs from everyday language is an important one, and a definition of academic language is needed. Cummins (1979, 1980, 1984a; Cummins & Swain, 1983) proposed such a theory; however, some aspects of Cummins's theory, like Bernstein's, seemed to link proficiency in a language variety with reasoning ability, and therefore aspects of his theory have been characterized as a deficit theory. Thus, some of the issues in the 1970s debate about minority students and standard English have reemerged in a debate about ESL students and academic English.

BICS and CALP

Cummins initially developed his theory to account for data reported by Skutnabb-Kangas and Toukomaa's (1976) finding that preschool children who immigrated to Sweden did not do as well academically as older children who had had some schooling before immigrating. To explain this finding, Cummins proposed that there are at least two kinds of language proficiency: Basic Interpersonal Communication Skills (BICS), which in some ways is similar to proficiency in the restricted code, and Cognitive/Academic Language Proficiency (CALP), which in some ways is similar to proficiency in the elaborated code. Cummins also proposed the *threshold hypothesis,* which states that BICS must develop to a certain level before CALP can be added to it. This hypothesis explains Skutnabb-Kangas and Toukomaa's results in the following way. Before the older children came to Sweden, they had developed both BICS and CALP in their native languages. When these children entered Swedish schools, they were able to transfer their academic language skills to the new school setting. On the other hand, according to Cummins, the younger children had not reached the threshold level of BICS development in their native languages, and so had not developed CALP. When these students entered the Swedish schools, they did not continue to develop BICS in their first languages because they were now surrounded by Swedish, both in school and on the street. Thus, these children did not reach the minimum BICS threshold required to develop CALP in either language. Cummins called this condition *semilingualism,* a term borrowed from Skutnabb-Kangas and Toukomaa (1976). Cummins (1979) claimed that when children are semilingual, "negative cognitive and academic effects are hypothesized to result" (p. 230).

Cummins also suggested that the threshold hypothesis explains why in Canada French-speaking children do not succeed in English submersion programs as well as English-speaking children succeed in French immersion programs. The difference between these two kinds of programs is that in immersion programs students are in classes only with other nonnative speakers and receive some instruction in their native language, whereas in submersion programs nonnative speakers and native speakers are mixed, and no bilingual instruction is provided. Cummins claimed that the English-speaking Canadian children (who lived in English-speaking areas) continued to develop BICS even after they began the mostly French curriculum, because they were surrounded by English outside of school. Thus, their English BICS reached the required threshold, and they could progress beyond semilingualism and develop CALP. However, the French-speaking children (who also lived in English-speaking areas) did not continue to develop BICS in French after they entered school because they were surrounded by English at school and on the street. Therefore, they could not progress beyond semilingualism and develop CALP.

More evidence for the existence of CALP came from Genesee's (1976) study of

English-speaking Canadians in grades four, seven, and eleven in French immersion and core French programs. He found that the students' IQ test scores strongly correlated with their scores on tests of academic French language skills (reading, prescriptive grammar, vocabulary, etc.); however, in general, their IQ scores did not correlate with their scores on tests of French oral production and listening comprehension. This finding implies that tests of listening and speaking measure BICS, whereas tests of the more academic skills measure CALP.

The linking of IQ scores with CALP points to the fact that CALP is more than just the ability to use appropriate linguistic forms; it includes the ability to reason as well, and therefore is reminiscent of Bernstein's elaborated code hypothesis. In fact, Cummins (1979) stated that children must progress beyond the threshold level of BICS "in order to avoid cognitive deficits" (p. 229). This seems to mean, in everyday terms, that children with CALP are smarter than children without it. It is true that Cummins (1979) also stated, "The fact that . . . minority language children may be more dependent on the school to provide the prerequisites for the acquisition of literacy skills does not imply that these children's basic cognitive abilities are in any sense deficient" (p. 240). But this observation apparently applies to children *before* they have entered a potentially damaging submersion situation. If language-minority children are put into submersion classes, where they cannot develop their native language beyond the threshold of BICS and develop CALP, they will not just fail to acquire proficiency in a language variety, they will also suffer "cognitive deficits." Thus, the BICS-CALP hypothesis, like the restricted/elaborated code hypothesis, links language proficiency with cognitive ability. It is this linkage that Labov criticized in Bernstein's theory. Therefore, as might be expected, the BICS-CALP distinction came in for some heavy criticism.

Edelsky et al. (1983) claimed that Cummins's evidence for CALP is flawed, and that his theory has undesirable implications for understanding why ESL students succeed or fail in school. They explained the success of immersion programs and the failure of submersion programs on the basis of social and political, not cognitive, factors, noting that one difference between the two kinds of programs is that submersion programs usually involve students of low socioeconomic status, whereas immersion programs usually involve students of middle and high socioeconomic status. They suggested that the former students are not motivated to perform well on school tasks because the culture of the school is different from and dominant over their own culture. The latter students, on the other hand, are more likely to see school tasks as legitimate and worthy of trying to do well.

Edelsky et al. also objected to Cummins's use of standardized tests to measure academic success because they believed that these tests lack *content validity,* that is, they do not really measure what they claim. They pointed out, for example, that the task of selecting the correct answer from several choices on a reading test is artificial. Reading ability can be measured only by asking students to do real-world tasks such as discussing or writing about a reading passage. Thus, according to Edelsky et al., Cummins did not measure the academic ability of his subjects, but only their test-taking ability. This argument suggests an alternative explanation for Skutnabb-Kangas and Toukomaa's (1976) finding that preschool children who immigrated to Sweden did not do as well academically as older children who had had some schooling before immigrating. Edelsky et al. say that what the former students developed was not CALP but an understanding of what teachers expect of students and strategies for meeting these expectations, what Saville-Troike and Kleifgen (1986) have called "scripts for school" (see p. 50). These scripts transferred to the new school setting. As Edelsky et al. (1983), who do not have a high opinion of typical school activities, put it, "We agree with Cummins that coping with school nonsense transfers from first to second language" (p. 6).

What, then, do Edelsky et al. (1983) make of the BICS-CALP distinction? They say, "The critical distinction, then, between interpersonal and 'academic' language proficiency is nothing so grand as the presence or absence of particular cognitive/linguistic abilities. Rather, one complex feature distinguishes the two: meaningfulness/artificiality" (pp. 9–10).

As a final comment on the Cummins/Edelsky et al. debate, note that Edelsky et al.'s comments are in the tradition of criticisms of school curricula made during the 1960s and 1970s by the "romantic educators" like Jonathon Kozol (1972) and Ivan Illich (1971), who deplored the artificiality and dreariness of most classrooms. Edelsky et al. (1983) invite their readers "to sit, as a child would, through one week of elementary school in a 'regular' classroom—to experience the tedium, the senselessness, the passivity, the absence of involvement with authentic text that accompany hour after hour of dittoed worksheet assignments" (p. 16).

To summarize, Edelsky et al. objected to the BICS-CALP hypothesis because it implied that nonacademic language could not be used for abstract reasoning (a claim that Labov had disproved) and because it was based on evidence from standardized tests, which, they said, lack content validity and are biased against minorities.

Cummins's and Swain's Revised Model

In a reply to Edelsky et al., Cummins and Swain (1983) modified the BICS-CALP hypothesis in an important way. In the revised model, they claimed that BICS differed from CALP along two independent dimensions, as shown in Figure 2.3. The vertical dimension in Figure 2.3 is the degree of cognitive difficulty. According to Cummins and Swain (1983), "The upper parts of the vertical continuum consist of communicative tasks and activities in which the linguistic tools have become largely automatized (mastered) and thus require little active cognitive involvement for appropriate performance" (p. 139). The revised model accounts for Larry's ability to reason clearly in nonacademic

FIGURE 2.3 Cummins's and Swain's Revised Model.

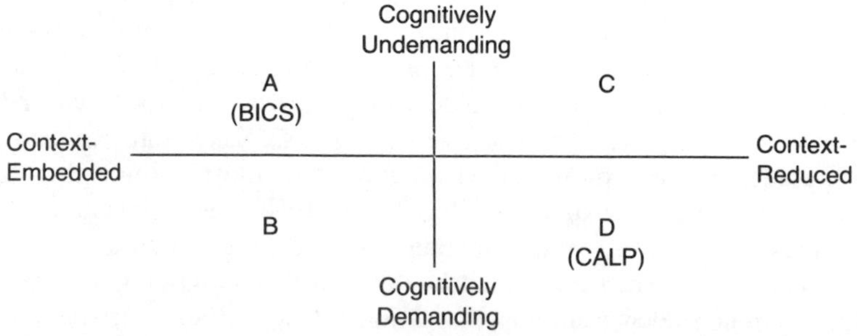

language since Larry's speech would be represented in quadrant B of Figure 2.3, as cognitively difficult language used in a contextually rich situation. Thus, the revised model does not imply that reasoning ability is associated solely with academic language.

However, the vertical axis in Figure 2.3 does appear to lump reasoning ability with general proficiency in the target language, for the lower end of this axis represents not only the ability to produce complex target language structures but also the ability to perform certain reasoning tasks, such as those described in Bloom's (1956) taxonomy of educational objectives (Cummins, 1984a). These include formulating hypotheses based on given information (as in Larry's hypothesis that God is white) and checking the consistency of hypotheses. (These "higher order" cognitive tasks are discussed in chapter 5.) The vertical axis in Figure 2.3 seems to imply that as one masters difficult linguistic structures, one also masters tasks requiring reasoning. Thus, like the elaborated code theory, the revised model still appears to include in the notion of language proficiency abilities that are more than purely linguistic.

Now consider the horizontal axis in Figure 2.3, which represents the ability to communicate with a greater or lesser amount of shared context. A communicative situation rich in shared context is a face-to-face conversation about the here and now. Such a situation is context rich in two ways. First, the meaning of the conversation may be made apparent by the objects in the immediate environment. One need not say,"Look, the cat's in the microwave!" but merely, "Look!" while pointing to the cat in the microwave. Second, in a conversation there are *feedback channels* through which the speaker may ask whether the listener agrees or understands, or the listener may signal agreement or understanding by nods, facial expression, and so on. Feedback enables the participants to make sure that the meaning is getting across. A communicative situation lacking in shared context, on the other hand, is an academic article in which all the cues to meaning must be linguistic.

An important aspect of the ability to communicate without reference to physical context is mastery of grammatical structures that make reference to and elaborate on the surrounding text, rather than the surrounding physical environment. Such structures include relative clauses, phrasal conjunctions, and nominalizations (see the discussion below). It is not entirely clear why knowledge of these structures should be placed on a separate axis from knowledge of other linguistic structures (recall that Canale and Swain [1980] expressed a similar reservation in regard to assigning cohesive syntactic devices to discourse competence rather than to linguistic competence). However, since certain structures are associated with decontextualized, academic discourse, perhaps knowledge of these structures should be given special prominence in a model of academic language proficiency.

The syntactic differences between face-to-face conversation and academic discourse were investigated by Biber (1986, 1988), who looked at a number of other genres including telephone communications, official documents, and fiction. Biber points out, first of all, that the differences in these genres do not simply correspond to differences between writing and speech. Academic language can be used in a lecture or even in a face-to-face exposition on an academic topic, as with Charles M.'s discourse on the supernatural. Nevertheless, the paradigm case of academic language is an academic book or article, and the paradigm case of informal language is a face-to-face conversation. Biber found that the linguistic differences between academic prose and face-to-face conversation tend to cluster into two groups, which he called "textual dimensions." Each end of a textual dimension is characterized by a complex of co-occurring features associated with a particular genre. Academic prose and face-to-face conversation are on opposite ends of the dimension Biber calls "informational vs. involved predication." Academic prose (along with official documents, press reportage, and biographies) is on the informational end of this dimension. The syntactic devices that occur with high frequency in academic prose include nouns, prepositional phrases, and attributive adjectives, as well as a diverse vocabulary. Such features, according to Biber, are associated with a dense infomational load. Face-to-face conversation (along with telephone communications, interviews, and personal letters), on the other hand, is at the interactive end of this dimension. The syntactic devices typical of face-to-face conversation include yes-no questions, *wh-* questions, emphatics, and present tense. According to Biber, these features are characteristic of language with a high degree of personal involvement and interaction.

The second textual dimension Biber identifies as differentiating academic prose from face-to-face conversation is "explicit vs. situation dependent reference." Situation-dependent reference is characterized by time and place adverbials, which refer directly to an external situation. Explicit (i.e., context-independent) reference is characterized by relative clauses, which serve to elaborate references internal to the text.

Biber identified five additional textual dimensions that distinguish various genres of English discourse. Academic prose and face-to-face conversation are not differentiated on some of these dimensions. For example, both these genres contain high percentages of suasive verbs *(demand, instruct)* and necessity modals *(should, must)* and therefore both occur at the same end of the dimension "overt expression of persuasion." But face-to-face conversation and academic prose are on the opposite ends of most of the dimensions Biber identifies, and so differ considerably in their characteristic syntactic devices.

Biber's research suggests that the horizontal axis of Cummins and Swains' revised model simplifies the linguistic differences between casual conversation and academic discourse by conflating several distinguishable dimensions into the single dimension of reduced versus shared context. This text has suggested that the vertical dimension similarly collapses distinguishable differences between cognitively easy and cognitively difficult language. The overall implication is that understanding academic English is a difficult task for any ESL student. I would like to suggest, however, that this difficulty can be mitigated by a factor that is neither strictly linguistic nor strictly cognitive, and therefore does not appear in Cummins's and Swain's model or in Biber's model. This factor is the amount of background knowledge the student possesses. The crucial role of background knowledge in understanding discourse is examined in chapter 3. For now, note that shared background knowledge can aid communication between the writer and reader in the same way that shared physical context aids communication between the speaker and listener. In both cases the speaker/writer can refer to information that is not present in the discourse. It is true, as Cummins and Swain observe, that in physically decontextualized situations the clues to meaning must be entirely linguistic, and Biber has shown that these clues differ considerably from those of face-to-face communication. However, such clues do not convey the meaning by themselves. Rather, they activate the appropriate background knowledge that the audience is presumed to have.[3]

Reduced context, then, depends not only on whether the communication is face to face or written, or informal or academic, but also on whether the audience possesses the background knowledge presumed by the writer/speaker. In the case studies we will see that students must develop strategies for dealing with texts for which they lack sufficient background knowledge, and that these strategies include inferencing and informed guessing. But such strategies, as well as mastery of the linguistic devices identified by Biber, are not so important for students who possess the background knowledge assumed by the text. Furthermore, no amount of proficiency in academic language can help a student who completely lacks background knowledge of a subject, as most readers can verify by browsing through a physics textbook. As will later be discussed, ESL students' difficulties with school assignments often have more to do with their lack of background knowledge about content subjects than with their lack of proficiency in the linguistic structures that characterize academic language.

To conclude, Cummins and Swain's (1983) revised model specifies three abilities that are important for academic success. The horizontal axis of Figure 2.3 represents the ability to use the target language structures that are characteristic of academic prose, and the vertical axis represents the ability to use general target language structures and to reason. However, it is not clear that these three abilities should be conflated to form the construct CALP. For one thing, the construct suggests that reasoning abilities are associated with mastery of certain linguistic structures, and for another it does not explicitly acknowledge the importance of subject-specific background knowledge. A later section proposes the construct of *academic language proficiency,* which refers only to mastery of the linguistic features of academic prose and thus to proficiency in a special variety of English. Academic competence, then, would include proficiency in this variety *in addition to* reasoning ability, background knowledge, sociolinguistic competence, and other abilities to be specified in chapter 5.

Linguistic Competence Revisited

The suggestion that the purely linguistic aspects of academic competence should be distinguished from other aspects is consistent with Cummins and Swain's (1986; Harley, Cummins, Swain, & Allen, 1990) most recent thinking. Cummins and Swain are educational psychologists, and in the tradition of that discipline they desired to "validate" three of the four proposed constructs of the communicative competence model (linguistic competence, sociolinguistic competence, and discourse competence) by designing tests that would measure each competence separately. As we saw in Spolsky's (1973) and Oller's (1979) criticisms of the separate abilities model, if scores on tests for the individual competencies correlated highly, then according to testing theory, the proposed competencies would not be distinct. Attempts to validate the model, however, have not been successful. Harley, Cummins, Swain, & Allen (1990) state, "The factor analysis . . . failed to conform to the hypothesized three-trait structure of proficiency" (p. 15).

What does emerge from Cummins's and Swain's (1986) analysis of standardized tests administered to French, Japanese, and Portuguese students living in Canada is that there is "a distinction between grammatical competence on the one hand, and sociolinguistic and discourse competence on the other" (p. 209). This result brings to mind Saussure's (1966) and Chomsky's (1965) claims that linguistic competence is a unique kind of knowledge that is learned differently from other kinds of knowledge, and Cook's

(1988) and others, claim that UG is operative in L2 acquisition. Cummins and Swain (1986) conclude, "Grammatical competence (and aspects of sociolinguistic and discourse competence that depend on grammatical knowledge) is acquired in different ways and is determined by different factors than is the case with most aspects of discourse and socio-linguistic competence" (p. 209).

Cummins and Swain propose a model of language proficiency in which grammatical skills are developed through exposure to and interaction in the target language, but discourse competence (which depends on knowledge of appropriateness conditions for speech acts, background knowledge, and other academic abilities) is developed through schooling. Differentiating purely linguistic abilities from other academic abilities helps to explain Cummins and Swain's (1986) finding that immigrant ESL students develop fluent oral English much faster than native English-speaking (NES) students in French immersion programs develop fluent oral French, as well as Collier's (1987) finding that ESL students submerged in U.S. public schools develop linguistic competence before academic competence. In both cases, the ESL students have many opportunities to interact in the target language outside of school, but they do not learn how to do academic tasks well because they are in a submersion situation. The NES students studying French, on the other hand, do not have opportunities to interact in French outside of school, but their schooling is much more effective because it includes some native language instruction and is geared to their abilities and not to those of native French speakers.

SPOLSKY'S PREFERENCE MODEL OF LANGUAGE PROFICIENCY

We conclude the discussion of language proficiency by reviewing a recent model proposed by Bernard Spolsky (1989). The model is perhaps the most ambitious yet proposed, and it provides a new and helpful way of thinking about proficiency in a second language.

According to Spolsky (1989), if you are asked whether you know a language, your answer may take one of three possible forms:

a. I only know a few words.
b. I can read professional material in it.
c. Not as well as my wife does. (p. 59)

Each of these answers corresponds to a different way of thinking about language proficiency, as embodied in the theories discussed in this chapter. The first reply refers to knowledge of language structure, including phonology, syntax, and lexicon (roughly, linguistic competence). The second reply refers to the functional ability to use the language for particular purposes, and in appropriate and effective ways (roughly, sociolinguistic and discourse competence). The third reply refers to an overall or general ability in the language (similar in some ways to Oller's [1983] unified competence).

Spolsky observes that it is difficult to reconcile the three ways of looking at proficiency into a single, comprehensive theory, yet each notion must be accounted for. The problem is that individual speakers may have very different capabilities in the three areas.

One person may have an extensive knowledge of linguistic structure yet be unable to communicate effectively with a professional colleague. Another may communicate effectively but with little structural accuracy. A third person, like Saville-Troike's (1984) subjects, may be able to speak fluently but be unable to use the language effectively for academic purposes. How can individuals with widely divergent abilities and skills all be said to be proficient in a language?

Spolsky proposes that the concept of language proficiency can be understood by using a *preference model,* as proposed in the semantic theory of Jackendoff (1983). He notes that the term *language proficiency* is like many other English words having a variety of meanings, some of which are only loosely related to each other. One example is *bird,* which can refer to creatures as diverse as an eagle and an ostrich. Another example, is *father,* which can refer to a genetic father, to an adoptive father, or even to someone who helped to create a nonhuman entity, as in "founding father." Jackendoff's theory explains how words, and the concepts they represent, can have multiple, related meanings.

The preference model of word meanings can best be explained by contrasting it to earlier semantic theories, for example, that of Katz and Postal (1964), which is associated with Chomsky's (1965) standard theory of generative grammar. Katz and Postal proposed that the basic meaning of a word can be broken down into a set of necessary and sufficient semantic/conceptual features. For example, the word *bachelor* contains the features "unmarried," "male," and "adult." These three features suffice to distinguish *bachelor* from all other words, and they show its relationship to similar words within the same semantic field. Thus, if the feature "male" is changed to "female," the word *spinster* is specified. Katz and Postal note that both *bachelor* and *spinster* have a number of secondary features (perhaps "irresponsible" and "lonely," respectively), but these features are not defining features of the words; that is, they are not necessary for picking out the exact concept to which each word refers. Katz and Postal's theory of meaning is a *categorical* theory: the meaning of each word (and concept) is discrete, and there is no possibility for fuzziness or gray areas of meaning.

Categorical semantic theories were challenged by Wittgenstein (1953), who pointed out that some words have a set of related meanings that are so diverse that there is no central core of meaning that can be specified by a set of necessary and sufficient features. Wittgenstein did not have in mind words like *bank* (side of a river) and *bank* (depository for money), since these are different words that happen to sound the same (homonyms). Rather, Wittgenstein referred to words like *father* and *game* (his famous example). The word *game* can refer to activities that may have very little in common, such as professional hockey and bouncing a ball against a wall. Wittgenstein proposed that although such activities may have no features in common, they do have different features of a prototypical game. Thus, similarity between the two kinds of games is like a family resemblance in which different offspring may have no features in common but may all have different features of their mother.

The theory that word meanings can be understood as a set of related examplars that share some features of a prototype has been developed by a number of scholars, including Labov (1972), Rosch (1973), Rosch & Mervis (1975), and Lakoff (1987). Rosch (1973) proposed, for example, that our concept of "bird" is based on a mental prototype of a creature that, among other things, lays eggs, flies, and eats worms. Notice that laying eggs is a necessary (but not a sufficient) condition for being a bird. Flying and eating worms are not necessary but rather are typical features of birds. Robins, which possess both the necessary and the typical features, are central members of the conceptual category "bird," but penguins and ostriches, which do not eat worms or fly, are more peripheral members. Labov (1973) made the additional point that neither necessary nor typical features of a conceptual category need be completely present or absent, but can be present to varying degrees and are thus *graded features*. For example, a typical cup is about as tall as it is wide, whereas a typical bowl is about half as tall as it is wide, but these ratios are not absolute, and there is a fuzzy, gray area in which vessels with intermediate ratios are not clearly cups or bowls.

Spolsky (1989) suggests that the concept of language proficiency is like the concept of "game" or "bird" because it has necessary and typical features, both of which may be present in particular individuals to a greater or lesser extent. Thus, different individuals can be said to be proficient in a language even though they exhibit a wide variety of abilities. Perhaps the prototypical learner in an academic setting can speak, read, write, and comprehend the second language with some facility, although not as well as a native speaker. However, there are also atypical learners (the penguins and ostriches among L2 learners), who may be able to comprehend but not speak the language, or speak grammatically but not always appropriately, or use the language effectively for interpersonal communication but not for academic tasks. According to Spolsky's model, all of these learners can be said to be proficient.

Spolsky characterizes L2 proficiency as a set of nineteen necessary and typical features (both of which can be graded). These features (which Spolsky calls "conditions") can be roughly divided into three groups (see Appendix). The first group describes the nature of the learner's interlanguage, specifying that it is systematic and that it must be based on some specific variety of native speaker language (New York City English, British Received Pronunciation, academic English, etc.). The second group of features describes the psycholinguistic nature of the learner's knowledge, which includes knowledge of discrete structural items such as words, phonemes, and syntactic patterns. Typically, this knowledge is mostly implicit (subconscious) but it can be to some extent explicit (accessible to introspection) as well, and it includes both unanalyzed knowledge (memorized chunks) and analyzed knowledge (productive patterns). The third group of features involves the learner's ability to use the language in particular ways, of which there are three general types:

1. The varying ability to use the four language modalities (listening, speaking, reading, and writing
2. The varying ability to use the language accurately and fluently
3. The varying ability to use the language effectively and appropriately.

The features of the preference model can be present in different combinations and different strengths in individual learners, as the features of *bird* can be present in different combinations and different strengths in individual species. In the previous discussion, we saw that different researchers have emphasized different features in their definitions of language proficiency, thus describing different "species" of learners. The descriptivist and audio-lingual school emphasized grammatical accuracy. The communicative competence school emphasized functional effectiveness in interpersonal communication. The academic language school emphasized functional effectiveness in academic settings, and some models within this school claimed that proficiency included aspects other than those specified in Spolsky's model, such as reasoning ability.

Spolsky's preference model is like a rough map of the landscape of L2 knowledge and skills. It lays out the basic features of this territory and suggests what researchers exploring the territory may expect to find. The main claim of the model is that different learners will have different features of L2 proficiency at different strengths. An implication of this claim is that certain "profiles" of proficiency will be best suited for particular goals. For example, students in a vocational English program for restaurant workers would ideally acquire the features of formal speech in the local dialect (specific variety feature). They would need both receptive and productive skills, but primarily in oral modalities (productive-receptive skills feature). They could employ certain unanalyzed chunks of the target language, such as politeness formulas (unanalyzed knowledge feature). They would need a good control of certain language functions like greeting, requesting, clarifying, and thanking (integrated function feature). These students would not need explicit knowledge of English (explicit knowledge feature), high overall proficiency (overall proficiency feature), or academic skills (academic skills feature). Chapter 5 considers a proficiency profile compatible with academic competence.

General Proficiency

Despite the fall of the unified competence theory, Spolsky (1989) maintains that the notion of a general or overall language proficiency is valid and useful. The first argument for this claim is philosophical: it is not contradictory to look at language proficiency as a holistic or gestalt ability made up of a number of identifiable discrete abilities, such as the ability to produce particular grammatical patterns (including the cohesive discourse devices), and the ability to understand and appropriately produce particular speech acts. In this sense general language proficiency is like the concept of "bird," which can be broken down into necessary and typical features that work together in a particular way to form a gestalt that is more than the sum of its parts. As Oller (1983) puts it, "The idea that global and particulate models were incompatible must have been quite wrong. . . . Both views are needed and . . . can complement . . . rather than contradict one another" (p. 36).

The second argument for general proficiency is that language is redundant. The implication of redundancy is that to an extent knowledge of a particular area (say vocabulary) can make up for a lack of knowledge in another area, and therefore the sum total of knowledge makes up an overall ability.

The third argument is that general proficiency can be operationalized (measured) by means of an integrative test such as the cloze test, in which subjects are asked to supply words or morphemes that have been randomly deleted from a reading passage. The equivalent test for listening comprehension is to ask questions about a passage that has been masked by a certain amount of white noise. It should be noted, however, that traditionally the content of the reading and listening comprehension passages on these kinds of tests is very general, like the content of similar passages on discrete point tests. Both kinds of tests are geared for students who have the general academic background assumed in an American public school curriculum, but not knowledge of the specialized fields. Thus, like standardized proficiency tests, cloze tests, as commonly used, should not be expected to predict the success of students in academic programs. It follows that students who have a high level of general proficiency (as determined by these tests) may have difficulty in such programs. In sum, the preference model of language proficiency allows for very different proficiency profiles for different learners. The concept of a general or overall proficiency, however, provides a rough way of comparing such individuals.

Academic Language Skills

Spolsky's model of L2 proficiency is the only one we have encountered that specifies that proficiency is necessarily gained in one or more particular language varieties, such as New York City English or Madrid Spanish. This is not to say that L2 learners will sound exactly like New Yorkers or Madrileños. But a learner's variety can be expected to have some features of the local variety to which the learner has been exposed, such as the New Yorker's [r] deletion and the Madrileño's voiceless interdental fricative. Spolsky (1989) claims that because many learners have studied the second language in an academic setting, knowledge of the features of academic language is a typical, graded feature of L2 proficiency. This claim is contained in the academic skills feature of the preference model, which states, "Learning of a second language may be associated to varying degrees with the development of academic language skills" (p. 44). Apparently, the academic skills feature does not in itself include literacy skills, because these are part of the productive/receptive skills feature and the dual knowledge feature. Rather, Spolsky uses the term *skills* to mean "knowledge," as *library skills* means "knowledge of how to use the library." However, it would be virtually impossible for a student to learn the characteristic features of academic language without mastering literacy skills. Nor does the academic skills feature imply superior reasoning ability. Thus, the feature seems to be similar to cognitive/academic language proficiency without the cognitive component (hence, simply academic language proficiency). Therefore, Spolsky's view of academic language appears to be compatible with the structuralist tradition, which views linguistic abilities as qualitatively different from other cognitive abilities. Chapter 5 argues that proficiency in this variety of language is one factor that, along with other nonlinguistic factors, makes up academic competence.

SUMMARY

During the twentieth century, the structuralist paradigm has dominated theories of language and language proficiency. Within the descriptivist/behaviorist school, language proficiency was viewed as the mastery of a large number of habits that corresponded to phonological and syntactic patterns and general vocabulary. Listening, speaking, reading, and writing were considered separate skills. This view favored the teaching and testing of small pieces of language.

Within the generative school, language proficiency was viewed as the knowledge of phonological and syntactic patterns and vocabulary, that is, linguistic competence. Chomsky (1965) claimed that children acquire competence in their native language because of a species-specific Language Acquisition Device, and Diller (1978) and Krashen (1981) extended these claims to L2 acquisition. These scholars believed that this theory implied that teaching should be meaningful and holistic. Recently, the contents of the LAD, namely UG, have been described; however, the pedagogical implications of UG are not yet clear. In both the descriptivist and the generative schools, mastery of linguistic structures was considered the most important factor in language proficiency.

Oller's (1976) unified competence theory, a reaction to structuralist views, de-emphasized knowledge of linguistic structure and emphasized background knowledge and reasoning ability, all of which were said to make up a gestalt language ability very similar to general intelligence.

The communicative competence school extended the structuralist paradigm. Hymes (1971) pointed out that knowing a language required knowing not only linguistic structures but also how to use these structures appropriately. Canale and Swain's (1980) model of communicative competence included Chomsky's linguistic competence but added sociolinguistic competence, strategic competence, and discourse competence. In practice, the tests and instructional methods associated with this school tended to emphasize socio-linguistic competence and de-emphasize linguistic competence.

Bernstein (1964) broke with the structuralist tradition, claiming that the linguistic structures associated with "elaborated code" are inherently more suited for cognitively demanding discourse, thus violating the structuralist axiom that no mature language variety is inherently superior to another. This implication was contained in Cummins's (1979) BICS-CALP model as well. Cummins and Swain's (1983) revised model attempted to delineate the various components of CALP.

Spolsky's preference model emphasizes that there are various kinds, not just degrees, of language proficiency. His model reasserts the structuralist position that knowledge of linguistic structures, general vocabulary, and language functions are features of proficiency, but reasoning ability and background knowledge of particular subjects are not.

NOTES

1. According to Green (1989), "Grice . . . hinted that he takes [the Cooperative Principle] to represent values universally assumed in human society. Grice does not actually claim universality for the Cooperative Principle" (p. 95).
2. In Canale and Swain (1980), discourse competence is considered a component of sociolinguistic competence. In Canale (1983) discourse competence is given equal status with the other three competencies.
3. In fairness, it should be noted that Cummins has strongly emphasized the importance of background knowledge to L2 academic competence. The point here is that background knowledge is not part of the way CALP is represented in the revised model. Cummins (1984a, 1989) has included background knowledge in his "iceberg" model of dual language proficiency. What is needed is an articulation of the two models.

CHAPTER 3
Theories of Understanding

SCHEMA THEORY

In chapter 2, I observed that background knowledge of content material is an essential element of academic competence and suggested that one reason that ESL students do not perform well on the content sections of standardized achievement tests, but do perform well on the English language sections of these tests, is that they lack the background knowledge that the tests assume. The crucial role of background knowledge in understanding a language, first or second, is emphasized in *schema theory*.

A schema is any mental representation, typically of an object or an event, that specifies general properties and shows how these properties are related to each other. Thus, a schema is an abstraction that leaves out the details of an instance. The schema for "bird" contains the information that a bird (necessarily) lays eggs and (typically) flies, but leaves out specific details like the color of the bird (Rosch & Mervis, 1975). A schema for an event is called a *script* or *frame*. This is a generalized scenario of a sequence of actions that fits a common situation, like going to the dentist or asking a question in class. Rummelhart (1980) argues that schemas are the basis for all understanding. He states, "schemata are employed in the process of interpreting sensory data (both linguistic and nonlinguistic), in retrieving information from memory, in organizing actions, in determining goals, . . . and generally in guiding the flow of processing in the system" (pp. 33–34).

Schema theory claims that understanding discourse involves more than just extracting information from a text. Much of the necessary information is supplied by the audience in the form of schematic background knowledge. The task of the speaker/writer is to prompt the audience to activate the appropriate schemas and to provide appropriate new information that can be integrated into the existing schemas.

The role of schemas in understanding a text can be seen by considering how a computer could answer questions about a simple story such as in (1).

1. John went into the restaurant and ordered a hamburger. He paid the check and left.

It would be comparatively easy to program a computer to answer the question, "Who went into the restaurant?" The program would have to have information about English grammar, such as Rule 1 in Figure 2.2, which states S→NP VP. The program would also have a rule that states that the first NP in S is normally the subject of the sentence. Then, the computer could search for the NP that is the subject of the VP "went into the restaurant" and come up with the answer, "John." This kind of "bottom-up" processing is possible because all of the information needed to answer the question is either in the grammatical rules of English or in the text of the original statement.

However, what if the computer were asked, "Did John eat a hamburger?" Because this information is not explicitly stated in the text, the computer could not find the answer in the same way that it found the answer to "Who went into the restaurant?" To find out whether John ate the hamburger, the computer would have to engage in "top-down" processing, which would involve activating a restaurant schema containing the information that customers normally eat the food they order. The computer would assume that this information, and all the other information in the schema, applied to the story by default unless the text stated otherwise.

Schemas, then, are units of organized information. The schema for restaurants contains information about waiters, cooks, and customers and their relationships to each other. Another type of schema contains linguistic information. The phrase structure rules in Figure 2.2 might be considered a schema for a sentence.[1] Like the restaurant schema, these rules specify what the schema describes (a declarative English sentence), the "participants" in the schema (the grammatical categories NP, VP, etc.), and the relationship among these participants (NP precedes VP, etc.).

Background Knowledge

Now consider the role of schematic background knowledge in accomplishing academic tasks. This aspect of schema theory has been most developed in regard to reading, although schemas fulfill the same function in listening comprehension. Before Goodman (1967), reading was thought to be entirely a bottom-up process in which the reader gathered information from the page, identifying letters and combining them to form words, which were combined to form sentences, and so on.

In place of this model, Goodman offered a top-down model of reading (although he did not use this term). This text has just described top-down processing as a complement to bottom-up processing, which is needed to infer information not explicitly stated in the text. Goodman (1967) pointed out that top-down processing can also eliminate the need for a considerable amount of bottom-up processing, and thus make the reading process more efficient. He described the process of normal fluent reading as follows:

> Reading is a selective process. It involves partial use of available minimal language cues selected from perceptual input on the basis of the reader's expectation. As this partial information is processed, tentative decisions are made, to be confirmed, rejected or refined as reading progresses. More simply stated, reading is a psycholinguistic guessing

game. It involves an interaction between thought and language. Efficient reading does not result from precise perception and identification of all elements, but from skill in selecting the fewest, most productive cues necessary to produce guesses which are right the first time. (p. 108)

In this model, the reader's guesses are formed largely on the basis of background knowledge about the subject of the text. The writer's job is to assess how much background knowledge the intended audience has about a particular subject and to provide appropriate new information. Obviously, American students have much more background knowledge than ESL students do about many subjects taught in U.S. schools.

The Role of Background Knowledge in Understanding Academic Material

Many studies have demonstrated the importance of background knowledge for understanding academic material. In a classic experiment, Bartlett (1932) asked English subjects to read a myth of the Indians of the West Coast of Canada, which is reproduced in its entirety below.

The War of the Ghosts

One night two young men from Egulac went down to the river to hunt seals and while they were there it became foggy and calm. Then they heard war-cries, and they thought: "Maybe this is a war-party." They escaped to the shore, and hid behind a log. Now canoes came up, and they heard the noise of paddles, and saw one canoe coming up to them. There were five men in the canoe, and they said:

"What do you think? We wish to take you along. We are going up the river to make war on the people."

One of the young men said, "I have no arrows."

"Arrows are in the canoe," they said.

"I will not go along. I might be killed. My relatives do not know where I have gone. But you," he said, turning to the other, "may go with them."

So one of the young men went, but the other returned home.

And the warriors went on up the river to a town on the other side of Kalama. The people came down to the water, and they began to fight, and many were killed. But presently the young man heard one of the warriors say:

"Quick, let us go home: that Indian has been hit."

Now he thought: "Oh, they are ghosts."

He did not feel sick, but they said he had been shot.

So the canoes went back to Egulac, and the young man went ashore to his house, and made a fire. And he told everybody and said: "Behold I accompanied the ghosts, and we went to fight. Many of our fellows were killed, and many of those who attacked us were killed. They said I was hit, and I did not feel sick."

He told it all, and then he became quiet. When the sun rose he fell down. Something black came out of his mouth. His face became contorted. The people jumped up and cried.

He was dead.

Although Western readers find this story bizarre, it is perfectly reasonable to the people from whose culture it is taken, since it fits in well with their schemas about how the world works. It is interesting that when Western subjects are asked to recall the story, they change it in important ways so that it fits their own schemas for a proper story. One English subject retold the story, twenty hours after hearing it, as follows:

The War of the Ghosts

Two men from Egulac went fishing. While thus occupied by the river they heard a noise in the distance.

"It sounds like a cry," said one, and presently there appeared some in canoes who invited them to join the party on their adventure. One of the young men refused to go, on the ground of family ties, but the other offered to go.

"But there are no arrows," he said.

"The arrows are in the boat," was the reply.

He thereupon took his place, while his friend returned home. The party paddled up the river to Kalama, and began to land on the banks of the river. The enemy came rushing upon them, and some sharp fighting ensued. Presently someone was injured, and the cry was raised that the enemy were ghosts.

The party returned down the stream, and the young man arrived home feeling none the worse for his experience. The next morning at dawn he endeavored to recount his adventures. While he was talking something black issued from his mouth. Suddenly he uttered a cry and fell down. His friends gathered round him.

But he was dead.

The writer of this summary has altered the story to fit an English speaker's schemas for how stories and the world in general work. For one thing, he has changed the role of the ghosts so that they are the enemies of the war party. For another, he has said that when the young man returned home, he was none the worse for his experience. But as we will see, he was half dead. In addition, the writer has left out the puzzling parts of the story, such as the connections between the Indian's injury and the termination of the battle.

In order to see how the story would be understood by someone having the appropriate background knowledge, I asked an anthropologist who was familiar with the culture of the Indians of the Northwest, but who had not heard this particular story, to read and react to the text. The anthropologist was not at all puzzled by the story and explained that it is about the death of a young man. The audience for whom the story is intended does not believe that death is a sudden, or even completely physical, event. Rather, the process of dying is mostly spiritual and does not affect the body until the final stage. The two young men at the river encountered death in the form of ghosts. Naturally they attempted to hide. One man was able to escape deadly contact with the ghosts, but his companion was not, and when he got into the canoe, the process of his dying began. The journey with the ghosts was a spiritual journey, and it resulted in his being mortally wounded in a spiritual sense, which did not cause physical pain. The battle ended, as is customary, when one of the combatants was injured, so the war party retreated. The young man then played out the remaining part of his life. He returned to his village and told his story, after which his body fell—the final event in the process of dying.

Background Knowledge and Language Proficiency

The comparison between Bartlett's subject's understanding of the story and the anthropologist's understanding points out the enormous difference that background knowledge can make in comprehending a text, and it raises an intriguing question. What is the relationship between general language proficiency (in Spolsky's [1989] sense) and background knowledge of a particular topic? Which ESL student can better understand a lecture on generative grammar, one with low general proficiency who knows something about Chomsky's theory, or one with high general proficiency who knows nothing about the theory?

First, let us consider the case of high-proficiency readers. Steffensen, Joag-Dev, and Anderson (1979) studied the effect of schemas on comprehension for students at a high proficiency level. Steffensen, Joag-Dev, and Anderson asked subjects from India and from the United States to read a report about an Indian wedding and an American wedding. They found, as expected, that the subjects spent less time reading the report about the kind of wedding they were most familiar with and that they recalled more material about that kind of wedding. They also found, as Bartlett had, that the subjects' recall of the passage produced distortions and elaborations that arose from their schemas for weddings. For example, the Indian passage stated that the bride's family gave gifts to the groom's family, a custom in India but not in America. One American subject changed "gifts to be given to the in-laws" to "an exchange of gifts." Another American subject incorrectly recalled that these gifts were "favors," distributed to all the guests.

Beyond the factual level, important differences emerged in the interpretation of the stories. The American story contained the information that the bride would be wearing her mother's wedding dress, an old American tradition. An Indian reader interpreted this to mean that the bride could not afford a modern dress. The subjects were also asked to rank the importance of different aspects of the stories. On this task the Americans rated information about the ritual and ceremony as important, whereas the Indians rated information about the social status and finances of the parties as important. Both groups of subjects better remembered details that they thought were important. Steffensen, Joag-Dev, and Anderson concluded that even when literal comprehension of a text is not a problem, the understanding of the text can vary according to a student's background schemas.

Steffensen, Joag-Dev, and Anderson's study illustrates the same general point as Bartlett's experiment: background knowledge is necessary for understanding discourse. However, there is an important difference between Bartlett's and Steffensen, Joag-Dev, and Anderson's results. Bartlett's subjects were puzzled by the story and indicated that they did not understand it well, but Steffensen, Joag-Dev, and Anderson's subjects did not realize that they had not understood some aspects of the story. This illustrates how culturally based schemas, as well as a lack of schemas, can interfere with full understanding of a text. We now consider the use of schemas by less proficient ESL students. After Goodman's (1967) theory of reading became well known, reading specialists tended to emphasize the top-down aspects of the reading process. According to Carrell (1988), "The introduction of a top-down processing perspective into second language reading had a profound impact on the field. . . . There has been a tendency to view . . . top-down processing perspective as a *substitute* for the bottom-up, decoding view of reading" (p. 4).

The importance of bottom-up processing, which depends to a large extent on general language proficiency, has lately been emphasized in the *interactive* model of reading (Carrell, Devine, & Eskey, 1988). In this model, readers, especially second language (L2) readers, are said to rely equally on schema activation and decoding. Within this framework, Clarke (1980) proposes the *short-circuit hypothesis,* which is that if general language proficiency is below a certain level, the interactive process breaks down and even students who have the appropriate background schemas, and who have mastered the interactive process of reading in their first language, revert to bottom-up decoding.

To test the short-circuit hypothesis, Clarke (1980) gave twenty-one native Spanish speakers a cloze test in Spanish and English. These subjects had a low level of general English proficiency, as determined by the *Michigan Test of English Language Proficiency*. On the basis of their Spanish cloze test scores, Clarke divided the subjects into good first-language (L1) readers and poor L1 readers. He then analyzed the reading strategies in Spanish of both groups. He found that 41 percent of the miscues made by the good L1 readers were semantically acceptable; in other words, even though these subjects failed to guess the exact word that had been deleted from the passage, they did guess a word that made sense in the context. On the other hand, only 25 percent of the miscues of the poor readers were semantically acceptable. Clarke interpreted this result to mean that the good readers were relying mainly on semantic cues, and therefore were using top-down processing, whereas the poor readers were relying mainly on syntactic cues, and therefore were using bottom-up processing.

Clarke then gave the subjects a cloze test in English to see whether the two groups of readers used the same strategies in their second language as they did in their first. He found that both groups provided fewer semantically acceptable miscues. The poor L1 readers produced 18 percent semantically acceptable miscues, a decrease of only 7 percent. However, the good L1 readers produced 22 percent semantically acceptable errors, a much larger decrease of 19 percent. Clarke says that these results show that the good L1 readers were not able to transfer their top-down strategy to L2 reading, and that they reverted to a bottom-up strategy. Their low general proficiency "short-circuited" the interactive reading process. He concludes:

> Perhaps there are not "good readers" and "poor readers" but merely good and poor reading behaviors which characterize most readers at different times; when one is confronted with difficult reading (whether because of complex language or unfamiliar content) one is likely to revert to poor reading behaviors. (p. 207)

Clarke suggests that the good readers abandoned the top-down strategy when confronted with difficult material because they were unwilling to tolerate inexactness and to take chances and make mistakes. Eskey (1986) describes this common L2 reading behavior as follows:

> [The second language] reader is typically an insecure reader who all too frequently believes that to comprehend a text, he must first comprehend every word in the text. He may therefore deliberately read very slowly . . . with frequent trips to the dictionary . . . a strategy which . . . practically precludes successful reading comprehension and practically insures a high degree of frustration. (p. 19)

In chapter 4, we will see that this description fits many of the subjects of the case studies. On the other hand, there were some subjects, such as George, described in case study 5, who were so overwhelmed by the amount and difficulty of their reading assignments that they resorted to very inaccurate top-down processing as the only way they could hope to finish their assignments.

Clarke's quotation makes the important point that the short circuit in the reading process can be caused not only by a lack of general proficiency but also by a lack of suffi-cient background knowledge. Therefore, as Grabe (1988) points out, successful reading seems to require that the student possess a critical mass of background knowledge and decoding skills. I would add that the L2 reader should also be able to vary reading strate-gies, relying more on top-down processing when relevant background knowledge is available and switching to more bottom-up processing when such knowledge is lacking. This point is pursued in chapter 5.

Scripts for School

Just as a restaurant script enables us to understand the story in (1), scripts for school enable ESL students to understand what goes on in a classroom even though they may have low general English proficiency. Saville-Troike and Kleifgen (1986) studied elemen-tary ESL classes containing students from eight different language backgrounds, all of whom spoke little English. They found that these students understood what was expected of them in the classroom and that they were able to follow the lessons to a large extent. These researchers attribute this high degree of understanding to the fact that the students were able to use top-down processing based on the scripts for school they had learned in their native countries.

One useful script was the initiation-response-feedback script for teacher talk in which the teacher asks a question or makes an observation that invites comment, the student responds, and then the teacher evaluates or expands on the response. This script was adhered to by all of the students except for kindergarten children who had no prior school experience. Saville-Troike and Kleifgen (1986) also found that many of the students had learned scripts for specific content material. One child from Iraq was able to recognize a Native American story about Coyote and the Rabbit as a typical trickster tale and was able to predict correctly that "The rabbits will try to play another trick on him and he will fail. Coyote will lose in the end" (p. 214).

Scripts for school are, of course, culturally based, and some of the differences between the scripts that the students had learned in their native countries and the American scripts caused misunderstanding, especially in the area of classroom discipline. Based on the practice in their native countries, the children usually thought that students should remain quietly in their seats listening to the teacher for most of the school day. When they found that in the United States students can move around the room and talk to other students, they mistakenly assumed that they were allowed to do anything they wanted. When their behavior got out of hand and they were sent to the principal's office, the students and their parents often felt that this punishment was too severe, since they expected teachers to handle their own discipline problems except in extreme cases. Other difficulties attributable to differing scripts for school included appropriate behavior for girls (who should be respectful toward boys) and appropriate subjects for study (which should include themes of moral values, filial piety, and loyalty to the nation).

The ESL students whom Saville-Troike and Kleifgen studied had a good deal of success in their ESL and content classes because they had considerable background knowledge about what is supposed to go on there. However, it should be kept in mind that in elementary school, especially in the lower grades, full understanding of content mate-rial is often not required to get along in the class. Chapter 4 discusses ESL students at higher levels, whose success depends to a great extent on a detailed and cumulative under-standing of new content material. These students often use strategies for doing academic tasks such as taking notes, participating in discussions, writing papers, and so on that are based on the scripts for school they learned in their native countries, but these scripts are often not effective for doing tasks in a second language and in a different academic culture.

BEYOND SCHEMAS—THE PHILOSOPHICAL BASIS OF UNDERSTANDING

The principal claim of schema theory is that we construct mental representations that allow us to understand what goes on around us. But schema theorists have not often addressed the question: mental representations of what? This question quickly leads to some fundamental philosophical issues concerning the nature of human understanding. A discussion of these issues is important for second language scholarship because it can clarify how the discipline fits into the larger framework of psychological and philosoph-ical inquiry. The ESL field needs a philosophical underpinning that is consistent with what we know about how students acquire language, understand academic material, and accommodate to a new culture. Another reason that L2 scholars should be interested in philosophical issues is that insights from language teaching can shed light on these issues. Language teachers deal with questions of meaning and understanding in a practical way every day, and in the history of science it has often been the case that the working knowl-edge of practitioners has contributed to theory. For example, Euclid's first four axioms (which might be regarded as the basis of mathematics) were not original with Euclid, but were a formalization of practical "rules of thumb" devised by Egyptian astronomers to predict the rise and fall of the Nile (Guba & Lincoln, 1989). We begin by considering a widely held philosophy of science: objectivism. This discussion will range far from the language classroom, but its relevance will be made clear in chapter 5.

Objectivism

In the first section of this chapter, it was stated that, among other things, schemas accu-rately represent objects in the physical world. This position, which is probably tacitly accepted by most reading scholars and psychologists, is based on the philosophy of *objec-tivism,* the dominant philosophy of science in the West for the last 350 years. One reason for its popularity is that objectivism provides a common sense answer to two fundamental questions regarding human understanding, the ontological question and the epistemolog-ical question. The ontological question asks, "What is the nature of reality?" and the epistemological question asks, "How do we know what we know?" The objectivist's answer to the ontological question is that the natural world consists of objects that have certain properties, such as weight and density, and that exist in certain relationships to each other, for example, "The rock is in the river" and "The bird is flying over the tree".[2] The objectivist's answer to the epistemological question is that the mind constructs an accurate model of reality that reflects the objects, properties, and relationships that exist independently in the world. However, according to objectivism, it is important not to confuse external reality with mental models of reality. Therefore, objectivism endorses the "independence assumption," which Lakoff (1987) states as follows: "No true fact can depend on people's believing it, on their knowledge of it, on their conceptualization of it, or on any other aspect of human cognition" (p. 164). Thus, objectivism posits a "God's eye" view of the universe, independent of human perception, in which all objects, properties and relationships are correctly characterized. In other words, to the question, "If a tree falls in the forest and no one hears it, does it make a sound?" the objectivist answers yes.

The objectivist epistemology is incorporated into model-theoretic semantics, which is the semantic theory assumed by generative linguistics, including Katz and Postal's (1964) semantic component for Chomsky's (1965) standard theory, and the more recent theory of categorical grammar (Oehrle, Bach, & Wheeler, 1988). Some psychological theories are also based on model-theoretic semantics, for example, those of Osherson and Smith (1981) and Smith and Medin (1981). These theories claim that correct human understanding depends on our constructing schemas that accurately reflect the physical world.

Social Constructionism

Objectivism has been challenged by the philosophy of social constructionism (Kuhn, 1970, 1977; Rorty, 1979, 1989). One disagreement involves the objectivists' dichotomy between two kinds of "facts," which Lakoff (1987) calls "brute facts" and "institutional facts" (p. 170). Brute facts involve the objects, properties, and relationships in the physical world and, according to objectivism, are true regardless of any human institution. Such facts include the height of Mount Everest and the atomic weight of gold. Objectivists believe that scientific theories are grounded in brute facts and, therefore, that these theories can be objectively evaluated. Theories that correspond to and predict the actual brute facts of nature are true; other theories are false.

Institutional facts, on the other hand, are set up by human beings. They include customs, like leaving a tip in a restaurant, or agreed upon states of affairs, like the fact that George Bush is president of the United States. Sampson (1980) provides the following illustration of the compelling nature of institutional facts. A professor is about to leave home to deliver a lecture, but he discovers that he has no pants to wear—they are all at the cleaners. The only thing he can do is to call the university and cancel the lecture. It will not occur to the professor that a practical alternative would be to wear one of his wife's dresses. The institutional fact that in our society men should not wear women's clothing is so powerful that to ignore it would cause considerable damage to the professor's reputation.

Thus, institutional facts, which include customs, values, traditions, and laws, make up a large part of day-to-day reality, and since these facts differ from society to society, social reality differs as well. Social constructionists such as Kuhn and Rorty have emphasized that cultural relativism is not just a matter of differences in comparatively small matters, such as what kind of clothing to wear. Rather, different schemas regarding the nature of authority, causality, history, family structure, ethics, and so on add up to very different internal models of the world, so that people in different societies understand and evaluate events in very different ways.

Language teachers are in a strong position to appreciate the social constructionists' claim that models of the world can vary greatly in different societies. When I was an ESL teacher in Ethiopia, I observed a profound difference between my American colleagues' and my world view and that of our traditional Ethiopian students, which became apparent when the first astronauts landed on the moon in 1969. The Americans were excited about this event and a bit self-satisfied. Surely the moon landing, which was reported in the Amharic-language newspapers and radio, would impress our students. However, many of the students were not impressed and wondered what all the excitement was about since within their model of the world, Ethiopian angels had regularly visited the moon for millennia.

According to Lakoff (1987), institutional facts have not been widely discussed by objectivist philosophers or model-theoretic linguists, but they pose a serious challenge to objectivism because they violate the independence principle. Obviously, institutional facts *do* depend on human understanding because they do not correspond to any physical objects. Social constructionists emphasize that the sum total of a society's institutional facts makes up a social reality that not only can differ drastically from one culture to another but also is in constant flux, as participants in social events act and interact, thereby "constructing" a new reality. One institutional fact that may be in the process of changing is the custom of referring to the body of water between Saudi Arabia and Iran as the "Arabian Gulf" instead of the "Persian Gulf."

Social constructionists also point out that different institutional facts in different societies are equally valid. It doesn't make sense to argue about whether a custom like that of the dowry is "true" in a universal sense. Different customs are appropriate to different societies, and therefore, in regard to institutional facts at least, truth is relative. ESL teachers can easily appreciate this point, since they teach students who, because of their cultural backgrounds, often interpret the same events in very different ways—for example, the war in the Persian Gulf.

Rorty (1979) claims that cultural relativism also applies to theories about brute facts, such as scientific theories. He points out that the statement "The earth revolves around the sun" is true for modern Western society but was not true for Western society before about 1600. The reason for this change was not just that the telescope allowed Galileo and other astronomers to observe the heavens more accurately. Galileo's principal critic, Bellarmine, did not deny the accuracy of Galileo's observations. What Bellarmine did deny was that great importance should be placed on these observations. In the medieval world view, when observational evidence conflicted with scriptural authority, observational evidence was set aside. What the Copernican revolution accomplished was much more than just establishing a different schema for the solar system. Rather, it established a different way of constructing knowledge, one in which observational evidence was valued over evidence from scripture and the writings of the Greek philosophers. Guba and Lincoln (1989) point out that argument and debate can occur only within the same world view or paradigm, in which basic assumptions are shared. Thus, the debate between Bellarmine and Galileo (as well as the debate between my traditional Ethiopian students and me over the importance of the moon landing) was at cross-purposes because basic assumptions were not shared.

Social constructionists agree with objectivists that knowledge of brute facts consists of mental representations that are somehow connected to perceptions of objects in the world. However, they claim that these representations are not accurate reflections of reality but are influenced by an individual's language and culture. Schemas for objects, like "bird" and "chair," do not exist in isolation, but are part of a complete model of the world that is represented in language as well as in the minds of speakers. Thus, our knowledge of what a chair is depends in part on our knowledge of what it is not; that is, how it contrasts with a stool, a pouf, etc. But the dividing lines between individual concepts in a semantic field like "furniture" do not necessarily coincide with naturally occurring "joints" in nature. Rather, these dividing lines are supplied by the lexicon of a language, and different languages supply different dividing lines. For example, different languages divide the color spectrum into as few as two and as many as eleven basic colors (Kay & McDaniel, 1978).

Social constructionists, then, deny that there is an essential difference between brute facts and institutional facts, and claim that no form of knowledge is firmly grounded in reality. There is no God's-eye view of nature. Language and mind do not reflect reality but rather create it. Thus, social constructionism proposes a relativistic theory of knowledge in which truth can be judged only in relation to a particular culture at a particular time.

Relativism and Scientific Theories

The relativistic theory of knowledge proposed by social constructionists makes a very controversial claim: even within the scientific paradigm it is impossible to choose between competing theories on an objective basis. Kuhn, perhaps the best-known philosopher of science, takes this position, challenging the objectivist conception of science as an enterprise involving the discovery of preexisting laws of nature that govern an objective reality. According to Kuhn (1970), scientific laws, like institutional facts, are "intrinsically the common property of a group or else nothing at all" (p. 201). The usual reply from objectivists to this claim is that different theories make different predictions and that we can decide which predictions are correct on the basis of observational evidence. But both Kuhn and Rorty hold that observational evidence does not offer a "privileged path to truth." They say that all observations of the world can be understood only in terms of a network of schemas (just as all written texts can only be so understood) and that all schemas are relative to the societies that constructed them. In other words, Kuhn and Rorty claim that scientific observations can be understood and described only in terms of the categories and vocabulary of some scientific theory. But all scientific theories constitute a self-contained paradigm that assumes that its categories and vocabulary are correct.[3]

An opposing view is offered by Russman (1987) who, following Popper (1970), claims that there *is* a neutral language of observation, which can always be invoked. To understand this point, consider an example from psychology that involves two conflicting paradigms. Suppose that a behaviorist and a cognitive psychologist observe a hungry dog who once got sick from eating poison meat walk away from a dish containing the same kind of meat. The behaviorist would say that the dog has developed a conditioned response in which the smell of the meat acts as a stimulus that elicits the response of walking away. The cognitivist would say that the dog has constructed a schema in which meat having a particular smell is identified as a food causing sickness. Notice that both of these descriptions assume the truth of their respective theories. The behaviorist's description includes the terms *stimulus* and *response,* which presuppose that there is an automatic connection between the two. The cognitive psychologist's description of the dog's actions includes the term *schema,* which presupposes that mental representations exist and can be inferred from behavior.

However, it is possible to describe the dog's actions in theory-neutral terms, using everyday language, as follows: "The dog encountered a type of meat that had once made it sick and walked away from the meat." It is also possible to express the predictions of the two theories in similar neutral language and thus to evaluate the theories. Such an evaluation might read as follows:

> Behaviorism claims that if an animal's actions in a particular environment result in harm, the animal will be less likely to repeat those actions in that environment. Thus, learning is a gradual process. This hypothesis predicts that it would be unlikely for the dog to reject the poison meat on the basis of just one previous encounter—it should require several bad experiences with poison meat for the dog to learn to avoid it. Schema theory, on the other hand, allows for some cases of immediate learning on the basis of innate schemas that can be triggered by a single experience. Therefore, the fact that the dog walked away from the meat on the second encounter supports the cognitive theory.

Notice that in the case of the dog and the meat, neither psychologist would deny the basic observational facts, despite their different conceptual frameworks. Even though behaviorism predicts that the dog will probably eat at least some of the meat on the second encounter, a behaviorist would not claim that in fact the dog did this. Everyone will agree that the dog rejected the meat regardless of his or her theoretical paradigm. Thus, despite the fact that phenomena can be described in a technical vocabulary that assumes the truth of a paradigm, there always remains a neutral, everyday vocabulary of observation that allows us to step outside the theoretical framework. In the next section we will examine the basis of this neutral vocabulary in more detail, and I will point out its importance for language teaching. For now, note that within a paradigm in which scholars agree that observational evidence is important, it is at least sometimes possible to describe this evidence in a neutral way, and thus to evaluate competing theories. This conclusion implies that the claim that understanding physical reality is completely relative to a particular group at a particular time is wrong.

However, the debate with the social constructionists about the relative nature of observational language is not yet finished. Rorty claims that even the vocabulary of everyday language, illustrated above, is not neutral: it is part of another more pervasive paradigm, one that cannot be escaped—namely the world model embodied in a particular language. Just as the vocabulary of a scientific theory assumes a particular view of reality, the vocabulary of a natural language assumes the view of the society that speaks that language, and this view forms the framework of thought itself for speakers of that language. Thus, according to Rorty, our internal model of the world is not constructed out of raw perceptual data, and the only way we can understand objects, properties, and relationships is in terms of schemas that incorporate the socially constructed categories of some language. Perception is influenced, or "mediated," by the language we speak, and there is no grounding of words in reality. Even simple observations such as "The dog ate the meat" are relative to a particular linguistic and cultural framework. An upcoming section attempts to show that these claims are not exactly right, but first we consider the effect that social constructionism has had on theories of education and teaching techniques.

Teaching Implications of Objectivism and Social Constructionism

Bruffee (1984, 1986) points out that both the objectivist and the social constructionist views of knowledge have analogs in teaching. The objectivist believes that knowledge about brute facts, and by extension "proven" scientific theories is authoritative: certain claims are true and others are false. The ultimate authority is nature, but next in authority is the scientist who understands nature, and there is no point in discussing or debating scientific facts. The classroom analog of this view is the lecture course, in which an authoritative teacher stands at the front of the room and supplies facts to the students. The flow of information is from the authority to the neophyte.

The social constructionist, on the other hand, believes that all knowledge, including scientific knowledge, is collaboratively constructed. Authority resides in a society of scholars who agree that certain assumptions and approaches are fruitful. Members of this society interact in conversation and by writing books, articles, letters, and, more recently, electronic mail messages. The process of expounding, criticizing, and revising ideas within a scholarly community has been called the "hermeneutic circle." In science, the hermeneutic circle includes reports of experiments, but experimental results are suggestive rather than conclusive. As Kuhn (1970) points out, no scientific theory is without exceptions and problems, and scholars must interpret experimental data and assess how new data affect a dominant theory. Sometimes when experimental results call a theory into question, scholars consider the results to be a special case or a convenient fiction that does not change the basic paradigm. For example, for at least fifty years after Copernicus proposed the heliocentric universe, astronomers accepted the utility of his model for calculating the location of the planets, but they did not believe that the model was literally true (Kuhn, 1959).

Bruffee (1984) says that the classroom analog of the social constructionists' model of knowledge is a community of scholars constructing the network of schemas for a particular area of knowledge. Such construction can be observed at professional conferences, where someone will read a paper presenting new data and members of the audience will ask questions or make comments that assess how the new data fit with previously known data and whether the new data support the dominant theory. The job of the teacher is to engage students in the ongoing conversation of an academic discipline. Bruffee (1984), who is a scholar of composition, states, "Our task must involve engaging students in conversation among themselves at as many points in both the writing and reading process as possible, ensur[ing] that students' conversations about what they read and write are similar in as many ways as possible to the way we would like them eventually to read and write" (p. 642). Notice that the metaphor of learning as conversation is appropriate for the many interactive techniques for teaching writing that ESL teachers have borrowed from the field of composition studies. The technique of conferencing with students (Graves, 1982) is an oral conversation. Dialogue journals (Peyton & Reed, 1990) and comments written by professors or peers are part of a written conversation. Indeed, the whole notion of writing processes (Emig, 1971; Hairston, 1982; Murray, 1968) implies a continuing conversation in which the student increasingly adopts the conventions, assumptions, and voice of a particular academic discourse community.

Experiential Realism

An alternative to objectivism and social constructionism is the philosophy of experiential realism, which stakes out a middle position regarding cultural relativism. This theory endorses the claim that mental models of institutional facts are entirely socially constructed, but rejects the claim of radical relativists[4] that mental models of basic physical reality can differ without limit in different societies. Instead, experiential realism holds that such models are constructed mainly by the human perceptual and cognitive apparatus when confronted by the physical world, although this process is mediated to some extent by language. Therefore, schema construction is similar in some respects in all societies because it is constrained by universals of perception and cognition and by the universality of certain basic aspects of human experience. Experiential realists say that human beings have a "concept making capacity" that allows us to learn about reality directly (in social constructionists' terms, *to construct* reality directly) and not only by means of language. Since this apparatus is universal in the human species and since basic experience with physical objects is similar in all societies, "directly known" knowledge is similar as well. Such knowledge provides a grounding for schemas of brute facts, and thus for at least some scientific theories. Evidence for these claims comes from studies of universals in language and language acquisition.

Johnson (1987) is the principal work on experiential realism, but Johnson's theory derives from and is compatible with the work in linguistics, psychology, and anthropology that has emerged mainly from a group of scholars at the University of California at Berkeley, including the anthropologists Berlin and Kay (1969); the psychologists Slobin (1985) and Rosch (1973; Rosch & Mervis, 1975); and the linguists Fillmore (1982), Lakoff (1987), and Talmy (1985a, 1985b). Thus, the theory of knowledge described here is not exclusively philosophical in nature, but is based on a broad cross-disciplinary perspective. It should also be said that this text's account of experiential realism is a selective summary of some of the writings of the scholars just mentioned, who do not necessarily agree on all matters, and none of whom, perhaps, would agree with everything said here.

First consider what is meant by the term *realism*. The only evidence we have that anything exists outside of ourselves comes from our senses. But what if our senses deceive us? Descartes considered the possibility that everything that appears real is in fact a dream, or is being conjured up by a deceiving demon. The position of *solipsism* acknowledges that some such possibility may well be true, and that we have no way of knowing whether anything outside of ourselves is real. But solipsists are hard to find among modern philosophers, perhaps because this position is not very productive. If it is accepted that nothing outside of ourselves is real, then there is little left to philosophize about. Thus, objectivists, social constructionists, and experiential realists agree that some kind of external reality exists. Some social constructionists have been accused of solipsism, but according to Johnson (1987), "It does seem perfectly clear that these people do agree that there are hunks of matter. . . . Both Rorty and Putnam grant the existence of an 'external world' " (p. 226).[5]

As we have seen, the major difference in the three philosophies discussed here involves the question of relativism: whether there is some grounding of mental models of brute facts (and thus of at least some scientific theories) or whether such models, like models of institutional facts, are completely relative to the languages and societies that have produced them and can vary without limit. Experiential realists claim that such models are grounded not in reality but in the human concept-making capacity, which allows us to construct at least two kinds of mental representations: *image schemas* and schemas for *basic-level objects*. Therefore, as Lakoff (1987) notes: "Since image schemas are common to all human beings, as are the principles that determine basic-level concepts, total relativism is ruled out, though limited relativism is permitted" (p. 268).

It is beyond the scope of this text to present the theory of image schemas and basic-level objects in full. Instead, I will attempt briefly to outline the theory in connection with some of the supporting evidence and refer the reader to more comprehensive discussions. The first kind of evidence for the existence of image schemas comes from the study of universals in L1 acquisition. In a number of cross-linguistic studies, Slobin (1973, 1985) found that certain kinds of linguistic structures seemed to emerge before others. He claimed that these structures reflect "prototypical scenes" in a child's experience. One such scene is the *manipulative activity scene,* which Slobin (1985) describes as follows:

> Manipulative activities involve a cluster of interrelated notions, including: the concepts representing the physical objects themselves, along with sensorimotor concepts of physical agency involving the hands and perceptual-cognitive changes of state and changes of location, along with some . . . notions of . . . causality, embedded in interactional formats of requesting, giving and taking. (p. 1175)

The manipulative activity scene is a gestalt made up of the parts Slobin describes. Certain parts of this scene can be marked grammatically. For example, in many languages direct objects are marked for the accusative case. But Slobin claims that children learn to mark "prototypical" direct objects, that is, objects that are physically manipulated (such as the object of the action of giving) before they learn to mark objects that are not manipulated (such as the object of the act of seeing). A similar situation occurs in the acquisition of Kaluli (Schieffelin, 1985), an ergative language that marks the *subjects* of verbs that take a direct object. Children first use the ergative marker with the subjects of verbs involving direct physical manipulation. According to Slobin, these facts suggest that at first the children do not mark grammatical classes, like "direct object" or "subject of ergative verb," but rather semantic classes, like the objects or actors in the manipulative activity scene. Slobin suggests that children understand the manipulative activity scene directly, or prelinguistically, based on their interaction with objects in the world as mediated by human perception and basic cognition, and that they map language onto this emergent concept. This kind of understanding, he says, is universal in the human species and accounts for "basic child grammar," a grammatical system shared by all children in the beginning stages of language learning. Slobin observes that the notion of basic child grammar is similar to Bickerton's (1981) notion of a universal "bioprogram" that accounts for similarities in unrelated creole languages.

Johnson (1987) points out that the concept of an agent applying force to an object is ubiquitous in human experience. We push the door and it opens; we throw a baseball and it flies; we slip and gravity pulls us down. According to Johnson (1987), such universal experiences give rise to the "force" image schema. This schema is an emergent gestalt that "exists for us prelinguistically, though [it] can be considerably refined and elaborated as a result of the acquisition of language" (p. 48). There is a temptation to diagram image schemas with line drawings, although such drawings simplify the gestalt concept and suggest that image schemas are primarily visual, which is not claimed. A drawing of the force image schema appears in Figure 3.1.

Further evidence that knowledge of basic physical relationships can be understood directly is provided by Talmy (1985a, 1985b), who claims that these relationships form a privileged class of knowledge that all languages tend to represent by grammatical rather than by lexical devices. One example is English prepositions. Prepositions are grammatical rather than lexical devices because they belong to a closed class of words that is relatively small and cannot be added to easily. Nouns and verbs, on the other hand, are lexical devices because they belong to open classes of words that are large and can be added to easily.

Talmy (1985a) says that prepositions assume image schemas that contain certain basic elements such as "figure" and "ground." For example, across, as in "The child swam across the pool," refers to a figure (the child), a ground (the pool), and a path traveled by the figure across the ground. Talmy claims that there are universal constraints on how image schemas can characterize the possible relationships between figure, ground and path. For example, the figure is typically smaller than the ground. Thus, "The towel lay across the body" sounds more natural than "The body lay across the towel." Furthermore, the absolute size of the figure and ground do not seem to matter. Thus, "The ant walked across the paper" and "The bus drove across the country" sound equally natural.

One aspect of the ground that languages typically encode grammatically is its state or constituent structure. *Through* refers to an image schema in which the ground is some medium, such as water or trees, rather than a flat plane. Thus, "The man walked through the field" cannot refer to a plowed field but only to a field covered with some substance such as wheat.

Some languages grammatically encode very fine distinctions in the ground. Atsugewi, a California Native American language, marks the characteristics of the ground with a set of suffixes that distinguish some fifty properties of ground geometries and the paths that relate to them. Among these suffixes are

-ic't	into a liquid
-cis	into a fire
-čis	down into a gravitational container (e.g., a basket or cupped hand)
-wamm	into an areal enclosure (e.g., a corral or a field)

FIGURE 3.1 The Force Image Schema.

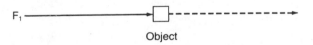

Object

But Talmy observes that despite its "semantic pyrotechnics," Atsugewi conforms to the general characteristic of language that certain properties of the ground are *not* marked. These properties include particular size, length, distance, texture, and material. Instead, grammatical devices schematize different qualitative or "topological" properties of the ground, such as the type of structural conformation, degree of subdivision ("partiteness"), number of relevant dimensions, and boundary conditions.

Talmy (1985a) characterizes the cognitive process of schematization as a "boiling down" of objects "in all their bulk and physicality" to idealized and abstract images. Like Johnson, he attributes the fact that such schematization appears to work in similar ways in all languages to the universal nature of the human perceptual and cognitive apparatus interacting with physical reality. "The explanation [for similarities] can be found in our very mode—in large part presumably innate—of conceiving, perceiving, and interacting with the contents of space" (p. 233).

According to Johnson (1987), image schemas underlie and permeate our language-based network of schemas for objects and events, and thus make possible our understanding of the world. They "provide a basis for and can connect up with our . . . networks or webs of meaning. Without them, we cannot explain the connections and relationships that obtain in our semantic networks" (p. 189). Johnson does not claim that all languages are built on exactly the same image schemas, but only that image schemas are substantially similar in all languages.

A second foundational notion of experiential realism is the notion of *basic-level objects*, the evidence for which comes mostly from studies of categorization. All languages categorize objects at various levels of abstraction. The least abstract category is one that contains a particular object. For example, the category "Montserrat" (my cat) contains one member. In English there are a number of more abstract categories to which Montserrat belongs: "Siamese cat," "cat," "animal," and "living thing." According to Lakoff (1987), languages may differ considerably in their systems of categorization, but most languages will have a word denoting a class of objects at the basic level, that is, at an intermediate level of abstractness. Thus, most languages will have a word that corresponds to "cat," but not necessarily to "Siamese cat" or "animal" or "living thing." Languages tend to have words for basic-level categories because it is at this level of abstraction that the properties shared by members of categories are most immediate and useful to human beings. The basic level of categorization for objects is distinguished from more and less abstract levels by three characteristics: (1) gestalt perception of overall shape, (2) the human capacity for physical interaction with the object, and (3) the ability to form a rich mental image of the object. It is possible to form a mental image of "Montserrat," "Siamese cat," and "cat," but not of "animal," so the basic level is the highest level of abstraction at which one can form a mental image.

Brown (1965), who first proposed the basic-level theory, noticed that basic-level categories are among the first to be named by children. This is so because the overall shape and manner of bodily interaction with objects at this level are salient to children. Brown observed that this latter characteristic is particularly important. He noted, "When something is categorized, it is regarded as equivalent to certain other things. For what purposes equivalent? . . . Flowers are equivalent in that they are agreeable to smell and are pickable. Cats are equivalent in that they are to be petted, but gently, so that they do not claw" (pp. 318–319).

Notice that the prelinguistic ability to conceptualize basic-level objects is also assumed in Slobin's account of the manipulative activity scene. In order for a child to understand that a force is acting on an object, he or she must first understand what an object is.

In addition to evidence from child language acquisition, evidence for a basic level of categorization comes from studies of folk classification of objects. Berlin, Breedlove, and Raven (1974) studied the system of plant classification in Tzeltal, a Native American language of southern Mexico, and concluded that it does not coincide with the English system at the subordinate (less abstract) or superordinate (more abstract) levels, but does coincide at the intermediate level. These researchers found that when an anthropologist pointed to a plant and asked what it was, the Tzeltal informant was likely to respond at the level of genus (maple) or species (sugar maple), but not at a level of greater or lesser abstraction. On the basis of their studies, Berlin, Breedlove, and Raven claimed that no language will have a unique system of categorization. Although they may differ in regard to superordinate or subordinate categories, all languages will include basic-level categories.

According to experiential realism, knowledge in the form of image schemas and schemas for basic-level objects is "preconceptual," that is, known directly, and not entirely by means of language. This theory explains how human beings who do not have language, such as infants and feral children, can understand the world. The claim that some aspects of language are mapped onto a prelinguistic understanding of reality is consistent with the experience of Helen Keller, who reported that before she learned her first word, *water*, she knew perfectly well what the cool liquid was and did not confuse it with milk or bread. However, as noted, Johnson acknowledges that directly known knowledge can be extended and built on considerably by different linguistic and conceptual systems, and so most knowledge is relative.

Thus, experiential realism claims that all societies are "plugged in" to physical reality by means of image schemas and schemas for basic-level objects. Johnson (1987) summarizes his position as follows:

> Things are only meaningful "objects" *for us* when we grasp them within some scheme, network or system of meaning structures. How we carve up our world will depend both on what is "out there" independent of us, and equally on the referential scheme we bring to bear. . . . There is thus no single, God's Eye way of carving up the world. But it does not follow from this that we can carve it up any way we wish. The inputs of sense perception do indeed *constrain* . . . knowledge, but they do not uniquely determine [it] [emphasis in the original]. (p. 202)

He continues:

> Shared understanding is not merely a matter of shared concepts and propositions. It is also a matter of embodied structures of understanding, such as image schemata, which constitute a large part of what we mean by *form* itself in our experience. Such structures . . . emerge in our bodily functioning; they are recurring patterns in our dynamic experience as we move about in our world. . . . [B]ecause of their internal structure they constrain our understanding and reasoning. Image-schematic structures of this sort are

not something imposed by our minds upon some infinitely malleable "stuff" outside us. Rather, they are definite, recurring patterns in an interaction of an organism with its environment. (pp. 206–207)

Let us consider a brief example of how two very different conceptual systems can be grounded in similar image schemas and schemas for basic-level objects. Lakoff (1987) describes an aspect of the conceptual system of Mixtec, an Otomanguean language of western Mexico. Mixtec does not express location with a set of prepositions or affixes, as do Indo-European languages, but rather with a metaphorical extension of body parts. Thus, the Mixtec translation of "the stone is under the table" is

yuu	wa	hiyaa	chii-mesa
stone	the	be—located	belly—table (the table's belly)

To take another example, "He is on top of the mountain" would be translated as

hiyaa-de	sini-yuku
be—located 3 ps. m.	head hill (the hill's head)

Notice that basic-level objects, such as *stone* and *table* are readily translatable into English. It may be that stones have many different associations and connotations for speakers of Mixtec and English (for example, perhaps religious connotations), but both languages have a word that categorizes these objects at the basic level. Undoubtedly, more abstract concepts would require considerable paraphrasing and explanation, and still might not be entirely comprehensible to an English speaker. Notice also that as Talmy (1985a) predicts, the Mixtec system takes into account only topological relationships; there are no grammatical devices that characterize the relationships of objects of a particular size or color, or to relationships that existed at a particular time of day.

Mixtec conceptualizes spacial locations by metaphorically projecting body parts onto objects. Other examples of this projection are the words *cii,* which can mean "belly" or "under," and *siki,* which can mean "animal back" or "on top of" (the objects of which must have a horizontal surface off the ground). But although the Mixtec system for representing topological spacial relationships is radically different from the English system, it is possible for English speakers to understand the Mixtec system, which seems unusual but not nonsensical. In fact, English sometimes makes use of the same kind of metaphorical projections. For example, we speak of the "face" of a cliff and the "foot" of a mountain. At a more general level, in English any object may be "in back of" another object. According to Johnson, these topological relationships are understandable to us because they can be interpreted by means of our own image schemas. English expresses these relationships by means of a system of prepositions and Mixtec by means of a system of metaphorical extensions of body parts, but both mappings are based on similar image schemas for basic topographical relationships.

Experiential realism seems to fit with the experience of living in another culture. In regard to brute facts, life is pretty much the same. Members of the new culture do not try to walk through walls or to drink out of closed containers. But in regard to institutional facts, things can be very confusing. In Catalonia you are supposed to queue up at a bus stop; in the Sudan you should not eat with your left hand; in Ethiopia you must not leave the table with your glass of mead empty. In order not to insult your host, you must leave a full glass to show that you could not possibly drink any more; otherwise, your host will just fill the glass again (as I learned one very bleary night).

Experiential realism also provides an account of how concepts beyond the basic level are formed. Johnson (1987) claims that basic-level concepts are used to understand more abstract concepts by means of metaphorical extension. For example, from my physical interactions with objects like packages and beer bottles, I know that objects often have to be opened in order to get at something inside. On the basis of this knowledge I can understand a professor who says, "Open your books to page 184." Opening a book isn't exactly the same as opening a package, but it is similar enough so that I can understand what the professor has in mind by means of metaphorical extension. Thus, the expressions "open your books," "open your eyes," and (extending even further) "open the meeting" are understood in terms of the basic-level experience of opening objects like packages and bottles. Metaphorical extension even allows me to understand my Spanish-speaking student who says, "Please open the light" (a literal translation of *abra la luz,* "turn on the light"). "Open the light" makes sense because turning on a light makes the inside of the room visible and accessible to me, like opening a box. It is possible to construct other grammatical expressions involving *open* that do not make sense because they diverge too much from our basic-level understanding of *open.* Such expressions include "open the mountain," "open the grass," and "open the sun." Although these expressions could be assigned a conventional interpretation, at present they are not interpretable because they are not grounded in the basic-level experience of opening a container.

In sum, the philosophy of experiential realism has two main tenets. First, much (but not all) knowledge is socially constructed. Second, some kinds of knowledge are known directly and are grounded in human perception and basic cognition, and therefore are similar in all societies. Notice that experiential realism does not endorse the objectivist claim that mental representations are true reflections of reality. Rather, it claims that some of these representations are true *in relation to human beings,* rather than in relation to a particular society. Another way of putting this is to say that schemas about physical reality are constructed not only socially but also biologically.

Teaching Implications of Experiential Realism

Experiential realism endorses the social constructionist model of knowledge in most respects and therefore has similar implications for teaching. The metaphor of education as an ongoing conversation in which students take a greater and greater part seems particularly appropriate for teaching a second language. This is, after all, precisely the metaphor that has guided the communicative approach to language teaching. The metaphor is especially appropriate in regard to teaching language through content, where an important goal is to acculturate students to the Western academic culture. However, as noted above, there is an unusual feature of the academic conversation. In an oral conversation all of the participants are present, but in the academic conversation many of the participants may be represented in writing or, as Bakhtin (1981) has emphasized, in memory.

A second similarity between the social constructionist and communicative approaches to language teaching is the role of the teacher as a "cultural broker." For a long time ESL teachers have known that it is important to introduce students to the English-speaking culture as well as to the English language. We have only recently realized that students need to be introduced to a specific academic culture as well as to the general culture, and that, in fact, becoming a member of the academic culture is the most important goal for many students. Nevertheless, the process of acculturation is similar, regardless of whether the target culture is general or academic. Oakshott's (1962) description of education reads very much like a description of how to attain communicative competence: "Education . . . is an initiation into the skill and partnership of [a] conversation, in which we learn to recognize the voices, to distinguish the proper occasions of utterance, and in which we acquire the intellectual and moral habits appropriate to the conversation" (p. 179).

It should be noted, however, that in introducing nonnative English speakers into the Western academic culture it is very important to take into account their own learning styles and their own traditions of academic conversation. Furthermore, just as adult immigrants to the United States may never become entirely acculturated, students who are already participating members of a different academic culture may find it very difficult to fully enter a new one. Case study 3 describes Duc, a forty-five-year-old lawyer and journalist from Vietnam, who had great difficulty functioning in an American college setting. Although Duc spoke good English, he was very uncomfortable in classes where he was expected to participate orally because this violated the Vietnamese academic tradition. He stated, "Because you [Americans] have been brought up in a different way, I mean in a free democratic process, you can feel strong in speaking, in relating, but whenever I respect somebody I feel myself tongue-tied."

Duc also mentioned that he didn't see the value of participating in class discussions. He said, "I feel I am there to learn, not for somebody to solve my own problems . . . and (as if) I think my friends can teach me more than the teacher." Therefore, Duc would probably be more comfortable interacting with instructors by means of a dialogue journal or a learning log. Perhaps he would be less reticent to participate orally in a small group of students that included a majority of international students, or to participate by means of computer conferencing (Smith, 1990).

We now consider the ways in which experiential realism differs from social constructionism and, therefore, has additional implications for teaching. As we have seen, experiential realism claims that the human sensory and cognitive apparatus constructs image schemas and schemas for basic-level objects that are similar for all human beings. This insight helps to explain why certain methods of beginning language teaching are successful and provides an answer to the question often asked of ESL teachers, "How can you teach English if you don't speak the students' language?" Most communicative language teaching methods introduce the target language in connection with basic-level objects and simple topological relationships. For example, in the Total Physical Response method (Asher, 1969), the teacher gives commands—"Stand up," "Turn around," "Put the pen on the book"—while demonstrating what the commands mean. The students then perform the actions themselves. No translation is necessary. These actions and objects are understood directly by students from all language backgrounds.

A second method that involves the manipulation of basic-level objects and topographical relationships is The Silent Way (Gattengno, 1972). In this method the objects and relationships are modeled by using colored rods while they are described in the target language: "The red rod is on the green rod," for example. The silent way exemplifies what is meant by direct or prelinguistic understanding because it is not necessary for the students' native language to mark the distinctions that can be taught with the rods. For example, many languages do not have separate words for *blue* and *green,* but as Rosch (1973) found, human beings can readily learn to mark these colors lexically, even though their language does not, because the two hues correspond to natural divisions imposed on the color spectrum by human optical physiology. A similar example is the relationship represented by the English words *in* and *on.* Both of these relationships are commonly expressed by the same Spanish word *en,* but this fact does not prevent Spanish speakers from perceiving the difference and learning to express the two relationships with different lexical items.

Thus, in the ESL classroom basic-level knowledge and image schemas provide a basis for communication available to everyone. An illustration of how ESL students can use basic-level knowledge to understand academic material was seen in Ceyong's case study. Ceyong could not understand the concepts from mineralogy on a purely academic basis, but she did understand them when she was able to feel the hardness of the rocks, weigh them, immerse them in water to determine their specific gravity, and so on.

A second illustration of communication grounded in basic-level knowledge and image schemas is provided by Saville-Troike's (1985) study of a multilingual classroom. Saville-Troike observed thirty-five ESL students, ranging in age from three to twelve years, who spoke eight different languages. She found that these children sometimes engaged in "dilingual discourse" in which each participant in a conversation used his or her own language, which was not spoken by the other participant. Despite the language difference, these communications were remarkably successful, as the following excerpts show (capital letters represent English translations of utterances in Chinese):

2. (Student C3 walks over to the teacher and shows her his broken balloon.)

STUDENT: LOOK. LOOK. MINE IS GONE. LOOK. LOOK.

TEACHER: Oh, it popped, didn't it. All gone. (p. 96)

3. (Student C4 looks through a balloon.)

STUDENT: I LOOK THROUGH IT AND IT'S ALL RED.

TEACHER: You're looking at the balloon? It's all red, isn't it. (p. 96)

4. (C4 is putting pegs in a pegboard.)

STUDENT: THIS ALMOST STOPS. THIS CANNOT FIT IN. THIS IS TOO BIG. I DON'T WANT IT.

TEACHER: That may be too fat to fit in there.

STUDENT: THIS CANNOT FIT IN.

TEACHER: Does it not work? Sure it doesn't. You're right.

STUDENT: FIND THE BIGGEST HOLE.

TEACHER: I don't think so. I don't think the hole is big enough. All these holes are just the same. If it's too big, it's too big for all of them probably. (p. 92)

The conversation in (2) concerns a basic-level object that can be seen by both participants. The conversation in (3) involves the color term *red*. According to Kay and McDaniel (1978), the vast majority of the world's languages have terms for a color that has as its most typical example what English speakers think of as prototypical red. In other words, *red* is a basic-level color term. (4) involves the basic-level shapes *square* and *round*, and the topological relationship *inside of*. Thus, one reason that dilingual communication was successful was that it involved basic-level concepts and image schemas. Saville-Troike (1985) observes, "When . . . dilingual communication was successful between children, there were always ample extralinguistic clues to meaning present" (p. 7).

The Cooperative Principle

The participants in dilingual discourse were able to understand each other not only on the basis of basic-level knowledge and image schemas, but also (as Saville-Troike points out) on the basis of Grice's (1975) Cooperative Principle (see page 25). As mentioned, the Cooperative Principle has a number of corollaries, which Grice calls "maxims." In the preceding dilingual exchanges, the teacher followed the maxim "be relevant" since she always commented on some saliant aspect of the physical situation. Saville-Troike (1985) notes, "When a mutually perceived state or event was unnatural . . . in some respect, it was understood to be comment worthy in both Chinese and English" (p. 5). Notice that this description assumes a mutual understanding of states and events that is not specific to either language. A major finding of Saville-Troike's study, then, is that the universal principles of conversation proposed by Grice govern the negotiation of meaning regardless of the linguistic code. But another reason that dilingual communication can be successful is that it involves universal basic-level concepts and image schemas.

In regard to higher-level teaching, and in particular to teaching language through content, the theory of image schemas and basic-level concepts in connection with the cooperative principle helps to explain why experiential teaching (teaching based on demonstration) is more effective than expository teaching (teaching based entirely on language). In a passage that anticipates some of the claims of experiential realism, John Dewey (1916) noted:

> When education . . . fails to recognize that the primary or initial subject matter always exists as matter of an active doing, involving the use of the body and the handling of material, the subject matter of instruction is isolated from the needs and purposes of the learner, and so becomes just something to be memorized and reproduced upon demand. (p. 184)

It is important to emphasize that language through content teaching must prepare students to benefit from expository as well as experiential teaching. Much of the academic conversation in which we desire students to participate is expository in nature. The point is that experiential teaching can provide an entry into this conversation. The goal of the language through content course should be to provide the most effective mixture of experiential and expository instruction. In general, ESL students will require considerably more experiential instruction than native speakers.

Conclusions

Experiential realism provides an epistemology that is compatible with effective ways of teaching language, at both the introductory and the advanced levels. According to this theory, most kinds of knowledge are socially constructed, and authority resides not in an objective standard of truth but in a community of scholars who share a paradigm that provides a particular vocabulary and a set of assumptions about what counts as a good argument. Scholarship is viewed as a continuing conversation, which continually results in a refinement of vocabulary and occasionally in a shift of paradigms, among members of this community. Education is viewed as increasing participation in this conversation. This model of knowledge implies that language instruction should be interactive and collaborative in ways that are compatible with students' learning styles and academic traditions. Experiential realism also claims that some knowledge about basic-level objects and topological relationships can be constructed by direct sensory experience and so is independent of language to some extent. Thus, experiential teaching that involves the observation and manipulation of such objects and relationships can provide an entry for ESL students into the English academic conversation.

NOTES

1. A generative linguist would not make this claim because it concerns how linguistic information is stored in memory and therefore is part of a performance theory, not a competence theory. However, a similar claim was made by the derivational complexity theory (Savin & Perchonock, 1965), which assumed a transparent relationship between a competence grammar and a theory of sentence production.
2. As Dowty, Wall, and Peters (1981) put it: "As a first approximation let us simply assume that the world contains various sorts of objects—call them 'entities'—and that in a particular state-of-affairs these entities have certain properties and stand in certain relations to each other" (p. 7).
3. Kuhn apparently does not hold as strong a relativistic position as Rorty, for he seems to place a higher value on sensory experience in evaluating scientific theories. Kuhn (1970) wonders whether "sensory experience [is] fixed and neutral. The [objectivist] viewpoint . . . dictates an immediate and unequivocal Yes! In the absence of a developed alternative, I find it impossible to relinquish entirely that viewpoint" (p. 126). We return to the issue of how sensory experience relates to models of reality in a later section.
4. It is not easy to identify "radical relativists." According to Smith (1988) even Rorty is "more positive than he acknowledges" (p. 218). Smith names Feyerabend (1978), Goodman (1978), and Barnes and Bloor (1982), in addition to herself, as self-identified radical relativists.
5. Johnson (1987) notes:
   It is often said . . . that Derrida and his disciples really do believe that there are nothing in the world but *texts*. . . . What they claim, however, is that matter is only *meaningful and comprehensible* by us insofar as it is grasped via "language" here used in a broad sense to include all structures of meaning and not just those that involve words (pp. 226–27).

CHAPTER 4
Case Studies of ESL Students in Content Courses

CASE STUDIES RESEARCH

Having discussed the theoretical background for a model of academic competence for ESL students, we now take a close look at what these students actually do in content courses. The naturalistic investigation of how adolescent and adult ESL students accomplish academic tasks in content courses is a fairly new area of research. There have been studies of elementary school children (Saville-Troike, 1984, 1985; Saville-Troike & Kleifgen, 1986; Wong Fillmore et al., 1985). There is a large literature on the learning strategies of students in ESL courses (O'Malley, Chamot, Strewner-Manzanares, Russo, & Kupper, 1985; O'Malley & Chamot, 1990; Oxford, 1990; Politzer & McGroarty, 1985; Rubin & Thompson, 1982; Wenden & Rubin, 1987). However, these studies focus mainly on the learning of language rather than on the learning of mainstream content material and, for the most part, gather data by means of students' self-reports rather than by participant observation (the relationship of the present study to the learning strategies literature is discussed later). I am aware of only one other naturalistic study of an ESL student in mainstream courses beyond the elementary level: Bensen (1989), a case study of an Arab student enrolled in an ESL Masters degree program.

As Yin (1984) points out, the case studies method of research is often used to investigate a new area of inquiry because case studies can provide rich pictures of individual subjects that are helpful for getting a first look at the nature of the new area of investigation, and for identifying questions for future research.

To investigate how ESL students deal with content material in mainstream courses, my graduate students and I made case studies of thirty-four ESL students. This chapter reports the results of that project. First, the research methods used for making the case studies are described. Second, two abridged case studies are presented, one of a high school student and one of a college student. Third, some generalizations based on all thirty-four case studies are made. Finally, a case study of an entire language through content course is presented.

CASE STUDIES OF ESL STUDENTS IN CONTENT COURSES

Subjects

Thirty-four nonnative speakers of English enrolled in content courses in Washington, D.C. area suburban schools were the subjects of this study. Ten of the subjects were in college, and twenty-four were in grades seven through twelve. Nineteen of the subjects were taking mainstream content courses enrolling a majority of native English speakers (NES). Six of the subjects were taking "sheltered" courses in which they studied mainstream material in classes enrolling ESL students only. These subjects included a college student taking freshman composition for international students; two high school students, one taking world history for ESL students and one taking literature for ESL students; and two intermediate school students, both taking social studies for ESL students. One of these subjects, Manh, was an exception in another way as well: he had suffered a stroke that had caused a learning impairment. Information about the subjects appears in Table 4.1. The subjects' first names were changed to a pseudonym in the same language, so that "Ann" might be changed to "Mary" and "Carlos" to "Juan."

TABLE 4.1   Subjects of the Study

Subject	Age	Sex	Grade	Years in U.S.	Country	Class
Enji	12	F	Intermediate	6	Kuwait	Social studies
Parmi	13	F	Intermediate	.5	Iran	English
Rosa	12	F	Intermediate	12	U.S.	ESL social studies
Hiroshi	13	M	Intermediate	3	Japan	English
Ana	13	F	Intermediate	2	Peru	Physical sciences
Anya	13	F	Intermediate	1	Yugoslavia	Social studies
Tim	15	M	Intermediate	5	Laos	Physical sciences
Jose	12	M	Intermediate	1	Puerto Rico	Social studies
Mark	12	M	Intermediate	2	Japan	Science
Ceyong	12	M	Intermediate	1	Korea	Science
Alexis	12	M	Intermediate	2	Greece	Study skills
Tri	17	M	High school	3	Vietnam	English
Nopadol	17	M	High school	2	Cambodia	Social studies
Marika	17	F	High school	2	Cambodia	Earth science
Sandra	18	F	High school	1	El Salvador	Cosmetology
Khan	19	F	High school	1	Vietnam	Biology
Ana	16	F	High school	2	Bolivia	U.S. government
Maria	14	F	High school	1	Peru	World history

(continued)

TABLE 4.1   (continued)

Subject	Age	Sex	Grade	Years in U.S.	Country	Class
Larry	13	M	High school	2	Korea	Biology
Carol	15	F	High school	3	El Salvador	English literature
George	13	M	High school	2	Colombia	ESL literature
Manh	16	M	High school	3.5	Vietnam	World history
Si-Young	14	F	High school	1.5	Korea	World history
Manny	16	M	High school	2.5	Cambodia	Earth science
Nazila	26	F	College	5	Iran	Religion in modern world
Duc	46	M	College	4	Vietnam	ESL methods
Zai	21	F	College	3	Malaysia	Middle english
Ahmad	20	M	College	1	Tunisia	Engineering
Fati	20	F	College	1	Tunisia	Speech
Joe	20	M	College	2	Somalia	Sociology
Elizebeth	19	F	College	3	Korea	Geography
Ellen	20	F	College	2	Korea	Religion
Lucy	42	F	College	6	Uganda	Psychology
Ali	22	M	College	3	Syria	History

Totals	Intermediate		High School	College
	11		13	10

Research Question, Data Collection, and Analysis

As is often the case in exploratory research, the initial research question was broadly framed: How do ESL students accomplish academic tasks in content courses? The definition of academic tasks was left open, but a provisional list included reading, note-taking, studying for tests, taking tests, writing papers, participating in class, and using reference tools. An early problem we encountered was what to call the behavior we were observing. For a time we considered adopting the learning strategies framework mentioned at the beginning of this chapter. According to Rubin (1985), a learning strategy is a process initiated by the learner that contributes directly or indirectly to learning. Direct learning strategies include questioning, memorizing, and monitoring. Indirect strategies include creating opportunities to practice the target language (p. 20). In general, these are the types of behavior that we expected to study; however, existing models of learning strategies were not entirely appropriate for our research for several reasons. One problem was that, as Bialystok (1983) observes, "There is little consensus in the literature concerning either the definition or the identification of learning strategies" (p. 100). Oxford (1990) adds, "Classification conflicts [of learning strategies] are inevitable . . . . [E]ven individual researchers often classify a particular strategy differently at different times, in light of new insights" (p. 17). A second problem was that the most widely known school of learning strategies research (represented in O'Malley & Chamot, 1990) constitutes a paradigm in the Kuhnian sense. The paradigm is based largely on what might be called "mainstream cognitive psychology" (cf. Anderson [1980, 1983]), and it is not entirely compatible with the theory presented here. For example, I have tentatively endorsed the claim that second language (L2) learning is fundamentally different from the learning of content material because it involves a genetically transmitted universal grammar (UG). However, Anderson claims that all types of learning, including L1 and L2 learning, are similar.

The strongest reason for not adopting the learning strategies framework for the case studies research was that, in the tradition of exploratory qualitative research, we did not want to impose predetermined categories of behavior on our observations. Rather, our goal was to write holistic descriptions of how individual subjects approached their courses. We were less interested in discovering our subjects' internal learning processes and more interested in describing the overt behaviors they employed to complete academic assignments (which, as we will see, did not necessarily result in significant learning). In addition, we did not want to have to handle the considerable theoretical baggage attached to the learning strategies framework, such as determining whether a particular strategy was direct or indirect, overt or covert, metacognitive, cognitive, or social, and so on.

In order to distinguish the ways in which our subjects accomplished academic tasks from learning strategies, we called the behaviors we observed "academic strategies." Academic strategies include study skills such as reading, dictionary use, note-taking, use of research tools, organization, and studying for tests. These skills are mainly used to enhance the student's knowledge of the content material. Academic strategies also include ways of completing assignments without high proficiency in academic English, and often with less than a full understanding of the material. These limitations require special ways of taking tests, writing papers, and participating in class discussions. The research question for the case studies, then, was "How do ESL students accomplish academic tasks in content courses?"

Case studies of the subjects were made by the author and by graduate students enrolled in an applied linguistics course. In most cases the graduate student researchers contacted their subjects by approaching a content area teacher and offering to tutor an ESL student in his or her class. In some cases, however, they tutored friends. In one case, a researcher tutored her son, and in one case a researcher tutored a student in her own social studies class.

The tutoring sessions made up a total of at least ten hours (although usually more) over a period of from six to ten weeks. In most cases, the sessions were recorded on audiotape. The researchers also wrote field notes immediately after the sessions, covering matters such as the setting of the interview, unrecorded comments, and the interviewer's reactions to the session. When the tape recorder interfered with the naturalness of the session, only field notes written after the session were used. Portions of the tape recordings were transcribed by the researchers. The researchers also observed the subjects in classes; interviewed their teachers; and made copies of their notebooks, workbooks, quizzes, papers, and other documents. In addition, many researchers kept a dialogue journal with their subjects.

The thirty-four case studies, tutoring session transcripts, field notes, documents, and other data were then analyzed by the author, who identified and coded seven frequently mentioned areas of interest: reading, dictionary use, note-taking, oral participation, organization, copying, and memorization. The coded portions of the documents were assembled into seven notebooks, one for each area of interest. By examining the notebooks, it was possible to compare the subjects' notes, tests, and papers as well as the researchers' observations about their academic strategies in each of the areas of interest, and to pick out common strategies, strengths, and weaknesses. As mentioned, this method of data collection and analysis is inevitably subjective, but it is a good way to get a first, overall impression of how ESL students approach their assignments in content courses.

The individual case studies contained a richness and texture that provided insights into the subjects' academic lives that cannot be captured in a summary of findings. Therefore, in order to convey these insights, as well as some of the variety and detail of the case studies, two representative studies—abridgements of the originals—are presented next. They are written in the first person by the researchers, although the author has edited, and in some cases rewritten, certain portions.

CASE STUDY 2—NOPADOL: A CAMBODIAN STUDENT ATTEMPTS TO LEARN U.S. HISTORY, BY ELIZABETH SCHEPPS

During the course of the day, I teach U.S. and Virginia history to forty-seven students in a Catholic high school. The classes are divided into twenty-one and twenty-six students, respectively. Of those forty-seven students, only Nopadol, an eleventh grader, is a nonnative English speaker. Since the beginning of the school year, I have observed his struggle to learn a rather difficult subject with this tremendous language handicap. It is not surprising that his grades have been among the lowest in either of the two classes. His average for the first semester was a 65 (70 is passing in our school and he did miserably on the semester exam—60). Nopadol is a challenge to any teacher and especially to me because I have been working with ESL students for four years.

When I began the research project, Nopadol immediately came to mind as a perfect subject. Not only could I tutor him on a regular basis (thus observing his learning strategies), but also I would be working with him on a daily basis in the classroom. When I asked him if he would like to cooperate in a research project, he readily consented. He is a very motivated student and desperately wants to prepare himself so he can attend a U.S. college. Part of this motivation is his own drive. He wants to be an electrical engineer. One of our most interesting sessions came about when he talked about how the tape recorder we were using operated. He recounted a story about the first time he took one apart; he could not get it back together, so he took it to a repairman who showed him how to do it. A second motivating factor is his cultural background. Nopadol is from Cambodia where he was reared to be an achiever. His schooling there was very strict. Students were often beaten—and they bore it because education was essential for success. Before beginning my research, I wanted to find out if Nopadol's problem was just language or if he was a slow learner. I rejected IQ tests as evaluation measures because they are so language-oriented. Instead, I talked to his other teachers and discussed with him his favorite subjects. Chemistry leads the list. His chemistry teacher said he was doing fine but does come in regularly for tutoring after school; note that chemistry is not as language-oriented as history. His next favorite subject is math, and he is passing in this course. The two subjects which are most difficult for him are religion and history. He is failing the former and barely passed the latter this quarter with a grade of 75 out of 100.

Note-Taking

Nopadol and I agreed to meet every Thursday after school in my classroom for one hour. The procedure we followed was to go over his notebook, discussing any points in the lesson he did not understand. This gave me a good opportunity to observe Nopadol's note-taking strategies. He also brought his textbook so we could look up answers to questions he did not understand. Every student in U.S. History is required to keep a notebook. Each day's lecture is dated, so it is easy to refer back to any particular lesson. Nopadol's notebook is well organized and very neat. Each page is titled by chapter and date. The notes are almost word for word what I write on the board. They are in outline form with practically no extra notation of something I say—just what I write on the board. One exception came on March 21, when I began the lesson by discussing the background of the Panama Canal before getting into the details. Nopadol had written down:

Panama Canal
Panama canal is not wind engut for a big ship, and it's not all the same levels so it take about one day to get to another side.

In the tutoring session, I asked him why he had written down this particular information. He said that it was very interesting to him, and he understood what I was saying. I was pleased to note his attempt at a new strategy, as well as his ability to get the main idea. It was not important to me at this stage that his English was not perfect, only that he had grasped the concept. Again on April 11, when I was discussing the economic reasons for the stock market crash of 1929, he had filled in my outline (the underlined phrases below) with his own interpretation. Note that he has understood the concept even if his English is incorrect.

Early 1929

<u>Prices went down</u>
In 1929 the prices is go down because people have few people can buy it. So they have tolow the prices down. then the people can buy it.

<u>Unemployment rose</u>
when the prices was went down they can not pay money much to the worker.

Looking through Nopadol's notebook, I could see that he rarely uses abbreviations unless I use them on the board:

No nation could discriminate against businessmen in collecting duties or RR rates.

I asked him why he wrote down "RR," hoping he had devised this abbreviation himself, but he said, "Because you did!" Sometimes my abbreviations are more of a hindrance than a help. He asked me what "V.P." meant. I had assumed every student would know this. It was essential to an understanding of the presidential succession. Another time, I had written "Gov." and he had mistaken it for *government,* not *governor.* The latter turned out to be a new vocabulary word for him, essential to an understanding of the concept I was teaching. I feel that not devising abbreviations slows him down and causes him to miss the part of the lecture given while he is writing. I have often seen him in the classroom reading the board and diligently writing down what he sees instead of looking at me and following what I am saying.

This strategy of note-taking is not unique to nonnative English speakers. My other students do it also, especially the average students. I think it gives them a sense of security. Only the top students tend to abbreviate and write down the things I say, especially the statements I repeat or emphasize with my tone of voice. Nopadol has not yet progressed to this point.

One surprising strategy on his part happened the day of the lecture on social reform. Nopadol said that he decided not to take any notes that day but just to listen to the lecture. He admitted that when he concentrates on copying down what is on the board, he often misses what is discussed. His intention was to copy his friend Matt's notes afterward. I noticed that these notes were missing from his notebook. He had every intention of getting the notes, but when he approached Matt, the latter was busy and answered in an exasperated manner that he did not have time to explain. I questioned Nopadol on the material to see if he had retained the main ideas of the lecture. Several days had passed and he remembered very little. Obviously this strategy had backfired, and he never tried it again. Nopadol admitted though that he certainly enjoyed the lecture more!

In conclusion, Nopadol's note-taking strategy is almost exclusively to copy what I write on the board. Although this strategy does not allow him to follow the thread of the lecture as well as when he just listens, he is usually able to get some understanding of the material by comparing Matt's notes with his own. Nopadol's notes do not seem to be a great help to him in studying for tests, although apparently having some notes to study works better than listening carefully to the lecture but taking no notes.

Studying with Peers

Nopadol appears to do better on his tests when his friend Matt helps him. Matt, who is very conscientious about his work, is one of the better students in the class. He is also one of twelve American friends Nopadol has at the school. During lunch, Matt will come over and talk to Nopadol, and a close friendship between the two has developed. Matt lets Nopadol borrow his notes, which often contain more extra information than do Nopadol's. One time I found that Nopadol had just this broad outline in his notebook:

> Sacco–Vanzetti case
> Unions—Steel Striked 1919
> Prohibition—18th Amendment
> Volstead Act

I knew that I had provided a more detailed outline in class and that the information he had was inadequate to study by. He said that he got tired toward the end of class that day, and anyway he could get the information from Matt! Besides loaning him his notebook, Matt also quizzes Nopadol before tests. Matt knows how to study, so he asks the pertinent questions. Sometimes I think that the friendship Nopadol has with Matt has been his greatest aid in learning as much about U.S. history as he has.

Background Knowledge

One reason Nopadol is not doing well in U.S. History is that he lacks so much background knowledge. All the American students have heard of George Washington and Abraham Lincoln and most are aware of the major events of the Revolutionary War and the Civil War. This background knowledge provides a framework onto which new knowledge can be fit, and Nopadol lacks this basic framework. However, in areas where Nopadol does have background knowledge, he does very well. This became apparent during one interesting conversation we had about international economics. Nopadol wants to go into the family business some day, so he is interested in economics. We were studying in class about the business cycle. I explained Adam Smith's theories on supply and demand and competition. This stimulated a discussion about competition between Cambodia and Japan. Nopadol realizes that "the government (Cambodia) try to make the country go up." Therefore, he prefers not to buy Japanese products—only Cambodian. His bias against Japan, which appears to be an even bigger competitor in Asia than in the U.S., showed up in a story he had seen on television about Japan stealing computer secrets. Another time we were discussing U.S.-Mexican relations, and he jumped in with a story he had seen on television about a young Mexican boy who had his green card but was illegally deported. He understood completely what had happened.

Test Taking

My first question with regard to Nopadol's test taking strategies was whether he uses his notes effectively on the tests. I cannot say that he does because he rarely passes a test. His test scores since we began the tutoring have been 52%, 64%, 52%, 64%, 60%, 75%, and 40%. These tests varied in the type of questions asked, so it is hard to compare them. However, on the test where he scored 75%, there appears to be some carryover from his notes. For example, his notebook had in the margin,

Big Four
1. Lloyd George—G. Britain
2. Clemenceau—want to make sure the German will not come to France
3. Orlando—?
4. Wilson—want to keep the world in peace.

With this information, he got the following questions correct on the test:

Matching
Clemenceau—French premier who attended the Paris peace talks

Multiple Choice
Wilson believed that the peace settlement should (a) award the Allies their territorial claims, (b) punish the Axis powers, (c) try to eliminate the causes of war.

What is puzzling is why he missed this question:

Matching
Lloyd George—English prime minister at the Paris peace talks.

I can see that "G. Britain" and "English" are two different words, but in our discussion, he appeared to know they were one and the same. He was very angry with himself on this one because originally he had the right answer—then he changed it.

My second research question regarding tests was whether Nopadol was better at certain types of questions than others. Most of my test questions are objective: matching, true/false, multiple choice, and identifications. Occasionally, I will ask for specific examples of a concept. I also ask essay questions. I wanted to analyze Nopadol's ability to handle each of these kinds of questions.

On three separate tests, Nopadol got 60% or higher on each of the matching sections. Below are two of the sets of questions. The correct answers are in parentheses.

Example I   Match the name with the description

(b)d	**1.** Bernard Baruch	**a.**	Democratic candidate for president in 1920
c	**2.** Clemenceau	**b.**	Head of the WWI Industries Board
a	**3.** James M. Cox	**c.**	French premier who attended the Paris peace talks
(d)b	**4.** Lloyd George	**d.**	English prime minister at the Paris peace talks
e	**5.** Herbert Hoover	**e.**	Head of the Food Administration

Example II   Match the name with the description

b	**1.** Warren G. Harding	**a.**	Carried all but six states in 1932
(e)a	**2.** Calvin Coolidge	**b.**	Believed Americans craved a return to "normalcy"
c	**3.** Herbert Hoover	**c.**	Administrator of Food Relief, WWI
(a)	**4.** Franklin D. Roosevelt	**d.**	Catholic, a "wet," Tammany machine politician
d	**5.** Alfred E. Smith	**e.**	"I do not choose to run."

On example I, discussed earlier, Nopadol had first selected answers he knew best. This is the strategy many students use. He knew Herbert Hoover because he remembered the information from Matt's notes which he had borrowed before the test. The second easiest was James Cox. He said he remembered this because I had discussed it in class the day before. The other correct answer was Clemenceau. In his notes, the information about Clemenceau had been written in the margin. He had realized that he didn't have this information so he had gotten it from Matt. He had gotten the George Lloyd question correct but then had changed it. He was very angry with himself. "Why did I change?" I think what confused him was the name Bernard Baruch. I know that I only mentioned Baruch in class. I did not write his name on the board nor was the information in the assigned reading. In this case, Nopadol's strategy of only copying my notes from the board put him at a disadvantage.

Example II is taken from a test on the chapter covering the 1920s. In his notes, Nopadol had listed the presidential elections of 1920, 1924, and 1928 in chronological order. We discussed in class the politicians that Nopadol got correct: Harding, Smith, and Hoover. However, Franklin D. Roosevelt, whom Nopadol did not correctly identify, was discussed only in the book. The definition for Coolidge was more difficult than the others because it meant piecing together several different ideas. Nopadol does much better on the straightforward questions. This may be another indication that his understanding of U.S. history is not deep because he lacks background knowledge.

On the third matching exercise he received his best score: 67%, missing four out of twelve. He missed three questions because the answers were to be found in a filmstrip or in the reading—not in the lecture. Nopadol did not understand the filmstrip, and he has difficulty picking essential information in the reading. His strategy is to pick out the subtitles, which are in bold type in the textbook. These subtitles do not give the main idea. In sum, Nopadol is able to answer matching questions when they are straightforward and do not demand much interpretation, and when the material is contained in notes which he reviews with his friend Matt. But when the questions cover the readings or filmstrips, Nopadol has more trouble because these ways of presenting information are more difficult for him to understand.

Multiple-choice questions appeared on five of the tests. These kinds of questions are generally longer and require more time to read. Nopadol is a slow reader, and I am convinced that the main reason for this is his lack of English vocabulary. A lack of sufficient time is a problem for Nopadol on these tests, so I generally allow Nopadol more time than the other students. The extra time does not seem to help if he does not know a particular word. He has never brought a bilingual dictionary to class. His scores on the multiple-choice section of these five tests were 60%, 70%, 50%, 83%, and 78%. Below are three examples of questions he missed because he did not know a key vocabulary word (the unknown words are italicized):

__(B) C__	After WWI, the public's attitude toward strikes and strikers was generally (a) sympathetic, (b) *intolerent,* (c) indifferent.
__(B) C__	The League of Nations *mandate* system concerned (a) international arbitration, (b) supervising regions taken from the defeated nations, (c) the payment of reparations.
__(A) C__	The Fifteenth Amendment *enfranchised* (a) blacks, (b) women, (c) eighteen-year-olds.

After each test we discussed his problems, and he admitted that he did not know these words.

Sometimes it is not just one word but a whole phrase that he does not know. In these two questions the same italicized phrase confounded him and he missed both questions.

__(B) A__	Railroads *contributed to the growth* of the cattle industry by (a) creating a bigger meat market, (b) providing a dependable means of transportation, (c) investing money in ranches.
__(A) C__	An important factor *contributing to the industrial growth* of the U.S. was (a) the large labor force available, (b) Great Britain's reliance on American goods, (c) the alliance of black and white farmers.

It may appear from the discussion so far that Nopadol is using only mechanical strategies on the tests, that he is just matching sentences from his notes with the test questions. This conclusion is suggested by the fact that he does so poorly on identification questions where no list of choices is given. However, I believe that Nopadol does have considerable understanding of U.S. history, though it may not be as deep as I would like. I have come to this conclusion because when Nopadol is able to express his answers in his own terms, drawing on what he understands instead of being asked for a discrete piece of information, he does well. The proof of this is how he answers essay questions. These are the kinds of questions he likes best. As you will see, I grade ESL students' answers on content, not on mechanics.

One of Nopadol's better essays was written after a field trip to the Pentagon. A colonel gave a lecture on the role of the U.S. military today. Nopadol's essay nicely captured the colonel's main points:

> The U.S. don't want to have the war with any nation in the wor. that includ Russai too. The U.S. try to make or cut the number of bom with the U.S.S.R However the U.S.S.R did not stop make the bom because they don't agrees with the U.S. Now the US.S.R. watch the U.S. who will becom the president. if a new president they will come and talk about in agint.

Nopadol wrote this and similar essays under time constraints and without notes. While the English may need reworking, he is able to communicate the main ideas, which is important to a history teacher.

My conclusion about the tests is that they are a good indication of Nopadol's English ability but are not a clear indication of how much history he knows. Until he can increase his vocabulary and thus understand the questions, he cannot pass the objective tests. However, Nopadol's ability to write intelligent essays suggests that his knowledge of history should be tested by means of essays and conversations instead of discrete point tests.

Conclusions

After tutoring Nopadol for three months, I cannot say that I have seen a lot of progress in his ability to handle a "language intensive" course like history. He is hampered by many things. First of all, he has little if any background in U.S. history. He is not used to working with the concepts. Second, he has very little interest in the subject. His bent is clearly toward the sciences and math. "I like the calculations," he says. Third, he has little time to study. A native English speaker needs to spend at least half an hour on U.S. history homework a night. But considering his reading ability, Nopadol would have to spend at least two hours per night. Naturally, he cannot devote this much time to one course since he must study for five other courses. Fourth, Nopadol rarely speaks English once he leaves school. Most of his social life takes place with his Cambodian friends. He is just not getting the input from his peers that is necessary to improve his vocabulary quickly. Fifth, Nopadol is not taking any ESL classes. He attended one or two in North Carolina but did not think they were of any value. His current course in English is a study of literature, grammar, and college-preparatory vocabulary. Sixth, Nopadol appears to be a fairly passive personality type. He does not actively pursue a knowledge of English. He prefers to learn current events from television rather than from a newspaper. He will go to his friend Matt for the answers rather than look them up. One year from now, Nopadol will be trying to get into a college to study electrical engineering. That may be enough time to improve his English sufficiently if he adopts his most effective learning strategies. He should make more effort to mix with Americans, particularly those like Matt who can help him with his notes and tests. In addition to watching television, he should read more, starting with the newspaper. This would help to increase his vocabulary. He should also ask his teachers the meanings of words he does not know in his text, just as he did with me. He should devote more of his study time to the subjects he finds most difficult. It is natural to pursue one's interests with enthusiasm, but almost any college program is going to require courses in various subject areas. If he concentrates on the strategies which have proven effective for him, he should be able to handle language-intensive content courses.

COMMENTS ON THE CASE STUDY OF NOPADOL

Although Nopadol attends a Catholic high school, it is in the same geographical area as the schools attended by Collier's (1987) subjects (see chapter 1), and therefore his case study sheds light on some of Collier's findings. Recall that Collier discovered that after three years of mainstreaming, the ESL students' reading test scores fell from the forty-fifth NCE to the thirty-fifth NCE, while the scores of their NES peers remained the same at the sixty-eighth NCE. This finding suggests that although eleventh-grade ESL students in the district have learned a good deal about content subjects, they are far behind their NES peers. This characterization fits Nopadol very well. He did not do well in the U.S. history course, but he was far from completely lost. He could follow the major points in the course but always seemed to be just below passing level.

A second finding is that Nopadol lacked effective academic strategies. He could not take notes on a lecture and follow the train of thought at the same time, but since the quizzes required that he know names and dates, he found it better to take the notes during class and try to understand them later. Also, Nopadol read much more slowly than the NES students and simply could not keep up with the reading for all his classes. It was for this reason that he relied much more on his notes than on the readings.

A third finding, one that emerged from many of the case studies, was that Nopadol did better on assignments in which he had some freedom to choose a topic and could avoid areas that he did not understand. He found multiple-choice tests especially difficult since he might miss an answer because he did not understand one vocabulary word.

A fourth finding concerned the role of background knowledge in Nopadol's learning. As Schepps points out, during their ten years of schooling in the United States, the NES students in her class had acquired a basic knowledge of the important figures and events of the Revolutionary and Civil wars, but Nopadol lacked this framework. In subjects such as international economics, where Nopadol did have adequate background knowledge, he did much better academic work.

CASE STUDY 3—DUC: OBSERVATIONS OF A VIETNAMESE GRADUATE STUDENT, BY DIANNA POODIACK

Background

It wasn't difficult to choose a subject for my research project in Applied Linguistics. I had met Duc the previous semester in a graduate class and had worked with him teaching writing in the Composition Tutorial Center (CTC). I often wondered how he survived as a graduate student in an American university; this project provided the opportunity to find out.

Duc was having a hard time in school. The previous semester he had received a "C" in Descriptive Linguistics (an unsatisfactory grade for a graduate student), and an incomplete in Proseminar in Composition. My main objective was to tutor him in Methods of ESL Teaching, but I also planned to check his progress in Modern English Grammar, and in completing the requirements for the incomplete in Proseminar in Composition Instruction.

Duc is a forty-six-year-old Vietnamese man, married, with three children ranging in age from thirteen to eighteen. A refugee, he has been in this country for four years, first living in Texas, then moving to northern Virginia. He began studying at Stonewall Jackson University after completing an A.A. degree in accounting at the local community college. His current goal is to earn an M.A. in English Linguistics. In Vietnam, he earned a B.A. in Pedagogy, an M.A. in International Law, and an M.S. in Political Science and Journalism. He took English as a foreign language in high school, and his coursework at the university for the B.A. in Pedagogy was primarily in British English. Currently, he is carrying six semester hours and is a teaching assistant in the Composition Tutorial Center, where he helps both NES and ESL students with their writing.

Duc's Educational Style

At the first tutoring session, it became apparent that Duc's greatest problems arose from the mismatch between the American style of education and the Vietnamese style. This mismatch resulted in three related problems: (1) Duc was reluctant to speak in class; (2) he was reluctant to ask his teachers questions, even in private, resulting in a breakdown in communications; and (3) he was reluctant to express his own opinions, even in writing. Duc had been a successful student in Vietnam, but he was unable to adapt to American ways. For example, in Vietnam students do not ordinarily participate orally in class either to ask questions or to express opinions (*Culture Capsules,* 1983). Duc knew that these activities were expected in his ESL Methods course, but he was afraid to participate orally. He mentioned in our first session, "Because you [native speakers] have been brought up in different way, I mean are free democratic process, you can feel strong in speaking, in relating, but whenever I respect somebody I feel myself tongue-tied." He explained to me that as a Vietnamese he had a great deal of respect for others based on age and expertise. In Vietnam, teachers are "fully respected." Thus, he felt an uneasiness here in talking for fear of "hurting" someone. He said he is often tongue-tied because he has *too much* respect for someone.

Duc believed that if you didn't agree with the teacher it meant you were criticizing her. He hesitated to speak in class not just because he was afraid of offending the teacher, but also because expressing his own opinions seemed too prideful. He believed that students who often participated did so to show off and dominate the teacher. He said, "I feel I am there to learn, not for somebody to solve my own problems . . . [as if] I think my friends can teach me more than the teacher."

In addition to cultural reasons for not speaking in class, Duc had the universal fear of being laughed at because of his imperfect command of a second language. He said, "The reason why I don't talk much in class because somebody before in my class laughed at some questions and the other student just ask the questions they fully know just to show off that they know and . . . just to dominate the teacher . . . and so I'm afraid asking."

Related to Duc's fear of talking in class was his general lack of confidence, which interfered with his own teaching in the Composition Tutorial Center. For example, one day when he was teaching, one of his students just "popped-in" the conversation (his words). When this happened, Duc said he couldn't go on: "I became somewhat tongue-tied." When I asked Duc why he lacked confidence, he gave me two reasons. One was that as a nonnative he didn't understand everything. The second reason was that, "Some people look down on us and make me . . . feel uneasy and make me become loss of confidence." Although he thought people looked down on him, Duc was still able to respect those people. But this caused problems, too. He said, "And the more I respect him, the more I cannot be me either."

Interaction with Teachers

Duc's respect for his professors bordered on fear and affected his communication with them. I believe that a lack of communication with the teacher was one reason Duc received an incomplete in the writing course. The requirements for the paper had been spelled out by the teacher in a private conference with Duc, but he had not understood what to do and had written the wrong kind of paper. He did not understand because he was unwilling to ask the teacher questions during the conference, as the following passage from my field notes suggests:

> I had the opportunity to discuss Duc's progress with the professor who gave him an incomplete last semester. She explained that she and Duc had gone over (and over . . .) what the requirements of the course were. She said he sat in the chair and nodded his head. She thought he understood, but when he passed in the paper, it was not what they had discussed.

I also have seen Duc nod as if he understood, when he didn't. When he and I discussed one of the questions on our methods mid-term, we talked about the answer at least three times. The first time Duc listened, wrote the answer, and seemed to understand. But the next night in class, he asked me for the answer again, then again in the next session. Each time I had the impression Duc understood. He did not ask for additional explanations and did not question me further. Had he not heard me and been afraid to ask me to repeat myself? Was this the same impression he gave his professor? And how many other instances occurred in Duc's classes that were similar?

Part of the problem Duc had writing the compositon paper was that he disagreed with the teacher's ideas, but he would not put that disagreement in writing. For this reason, he had changed the topic of his paper. He explained, "Because I was afraid . . . I had to choose another topic because to avoid [the professor's] criticism if I was trying to criticize policy . . . that's why I chose another topic."

Duc's reluctance to disagree with the professor also affected his performance in the teaching methods course. In this course, Duc strongly disagreed with Krashen's (1982) idea that second languages are internalized through acquisition rather than through learning. He explained, "But if I do not *know* the rule, how can I acquire it?" We talked about his bringing this question up in class. Duc felt that if you didn't agree with the teacher, it would be "criticizing" her. He felt he might hurt the teacher if he went against her views even on a take home exam. Besides, he said, the purpose of the exam was to test his understanding of the text, not to present his own ideas. Although Duc agreed that this teacher was very supportive, and strongly encouraged original thinking, he was still afraid to express his own views. This fear of expression appeared even in our last session when Duc said, "I'm afraid to write something imaginative. I'm afraid she'd think I fabricate the evidence."

In conclusion, I think that Duc's major problems were caused by his culturally based learning style, which prohibited him from speaking in class, from communicating with his teachers, and from expressing his own ideas. I have learned a lot from working with Duc. Perhaps the idea that is clearest to me is that it is absolutely necessary for teachers of ESL students to be aware of the complexities of their students' learning processes and of the individual students themselves.

COMMENTS ON THE CASE STUDY OF DUC

The case study of Duc shows the enormous difficulty ESL students can have adjusting to a new school culture. Duc's comments indicate that for him learning new scripts for school was not just an intellectual exercise but a deeply personal matter that went to the heart of his culturally based beliefs about how human beings ought to relate to one another. Duc characterized his feeling toward his professors as one of respect, but apparently he felt a good deal of fear as well. This fear made it impossible for him to interact effectively with his teachers.

Duc's comments also show that he did not respect students who participated orally in class, even though he understood that this participation was expected and required. He says that students who speak in class, "ask questions they fully know, just to show off . . . ." It appears that for Duc to adopt the kind of behavior he knew was expected of him would have required him to change his basic system of values to some extent. Duc was unwilling or unable to do this, and as a result he finally dropped out of the program.

As we will see in the next section, many of the Asian students in the case studies showed a reluctance to participate orally in class and to ask questions of teachers in private, even when they did not understand what they were supposed to do. However, at the intermediate and high school levels, this passive and respectful style of behavior was not as disastrous as it was for Duc. The case studies suggest that intermediate and high school teachers, who can teach as many as 150 students in a day, reward students who are respectful and work hard, even if these students have not done passing work. Perhaps Duc's style of interacting with teachers would not have caused problems for him in many academic situations, as is suggested by the fact that Duc had successfully earned an A.A. degree in accounting at a community college. But in the small graduate program in which Duc was enrolled, the professors required a great deal of personal interaction and participation as well as a high level of academic work. Duc's inability to interact with his professors beyond a superficial level was therefore a great disadvantage.

GENERAL FINDINGS OF THE CASE STUDIES

We now consider some general findings from the thirty-four case studies.

Reading

Reading is perhaps the most important academic skill. As Cummins (1979) notes, "The primary academic task for the child is learning how to extract information efficiently from printed text, and subsequent educational progress largely depends upon how well this task is accomplished" (p. 237). The case studies included many examples of students struggling with reading assignments that were far above their level. One such student was Enji, whose teacher was not aware of the difficulties she was having. One reason for this was that Enji, like many of the subjects, was a "word caller"; she had good decoding skills, but she often did not understand the words she was reading. Enji could read aloud materials at the seventh-grade level, but her comprehension was at the fourth-grade level. Enji's main problem, as measured by the Mann and Suiter *Developmental Paragraph Reading Inventory,* was vocabulary. Not only were many words unfamiliar to her, but also she was confused by new uses of known words, a common problem. For example, a book that Enji was using to write a research paper contained the following sentence:

> The classical conformation of the Arabian is a small, fine head, deep chest, high set tail, clean, hard legs.

In her paper Enji wrote,

> [The Arabian] has a small, fine head, deep chest, and a high set tail. It is always clean. It has hard legs.

The researcher noted, "I tried to explain to Enji that "clean, hard legs" meant that the Arabian's legs were trim and well formed, but she insisted that *clean* meant "not dirty.""

The student with the most difficulty in reading was Manh, the stroke victim, who apparently understood very little of what he read. To answer questions he did not understand, Manh would find a key word or phrase in the question, then try to find the same word or phrase in the text and copy down the whole sentence in which the key word or phrase appeared. For one tutoring session Manh's teacher had assigned several chapters of

The Adventures of Ulysses by Bernard Eislin with three pages of questions to be answered. After each question, the teacher had listed the page on which the answer could be found. Manh answered one of the questions as follows:

Q: Describe Lotusland.

A: Lotusland where Ulysses and his men blown by the gale.

Notice that Manh's answer is inappropriate grammatically as well as semantically. However, sometimes Manh was able to modify a copied sentence so that it would be grammatically appropriate, as in the following example:

Q: Why did Ulysses awake from his sleep?

A: Because it seemed to him that in his sleep he had seen the whole voyage laid out before him.

Manh had copied this answer word for word from the book but added the word *because*. This strategy paid off because although the answer is semantically inappropriate, the teacher marked it right. Below we will see more examples of how teachers sometimes pay attention only to the surface aspects of students' work.

Jose was another student who had great difficulty with reading. His tests indicated that he read at the early second-grade level, but his social studies text was at the fifth-grade level. However, Jose had found a good strategy for dealing with this difficult text, namely using visual material. His researcher observed, "Quite often, while reading, he flipped through the book pages to show me a picture of what he was reading. Grain elevator? He remembered and showed me a picture. He showed me his worksheets. He had completed only the sections where visuals were involved."

The good readers among the subjects shared a number of strategies, some of which illustrate the points made in the discussion of reading in the opening section of chapter 3. One of the good readers was Hiroshi, who chose for his outside reading book *The Adventures of Tom Sawyer,* a difficult book for any thirteen-year-old. His teacher asked the students to spend twenty minutes a day on their outside reading, but Hiroshi had to read for an hour a day in order to finish the book on time. It is clear that he would not have been able to understand crucial aspects of the story without the extra help from his researcher. One key to Hiroshi's success with *Tom Sawyer* was his ability to tolerate less than a complete understanding of the text and just concentrate on understanding the main points. Hiroshi underlined unknown words and later asked his tutor what they meant. He was also able to focus his attention on the important episodes in the book and skim the unimportant ones. His researcher noted:

As the sessions went further on, Hiroshi showed a great eagerness to read by himself. . . . He did not come to me as often as I had expected him to. [He] seemed to have an intuitive feel for which passages were important in plot development.

A second key to Hiroshi's success with *Tom Sawyer* was his interest in the book: "He identified with Tom in many ways. . . . Hiroshi loves to joke and occasionally play tricks on us."

Choosing a book of interest worked well for Joe, a college student, who like all the subjects, found reading very time consuming. His researcher observed: "Although Joe reads his sociology text every night, he still remains a few chapters behind at all times." For one assignment, Joe had to choose between analyzing a short article, "The Pursuit of Loneliness," or reading the five-hundred-page *Autobiography of Malcolm X*. Joe was inclined to choose the article because he "was worried about his reading capacity." However, his researcher felt that the *Autobiography* (which was written in collaboration with Alex Haley, the author of *Roots*), would be livelier and more interesting, so Joe decided to try the longer work. The researcher described the paper Joe wrote in connection with this assignment as follows:

> Joe's brief paper was well presented. He gave concrete references to the life of Malcolm X and also related the theories to his sociology text. . . . He admitted that he had skimmed certain parts of [the book], but he did like it well enough to read it from cover to cover. . . . Joe said that it was more enjoyable than his textbooks and thus he read it with ease.

Both Hiroshi and Joe succeeded on longer reading assignments because the material was of interest to them and because they could skim the less important parts.

The best reader was Duc, who used the strategy of rereading. To study for the midterm in his ESL methods class, he first read the material, underlining important points and writing notes in the margin. Next, he summarized the important points in his notebook. Duc modified this strategy for his reading assignments in the grammar class, where the text was more difficult for him. Unable to completely understand the material on a first reading, he was content to "grasp a notion of the subject matter. He then read the book a second time to gain something more, and then a third time to master the material." Duc's approach to reading illustrates Saville-Troike's (1984) observation that some of her good students "shared an active and competitive coping style" and "initiated independent learning activities" (p. 215).

Dictionary Use

The subjects showed great variety in the ways they used dictionaries. Many of them overused the dictionary. Ahmad, for example, looked up every unknown word in his Arabic-English dictionary. His tolerance for ambiguity was very low, as shown by the fact that he looked up even easy words like *toy*. He felt that the dictionary was the key to mastering his problems with English vocabulary, and had filled three notebooks with words he had encountered in his classes along with their Arabic translations. Ahmad explained how he approached a reading passage this way: "First, I look up the meaning of the difficult words in the dictionary. Second, I read the passage twice." Ahmad's strategy for using the bilingual dictionary was effective but not optimal. He did understand the material, but if he had not relied on the dictionary so much, he could have read more efficiently.

As we have seen, Hiroshi could use the dictionary more efficiently because he was able to live with some ambiguity and so looked up only the words that were important. Si-Young used this techinque as well:

RESEARCHER: Do you look up all the words in a dictionary?

S.-Y.: Not all.

RESEARCHER: How do you decide which ones to look up?

S.-Y.: If I read a sentence and I don't understand a word, then I keep reading and the word just comes out . . . so many times. Then I have to look it up . . . Because it might be important. That is why it repeats.

In general the students preferred bilingual dictionaries when they could get them; however, some could not find a useful dictionary in their language. Marika, for example, had a large, expensive Cambodian-English dictionary, but it contained only words used for everyday conversation, not scientific words. Perhaps one reason most students preferred bilingual dictionaries was that often they did not understand the definitions in monolingual dictionaries. For example, when Manny and his researcher were preparing for a test, they encountered the word *erosion*. Looking up the word *erode*, Manny found the following: "The wearing away of the earth's surface." Manny did not understand *wearing away*, and had to look it up. Similarly, Hiroshi looked up *pride* to find "an undue sense of one's own superiority." His researcher notes, "Probably *undue* and *superiority* are even harder than *pride*." Some of the students, however, found monolingual dictionaries very helpful, if they could find one right for their level. Jose often used the glossary in his social studies book, which, of course, was written at the same level of difficulty as the book itself.

Unfortunately, sometimes the students used dictionaries to complete assignments without really understanding the material. For example, Alexis had to write definitions for *feudalism, knight, lord, peasant,* and *squire*. The definition of feudalism was "the social, political, and economic system of the middle ages." Alexis did not understand this definition very well, but he resisted his researcher's attempts to have him write his own definition and copied the one in the dictionary. Perhaps Alexis used this coping strategy because it allowed him to finish the assignment within a reasonable amount of time. His researcher noted, "Looking up words was very difficult for him, and it sometimes took him five minutes to find a word."

Note-Taking

Taking good notes from lectures is a complex linguistic task. It requires that the student (1) comprehend the stream of speech, (2) separate important from unimportant information, (3) provide some sort of logical framework for the important information sometimes, but not always, provided by the lecturer, and (4) write down the important information in its logical framework. Even our best subjects had difficulty accomplishing all of these tasks at once. Duc was a good note taker, but when the teacher spoke too rapidly, he could not keep up taking notes in English and had to fall back on writing in Vietnamese. He also sometimes had trouble understanding unfamiliar dialects of English.

The most common problem for the good note takers was unfamiliar vocabulary words or idiomatic expressions. For example, Lucy's psychology professor had attempted to illustrate *stimulus* and *response* by observing that a government's withholding taxes from wages can act as a stimulus that induces in workers the response of working only for cash or "off the books." Because Lucy did not understand that phrase *off the books*, she missed the point of the example. Duc tried to figure out the meaning of unknown words from context while the lecturer was speaking, but in doing so he missed parts of the lecture. He remarked that he considered his need to understand every word a liability, and he wished he could tolerate some ambiguity and just follow the main ideas. But he felt compelled to try to figure out unknown words, even if he knew they weren't important. Elizebeth shared Duc's frustration at not being able to understand all the words in lectures. She said, "I usually didn't miss the main parts. . . . Some details I miss. I'm curious about the details. I want to understand her lectures perfectly. It's impossible for me to understand perfectly, for me right now." However, Elizebeth had developed an effective strategy for dealing with unknown words in lectures. She did not slow down to try to figure out their meaning, but rather transcribed them in the Korean syllabary and later asked friends what they meant. In addition, Elizebeth kept a tape recorder at hand, which she would turn on only when she did not understand what was being said. She explained that she did not record the entire lecture because she did not have enough time to listen to it all again; she just needed to replay the difficult parts.

Three of the college students—Lucy, Ahmad, and Joe—did not take extensive notes. In Lucy's case this was partly because she had trouble hearing the lecturer, who (according to the researcher) "had the type of voice that is very uneven in its sound and is very difficult to hear. Lucy was relieved that I had difficulty hearing him also." Nevertheless, in one lecture the researcher took four pages of notes while Lucy took only one page. Lucy's way of compensating for missing lecture material was to rely on the textbook, a common strategy. In fact, she trusted the book more than the lecturer. For example, the textbook had misprinted the abbreviation for *computer assisted instruction* as *CAT* instead of *CAI*. When the professor wrote CAI on the blackboard, Lucy assumed that the professor had made the mistake. Her researcher notes, "She believed this even though the professor had stated that CAI stood for Computer Assisted Instruction." Ahmad relied entirely on the textbook; in fact, he took no notes at all, not even those written on the blackboard. When asked why, he replied, "I don't need it. I have my books."

We found that there is a great difference between taking notes in college and taking notes in intermediate school and high school. In a precollege setting the teacher almost always writes some or all of the important information on the board. Thus, it was possible to copy and study from a set of notes that were not fully understood. In fact, the strategy of simply copying everything on the board, whether it was understood or not, was the most common strategy among the precollege subjects. We have seen that Nopadol diligently wrote down everything on the board instead of looking at the teacher and following what she was saying (the researcher noted that this strategy is used by many native speakers also), and that he did better on tests when he had notes to study (even if he did not understand everything in them) than if he dispensed with note-taking in order to understand the lecture better.

Some teaching techniques encouraged the use of verbatim note-taking. For example, Ana's science teacher came in early each morning and wrote on the board exactly what she wanted to see in each student's notes. In addition, the teacher said that she based her tests exclusively on what appeared on the board or in the text. Similarly, Mark's teacher wrote several pages of notes on the board, which the students copied. Mark would memorize these notes without understanding them. Using this strategy, he was able to get only barely passing grades. However, a few weeks after the tutoring sessions began, Mark did well on a test, missing only two questions out of twenty. He excitedly explained to his researcher that he had developed a new study technique. After seeing how the researcher used a tape recorder during the tutoring sessions, Mark had gotten one of his own and had recited his notes into it. Then he replayed the tape "perhaps 30 times." Although this technique had not improved his understanding of the material, it had improved his ability to memorize his notes and so improved his test scores. On the other hand, some students preferred to listen to the lecture for understanding instead of taking notes. This strategy usually worked whenever the lectures closely paralleled the material in the book and the tests covered only this duplicated material.

Organization

The more successful students were well organized and neat. We have seen how Duc attacked difficult reading material: first, he read to get an overall idea of the subject matter, then he read to get more detail, and finally he outlined and took notes on everything. Elizebeth also attacked difficult material by using total organization. For her geography notes she copied everything the professor wrote on the board in ink. After these entries she wrote down as much as she could understand of the lecture in pencil. Finally, she tape-recorded the parts of the lecture she could not understand so that she could go back later and listen to them again. Like Duc, Elizebeth was a very motivated student who used creative ways to understand the lecture material even when her elaborate note-taking system broke down. One day she was sick but attended class anyway. However, she could not concentrate enough to take notes, so she attempted to record the entire lecture. Unfortunately, her tape recorder malfunctioned and did not record anything. Since the subject of the lecture was the geography of South America, Elizebeth went to the library and checked out some maps, which she studied in great detail with her researcher. She subsequently received 100 percent on the quiz covering that material. Manny's note-taking strategy was similar to Elizebeth's. He would rewrite all his notes, usually three or four lectures at a time, because "I want to make it look nice, and it's easy to read."

The students who were well organized were usually very interested in the course material. Elizebeth remarked, "I love mapping and learning information about new countries. I'm pretty exciting about it, but I know I have to study a lot. I think it's really fun."

On the other hand, the students who were less organized and methodical about studying seemed less interested in their schoolwork and, unsurprisingly, were less successful. Alexis, who spoke very fluent English (his researcher never noticed an error in his casual conversation), was doing poorly in all his subjects and was failing math and world studies. Alexis's notebook was so messy his teacher had to put it in order for him, and on three occasions he had to look through all his books and papers to find an assignment. Alexis may have used disorganization as an excuse for not doing assignments. He was habitually "losing" assignments that were due and often could not find examples of papers or quizzes on which he had not done well. He often "forgot about" tests he had to study for and assignments that were due. In addition, he was often late to class. Alexis's lack of motivation is illustrated by an incident involving a dictionary. Alexis did not have a dictionary and needed one to do his assignments. He asked his researcher where he could get one and she made several suggestions, but despite repeated urging he never did follow through and buy one. On two occasions he asked to go to the library rather than participate in the tutoring sessions, and he once told his researcher, "I'd rather do this at home." When asked what his favorite class was, he replied in a flat tone of voice, "I don't know, none of them."

Sandra was able to use her organizational skills to great advantage, but in her case they were used to compensate for a lack of understanding. The textbook in Sandra's cosmetology course was written at the high school level, but on a reading test administered six months before the course began, Sandra had scored at the mid-second-grade level. To see how well Sandra understood the textbook, the researcher asked her to read a passage she had previously studied, dealing with facial makeup. Sandra read fairly fluently, pronouncing all the words more or less accurately and with correct intonation. However, when the researcher asked her what some essential words meant—such as *cotton swab* and *sponge*—Sandra did not know. When the researcher pointed out to the teacher that Sandra did not know the names of commonly used items, the teacher was amazed. However, Sandra managed to get an A in the course mainly by keeping all her written work in immaculate condition. Her notebook was divided into subject areas in which every assignment, worksheet, and test could be found. Each page was numbered with dark marking pen in the upper right-hand corner. Sandra never handed in a rough draft of a paper, even when this was allowed; instead, she insisted on recopying everything. All the headings and key words in her papers were underlined or written with colored felt-tip pens. Sandra's beautiful notebook made a hit with the teacher, who gave it an A+ and asked her to help other students organize their notebooks.

Speaking in Class

Few teachers of ESL students will be surprised to hear that most of the subjects, even those who spoke very good English, were reluctant to speak in class. This reluctance had at least three causes: the students' cultural backgrounds, their fear of being laughed at because of imperfect English, and their fear of divulging a lack of knowledge about the subject matter.

Many of the subjects came from countries where students do not orally participate in class. For example, according to the publication *Culture Capsules* (1983), Vietnamese schools are different from American schools in the following ways:

1. Teachers lecture usually for the whole period.
2. Students are expected to be silent during class. There are no or very limited class discussions.
3. Students do not interrupt the teacher's lectures to ask questions.
4. Students take notes on what the teacher says.
5. Much memorization work is done. Students must sometimes memorize their notes from the lectures.

As we have seen, these traditions partly explain why Duc, who spoke good English, felt tongue-tied in class. He said that asking questions would seem disrespectful to the teacher, and expressing his own ideas would seem too prideful: "I feel I am there to learn, not for somebody to solve my problems."

Zai, a Malaysian student who spoke excellent British-accented English, had very strong inhibitions about speaking in class that were culturally based. She insisted that American teachers should respect the Malaysian reluctance to speak in class as an almost religious prohibition and should grade Malaysian students only on their written work.

The most commonly expressed reason for not speaking in class was fear of being laughed at. We have seen that Duc had this fear: "The reason why I don't talk much in class because somebody before in my class laugh at some questions." Similarly, Manny never raised his hand in class, although he frequently knew the answers, because "They made fun. They laugh at me. My English not so good." However, Manny and several others had an effective way of asking questions. Manny would approach the teacher before or after class, or during class if there was a time when he could go up to the teacher's desk, and ask the question privately. Jose also used this strategy, but showed some reluctance to do even this. His researcher asked him to ask the teacher if it was acceptable for them to work together on worksheets. Jose shook his head, "No." Then the researcher suggested that she ask, and he smiled and said, "Yes." The researcher felt that Jose's anxiety about asking questions might have been heightened by the fact that his teacher sometimes called on him in class when he had not raised his hand, something she did not do to other students.

As we have seen, Ceyong talked to no one in her science class except her Japanese friend, with whom she spoke in Japanese. Ceyong wrote in her journal that she had once been laughed at by an American when she had said something in English. Her Japanese researcher noted, "I could understand her feelings because I had the same kind of experience and most Asians including me are so afraid to make mistakes." However, Ceyong was talkative in her ESL class, as were a number of the other students who were mostly silent in their content classes.

Tri, a Vietnamese student, explained his reluctance to speak in class in terms very similar to Duc's: he said that it wouldn't be fair for him to interrupt the whole class to ask a question because he was the only nonnative speaker. Tri also shared Duc's opinion of the value of class discussions: he did not take notes on these discussions because he felt that the students' contributions were unimportant. However, Tri's researcher believed that his reluctance to speak in class was also partly to conceal his lack of understanding. Tri did not understand many of the basic concepts in his literature class, partly because he lacked the necessary background knowledge. For example, in the tutoring session covering Frederick Douglass's "What the Black Man Wants," Tri did not know the following essential vocabulary words: *abolitionist, campaign, elective franchise, autocratic government,* and *woman suffrage.* Yet in a one-on-one discussion of this material with his teacher, Tri politely agreed and nodded affirmatively to her comments and questions, even if the right answer to the question was no. Similarly, Khan's researcher felt that Khan's silence was partly caused by her lack of understanding. This lack was shown by Khan's low scores on tests; by her teacher's comment, "basically nothing was processing in Khan's head"; and by the fact that Khan eventually had to drop the class. Khan's researcher observed that when the class was engaged in a teacher–class dialogue about osmosis, diffusion, and the steps of the scientific method, Khan was busy copying definitions of these terms from her textbook into her notebook, so that she could memorize them later. This was about all she could do in a class that was basically above her level. Saville-Troike (1984) noted that her younger ESL students also had difficulty understanding teacher–class dialogues, observing that "In these . . . we saw most of the limited English-speaking children entirely unable to cope: staring out windows, doodling, poking their neighbors—one even crawling under his desk in retreat" (p. 212).

Coping Strategies

As we have seen, the students were often given assignments they were unable to complete in a meaningful way. When this happened, they often employed *coping strategies* in an attempt to do the assignments in a mechanical way. The two most common coping strategies were copying and memorization.

Copying.   Copying took a number of different forms: looking for key words in the readings that were also present in the questions, then copying the sentence; looking for sentences in the readings that were affirmative versions of the questions, then copying the sentence; and copying larger passages from encyclopedia articles and other sources.

The strategy of looking for a key word or phrase often produced sentences that were grammatically awkward in the context of the question or that included extraneous information. For example, Manny answered a question as follows:

Q: What did people notice about the shape of continents?
A: Notice how the continents seem like pieces of a jigsaw puzzle that might just fit together.

This answer is copied word for word from the book. Although Manny did not know what a jigsaw puzzle was, he was able to locate the appropriate sentence from the text because of the key words *notice* and *continents*.

Manh also used the key word strategy, which produced the right answer for him about 50 percent of the time. However, it also produced some incongruous answers:

Q: Why did Ulysses decide to put his ships in harbor?
A: Ulysses wished to put as much open water as possible between him and the Island of Winds, but after six days he realized he would have to put his ship into harbor.

Here Manh had found a sentence with the key word *harbor* that had nothing to do with the question.

It is interesting to compare Manh's copied answers with his meaningful answers. For example, after much help and encouragement from his researcher during a one-hour session, Manh wrote the following definitions:

looting	The thief taken something
skillful	It skillfull to do something well.
archer	it helps people to make animal die by bow and arrow
overboard	something drop in the water from the ship.

Manh's researcher remarked, "I know most teachers would look at the above definitions and just cringe. . . . I know that for myself they were the most beautiful lines I had ever seen. They were meaningful, and that is what counted."

Ana used the strategy of finding affirmative versions of questions to complete a workbook exercise. For example, she got the following question right:

> One liter contains _____ cubic centimeters.

In the science book, the corresponding information appeared as follows:

> One liter contains 1000 millimeters or 1000 cubic centimeters.

However, Ana had trouble when the question was not worded very similarly to the information in the text. She provided no answer to the following question:

> Metric units can be changed by multiples of _____.

In the book this information appeared as

> Prefixes are used to change the units by multiples of 10.

Both the college and the precollege students copied larger sections of discourse for essays and papers. Marika, for example, had to do an extra-credit paper in earth science because she was failing the course. Her teacher assigned her the topic "icebergs as a water source" and told her that she had to write five pages and use three references, which she did. Marika's teacher liked her paper, used it as the basis for a class discussion, and reported to the school counselor that he was "pleased with Marika's progress." Marika was reluctant to show the paper to her researcher, but after being asked three times she finally did, remarking, "Please do not say anything about the paper." The researcher could tell immediately that most of the paper had been copied, and she verified this by checking the paper against the source material. This researcher had been Marika's ESL teacher the previous semester and had worked very closely with her during the earth science course, so she had a good idea of what Marika did and did not understand. She remarked, "It seemed to me the paper did very little to increase Marika's knowledge of earth science."

On the other hand, some of the researchers felt that copying could aid learning when the copied material was well understood. An example was when Fati had to write a biography of an artist for her art history course. The researcher helped Fati find some reference books, but did not help her write the paper because Fati said she knew how to do that. When Fati's paper was returned, it had received the grade D+ and the following comment was written on it:

> Clearly a lot of work was put in on this. Unfortunately, it contains not a word of your own. In the U.S. one does not copy other people's ideas and call them his.

Manny's Sentence	Sentence in Textbook
1. The sun located toward the edge of the milky way galaxy.	Our sun is located toward the edge of the Milky Way Galaxy.
2. almost every energy of the earth comes from the sun.	Almost all of the energy on the surface of the earth comes from the sun.

FIGURE 4.1   A Comparison of Manny's Sentences with Sentences in His Textbook.

Fati had nicely put together passages from a number of sources, but had made no effort to change the wording of the originals. Fati's researcher believed that Fati had done this to make the task of writing the paper easier and that she did not understand the concept of plagiarism. The researcher, who shared Fati's Arabic background, spoke to the professor, who agreed that no dishonesty had been intended.

Several students used a kind of partial copying strategy in which only sentences or phrases were copied and the copied material was fully understood and might even have been processed through the student's interlanguage system. For example, Manny was asked to read a passage on the sun and pick out four important points. A comparison of Manny's answers with the sentences from the originals is found in Figure 4.1. Manny's sentences do not appear to have been mechanically copied from the original. In sentence 1, Manny appropriately changed *our* to *the*. In sentence 2, he neglected to capitalize *almost*, changed *all* to *every*, and deleted the phrase *on the surface*. Similarly, Hiroshi used the semicopying strategy in his report on Hank Aaron. One of his sentences was:

So said Aaron to a mass of reporter in the moment after the finish of the game in which he hit his 715th home run.

The absence of *s* on *reporter* and the awkward phrase *in the moment after the finish of the game* appear to come from Hiroshi, but the rest of the sentence, with its stylistic beginning and its sophisticated relative clause, do not. Hiroshi's researcher remarked, "I do not think this sort of copying is cheating. Quite frankly, I think it is a positive way of exposing L2 learners to a higher level of learning, provided that the subject matter is understood by the learner."

Memorization.   Memorization is a favorite strategy in many countries; when students from these countries enter American schools, they continue to memorize. An example from the literature is when Chamot and O'Malley (1984) taught ESL students to remember vocabulary words by means of the cognitive strategies of "grouping" and "imagery." Grouping was taught by asking students to divide a long list of words into groups and label the groups according to their semantic similarity. Imagery was taught by having students close their eyes and create a vivid image that incorporated the words they had grouped together. However, the students who received this training were not able to learn the words on a twenty-item list better than a control group. Chamot and O'Malley

(1984) attribute this lack of success to the fact that "the Asian students preferred to rely upon rote repetition which seemed to have worked successfully for them in the past" (p. 5). Similarly, one of the researchers in the present study reported that in her schools in Palestine, "We used to memorize the whole lesson word by word. . . . I still suffer from this memorization strategy that our schools emphasize."

Many of the subjects in this study memorized definitions and even whole pages of text in order to prepare for exams. One was Ana, who memorized as much as she could of notes copied from the board, even though she did not understand them. Another was Mark, who as we have seen, used a tape recorder to help him memorize. Mark attempted to memorize fifteen or twenty words and their definitions for his weekly vocabulary tests by writing them many times. He was usually able to supply these items more or less accurately, in spite of not always understanding what he was writing. His lack of understanding is shown by the fact that he sometimes miscopied from the board, memorized the error, and then wrote the resulting nonsense on the test. For example, the following definition appeared both in Mark's notes and on his test:

   prey—an organism that is lucnted [should be *hunted*] by another organism.

Another problem was that sometimes Mark couldn't remember all of a definition. For example, he wrote in his notebook:

   humus—parts of soil made up of decayed leaves

But on his test he could only remember the following:

   humus—parts of soil made up

Mark also confused several definitions. In his notebook he had written:

   growth—the process by which organisms gets larger
   life cycle—the stages of development organisms pass through as they mture: birth,
         growth, maturity, death

On his test, however, he wrote:

   growth—maturity, death

It is interesting that none of these answers was marked wrong by the teacher, a fact that suggests another coping strategy: hand in whatever you can and hope that it gets by.

Like copying, memorization could be used for learning as well as for coping. For example, Ahmad used memorization as a way of learning new vocabulary. Recall that he would look up all the unfamiliar words in a reading passage in his bilingual dictionary and write the Arabic translation above the English word. He would also write the new word and its translation in a notebook and memorize the contents of the notebook. Although this strategy slowed down his reading tremendously, he did learn a lot of new vocabulary words. Fati memorized much of her oral report, which she understood very well, and therefore was able to deliver the report from notes rather than reading it. However, apparently she also memorized words and phrases she did not completely understand in order to make her classroom comments more impressive. Her art history professor commented, "Fati seemed to like these big words and long phrases that she had on her mind, but when she is asked to summarize what she has been saying, she does terribly."

Conclusions

The preceding discussion points to a conclusion similar to that of Saville-Troike (1984):

> Perhaps the most important point . . . is the extent to which there were individual differences among the subjects. . . . The diversity is particularly apparent in our study of children from different language and cultural backgrounds. . . . To the question of what really made a difference consistently for all of the children in this study, the only answer must be: very little. (p. 215)

The subjects of the present study approached academic tasks in ways that were influenced by their own academic backgrounds and cultures, their individual learning styles, and the nature of the assigned tasks. It can be said, however, that all of the subjects found their academic work very difficult and that those who succeeded did so by devoting much time and energy to their studies.

A second finding is that some of the subjects' academic strategies were more effective than others. For example, Duc had trouble taking notes because he insisted on trying to figure out the meaning of every unknown word from context and therefore missed some important information. Nopadol had the opposite problem. He insisted on writing down all the information on the board and therefore could not understand the lecture. However, Elizebeth developed effective note-taking strategies. The implication of this finding is that even good students like Duc may develop less-than-optimal academic strategies when left to their own devices. Therefore, they need explicit academic skills instruction.

Perhaps the most important finding of the study is that when students are faced with material that is beyond their ability to comprehend, they develop ways of completing their assignments without understanding them, thus concealing their lack of understanding from the teacher. The most common of these coping strategies are memorization and copying. It is important to note that these strategies can be used in meaninfgul as well as in mechanical ways. In sum, all of the subjects were given assignments involving academic material that they did not fully understand, and their task was to use their limited resources as efficiently as possible. All of the subjects developed ways of dealing with difficult material, but with varying degrees of success. Therefore, the goal of the ESL teacher in academic settings should be to show students how they can use limited resources to accomplish academic assignments most effectively.

CASE STUDY 4—THE PRECOURSE: TEACHING ACADEMIC STRATEGIES IN A LANGUAGE THROUGH CONTENT COURSE

The previous three case studies have focused on individual ESL students in content courses. We now consider an entire class of college-level ESL students studying descriptive linguistics. These students were enrolled in a type of language through content course that this author has called a *precourse* (Adamson, 1990).

Brinton, Snow, and Wesche (1989) distinguish three types of language through content courses: theme-based courses, sheltered courses, and adjunct courses. Theme-based courses are the most common. They involve studying popular topics, like drug abuse or pollution, using general-audience materials such as newspapers or magazines. Theme-based courses can also cover selected academic subjects like sociology, biology, and economics, using one of the ESL textbooks that contains chapters from college texts that have been adapted for ESL students. Sheltered courses, common in high schools, enroll only ESL students in special sections of a regular credit course. Sheltered courses are taught by content teachers or are team taught by a content teacher and an ESL teacher. Adjunct courses enroll ESL students for credit in a regular academic course and in an associated ESL course where the content material is reviewed and academic strategies can be taught. A precourse combines elements of an adjunct course and a theme-based course. Students enrolled in a theme-based course join a regular content course for less than a full semester and are tutored in the content subject and in academic strategies by their ESL teachers.

My colleagues Phyllis Duryee and Melissa Allen and I set up a precourse at the university level (see Adamson, Duryee, and Allen, 1990). The precourse worked as follows. I was teaching an undergraduate linguistics course, Introduction to Linguistics, at a medium-size southern university. I devoted about three weeks of the course to the study of L1 and L2 acquisition. This unit was appropriate for ESL students because the material was introductory and not technical. For this unit (taught during the fifth, sixth, and seventh weeks of the course) eighteen ESL students, who were simultaneously enrolled in a theme-based ESL course, joined the thirty-five regular students. The ESL students and their two instructors attended the course for three hours a week. For an additional two and one-half hours a week they met in their ESL classes to review the content material and to learn academic skills. Two groups of ESL students participated in the project. One group (whose median TOEFL score was 567) was in an advanced ESL course, and one group (whose median TOEFL score was 547) was in an intermediate ESL course. The ESL students participated fully in the linguistics course: they attended the lectures, participated in the discussions, wrote the one-thousand-word research paper, and took an exam on the material they had studied. During the ESL classes, the instructors taught academic skills in connection with the content material. The following is a brief summary of the techniques the ESL instructors used.

How Academic Strategies Were Taught

Note-taking.   The ESL instructor's notes on the lectures were photocopied and passed around. In a class discussion that focused on the content of the lecture, the instructor went over the notes point by point while the students highlighted, modified, and added to their own notes. The instructor then collected the students' notes and added comments and corrections, after which the students rewrote their notes. In a second type of exercise, the students went over their notes in small groups, underlining important material and adding material they had missed. The instructor of the advanced ESL course commented that she thought this was the most helpful note-taking exercise.

The instructor of the intermediate course thought that the most useful note-taking exercise was showing students how to review and expand their notes immediately after the lecture. To do this, she used the divided-page technique (see chapter 7), in which the students take notes on the right side of the paper and, as soon as possible after the lecture, expand the notes on the left side of the paper. This exercise seemed especially helpful to students like Lucy, who did not take extensive notes because they attended to the meaning of the lecture.

Preparing for Tests.   To prepare for the midterm exam, the students took a practice test. The class then critiqued typical answers, both good and bad, which were displayed on an opaque projector. Figure 4.2 shows a typical practice question, a student's answer, and the teacher's response, which brings out additional information.

Writing the Paper.   A course requirement was to write a one-thousand-word paper describing the language of a first or second language learner. This assignment required the students to find a subject; tape-record a fifteen-minute conversation; transcribe the conversation in English orthography; and comment on the data by using some of the concepts studied in the course, such as transfer from the first language, the two-word stage in child language acquisition, and the order of morpheme accuracy. The students were very dubious about their ability to do this assignment. The ESL instructors also saw that the assignment would be difficult, so they devoted more time to it than to any other assignment. One practical problem for the students who had recently arrived in the United States was finding a suitable subject. The teachers helped by finding beginning-level students at the English Language Institute who could be used as subjects, and by making appointments with them for recording sessions. In addition, the teachers did the assignment along

FIGURE 4.2   Part of the Practice Test for the Precourse.

Sample Questions

1. List three of the criticisms or critical comments which Dr. Adamson made about the Aitchison article.
2. What is lateralization?
3. Have Victor and Ishi had an important impact on today's thinking regarding language acquisition?

Student's Answer

3. ishi had a hard time to learn and he died because of the disease and the scientists tried to teach him how to speak English but it did not work. also Victor could not learn French and Victor died too. I think the reason that scientists could not find out about them maybe was because that they had not got enough and new equipment. Genie's case they had new technology and they had an operation on her brain that is why they could help her.

Teacher's Comment

Also no one knew the background of Victor or Ishi. Since they might have been brain damaged or retarded, their lack of language acquisition is not strong evidence for the critical period hypothesis.

with the students, demonstrating the process of tape recording and transcribing (this had been described but not demonstrated in the regular class). The teachers provided supplementary lessons on how to analyze the data and distributed a model outline for the paper. They also reviewed the students' drafts for content, organization, and mechanics.

Oral Participation.   In the ESL classes, the students had the opportunity to participate in real academic discussions in a reduced-risk environment. They participated enthusiastically in these discussions because they were dealing with real course material, not the specially edited ''canned lessons'' that are found in texts for theme-based courses. These discussions gave the students enough confidence to participate effectively in the regular class. In fact, the ESL students' enthusiasm and eagerness contrasted sharply with the laid-back attitude of many of the regular students.

Analysis of the Precourse

To assess how well the students followed the content material and whether the precourse helped prepare them for academic courses, all the documents the students produced, including class notes, term papers, midterm exams, practice tests, and worksheets, were copied and analyzed. In addition, the students were asked to keep journals in which they wrote their reactions to the precourse. At the end of the course, a questionnaire asking for the students' evaluations of the project was administered. The ESL students' grades for the precourse module were determined by the ESL teachers, but the content teacher also graded a sample of the ESL students' exams and papers in order to compare them to those of the regular students.

The ESL students as a group did not do well on the open-book, open-note exam, which required them to answer five of eight short-answer questions and one of three essay questions. To compare the ESL students to the regular students, the content instructor graded the intermediate group's exam. This group's median score was 51 out of 100, where 60 was the lowest passing grade. Some of the low scores seemed to reflect a lack of test-taking ability rather than a lack of knowledge. For example, Yuri wrote acceptable answers on the short-answer section, but she answered all eight questions rather than choosing five. As a result, she did not have enough time to write a good essay. Six ESL students did not attempt to answer all five of the short answer questions, probably because it took them longer to write answers than it took the regular students. In general, the answers that these students did write were acceptable.

It is difficult to generalize about the ESL students' problems with the exam. There was some use of coping strategies. Figure 4.3 compares Mahmet's answer to essay question 1 with the relevant passage from the text. Notice that Mahmet did not just copy the passage word for word. In some places he summarized it, and apparently he understood at least part of what he wrote. For example, he appropriately added the conjunction *but* to connect the first and second sentences in the text. Also, he sensibly summarized the wordy passage, ''The rapidity with which she acquired the complex grammar of English provides some support for the hypothesis that . . .'' with the phrase ''It appears that. . . .'' However, the last sentence in his essay shows that Mahmet did not understand everything he wrote. He interpreted *because* as a connector between the first sentence in the final

CASE STUDIES OF ESL STUDENTS IN CONTENT COURSES 99

Mahmet's Answer

Another case similar to some extent to that of Genie is that of a child who was not exposed to language until she was six-and-a-half years because of imprisonment with a mute and totally uneducated but within twenty-two months she progressed from her first spoken words (ball, cow, bye . . .) to asking such questions as "Why does the paste come out if one upsets the jar?

It appears that language learning mechanism is more specific than general, and language capacity of the right hemospher must be limited in time or amount of learning. Because don't have no grammatical description of right hemospher spech.

The Relevant Passage from the Text*

Another case, similar to some extent to that of Genie, is that of a child who was not exposed to language until she was six-and-a-half years old because of her imprisonment with a mute and totally uneducated aphasic mother (Mason, 1942). Within twenty-two months, she progressed from her first spoken words ("ball," "cow," "bye") to asking such questions as, "Why does the paste come out if one upsets the jar?" The rapidity with which she acquired the complex grammar of English provides some support for the hypothesis that the language learning mechanism is more specific than general.

This case is also consistent with a two-to-puberty critical period theory. The language learning capacity of the right hemisphere then may be limited either in time or amount of learning. Because we have no grammatical descriptions of right hemisphere speech, we cannot predict how far Genie will progress from comparisons with such cases.

*From V. Fromkin, S. Krashen, S. Curtiss, D. Rigler, and M. Rigler, "The Development of Genie: A Case Study of Language Acquisition Beyond the 'Critical Period,' " in *Language: Introductory Readings*, ed. V. P. Clark, P. A. Eschholz, and A. F. Rosa (New York: St. Martins, 1985), p. 128.

FIGURE 4.3 Mahmet's Answer to the Exam Question Asking Him to Discuss the Critical Period Hypothesis Compared to the Relevant Material From the Textbook.

paragraph and the first clause in the following sentence, an interpretation that makes no sense.

A more typical problem is Mouna's essay (see Figure 4.4), which will be compared with Turi's essay (see Figure 4.5). Both of these students are Iranian females, Mouna an ESL student and Turi a regular student. There is not a lot of difference in the quality of the two pieces of writing (Turi's essay received a C− and Mouna's received a D+), but that difference illustrates some important test-taking strategies. Here are some of the differences:

1. Turi's handwriting is a lot better than Mouna's. This shouldn't make a difference, but in the real world, where overworked professors have to grade fifty-plus papers in two weeks, it does.
2. Mouna's essay is longer and less focused. Turi's is concise and better organized.
3. Mouna's essay challenges some conventional ideas. This can be an important aspect of a good essay, but a potentially dangerous one because the student must show that she understands the conventional ideas and that her own views are better. Unfortunately, Mouna fails to do this. She disagrees with Lenneberg's

The critical period for language acquisition is when one reaches puberty and has not learned a language then in Lennenburg theory it is stated that he never will. I don't believe in Lenneburgs theory because even if one never learned a language their brain does not ceaze to function. If a person had been in a wheel chair and can now walk with the help of artificial legs does he not learn all over again I believe the same in terms of language. Genie who was isolated virtually after birth learned to speak of course not to the same extent as a natural child but this is because of ii psychological effect.

ii) A child must learn to imitate if he is to learn. Genie did not even see anybody accept her mother for a couple of minutes. Genie also could not talk because she could not breathe large quantities of air in and out in order to speak. This brought her a lot of physical pain. another reason why I disagree with Lenebgurgs theory is because Genie had large quantities of vocabulary just like a child She went through both 1st and 2nd stages again just like a child. Genie acquired 4 possessive morphemes. Even though Genie did not acquire the subject and object she had a large knowledge of vocabulary and no syntactic knowledge.

FIGURE 4.4   Mouna's Essay Discussing the Critical Period Hypothesis.

claim that normal language acquisition cannot occur after the critical period. To justify her opinion, she uses the analogy of a crippled person who learns to walk using artificial legs. But the two cases are not comparable because language acquisition is a cognitive ability and walking is a physical ability. Moreover, even if cognitive and physical abilities could be compared, the analogy would not support Mouna's case because walking with artificial legs is very different from walking normally, and Lenneberg's claim is that after the critical period human beings cannot learn to speak normally. Thus, Mouna has failed to refute Lenneberg's claim. Turi, on the other hand, just presents Lenneberg's views and cites the case of Genie as evidence for those views. This is a less ambitious but a safer strategy.

FIGURE 4.5   Turi's Essay Discussing the Critical Period Hypothesis.

The critical period for language acquisition occurs between the ages of 2–3. until 14. Lenneburg says that after this age, which is the beginning of puberty, children's ability to learn language slows down, the individual becomes less sensitive to stimuli. The basics of a language are not taught during the "critical period," therefore it to late.

Taking the example of Genie, her case is the evidence proving that language acquisition occurs within the critical period. Genie has lived in isolation during the critical period, therefore the development of language in her case has been limited, although she acquired stages of language beyond the "critical period."

Genie hasn't been exposed to any language learning during the "critical period." She started learning english at the time of a second-language acquisition, which is out of the critical period. Normally, the process of lateralization occurs after the critical period (and the language acquisition), but Genie's case proves that lateralization can precede language acquisition.

Genie's case shows that at some degree, language acquisition seems to be possible beyond the critical age.

In sum, Turi did not write a very good answer because parts of it are confused and because it lacks critical analysis. It is a safe answer. Mouna, on the other hand, has attempted to be analytical and independent, but she has not pulled it off. She shows more involvement and curiosity in the issue of a critical period and therefore is possibly a more promising scholar than Turi, but she has not yet learned how to make a convincing academic argument.

Comparison of the Exams and the Papers

The ESL students did much better on the papers than on the exams, and, in general, their papers compared favorably with those of the regular students. Some of the reasons for this are expected. First, the students had all the time they needed to write the papers, but they were pressed for time to write the exams. Their need for more time on the exams is suggested by the fact that six students did not attempt all five short-answer questions, and by the fact that the ESL students' essays were much shorter than the regular students' essays. One reason that the ESL students needed more time on the exam is that they seem to have been very dependent on their notes and on the text. We have seen, for example, how Mahmet summarized the text. There were also many answers that closely paralleled the students' notes. Thus, Hirsham copied misinformation from his notes onto the exam, where he wrote, "The child produces all sounds of world [languages] during babbling." Neither his notes nor his exam included the professor's comment that this claim is no longer accepted.

A second expected difference between the papers and the exams was that the papers were clearer and more grammatical. This difference, of course, reflects the fact that the papers were commented on by the ESL teachers and then rewritten. The papers did contain many minor grammatical errors that left no doubt that their authors were ESL students, but the exams contained incorrect grammar and vocabulary usage that sometimes obscured the students' ideas. For example, in the following passages from the exams, it is impossible to tell what the students had in mind:

- The critical period is a stage in biological process where the two hemispheres of the brain get each one its function. So both parts would be combined. Lennenberg called to the critical period hypothesis.
- The difference between the subject and object in normal children is of 95% accuracy.
- During the critical period, a person can learn the most because the brain at that time will be develop and feel by the language that can not be forgotten.

Some less expected patterns also emerged from comparing the papers and the exams. One point is that when students understand the material of a course, they do better on assignments that allow them some options. The case studies showed that ESL students often do better on essay questions than on multiple-choice questions. This is so because they can frame the answer to an essay question to take maximum advantage of what they understand; however, they can miss an entire multiple-choice question because they do not know one vocabulary word. On the paper, the students had considerable control over what they wrote. They were free to form their own hypotheses based on their own data and to express these hypotheses in their own ways. Furthermore, many of the ESL students studied the English of a speaker of their own native language and were able to analyze their subject's errors in terms of transfer. In this area, the students were real experts. Conversely, a general weakness of the papers was a lack of reference to the research covered in the lectures and readings, a subject about which the students understood much less.

A characteristic of both the papers and the exams was a tendency to speculate or philosophize from personal experience. An example from the exams, previously mentioned, is Mouna's comparison of language acquisition after the critical period to learning to walk after an injury. An example from the papers is Tesfaye's statement, "Language is acquired through interest . . . because if someone is not interested in learning a language, then he will never, and if he is interested in learning but doesn't show effort, he'll never learn." This kind of vacuous philosophizing is perhaps more tolerated on an exam than on a paper.

Students' Reactions to the Precourse

Two conclusions emerge from an analysis of the questionnaires, informal discussions with the students, and interviews with the two ESL instructors. First, the precourse was very hard for the ESL students. The instructor of the advanced ESL class, comparing the precourse material to the theme-based material the students also studied during the term, remarked, "[The precourse] was exhausting to the students. It was demanding because there was no variation in the subject matter. It demanded 100%." She thought, however, that the precourse should have been longer, perhaps seven weeks. The teacher of the intermediate group, on the other hand, thought that three weeks was about right for her students.

Second, the students were enthusiastic about the precourse because they thought that it prepared them for academic courses. The intermediate teacher stated, "What I really liked was that they became really excited about the project; they certainly got involved." She explained that this involvement was a result of its being a "real course," having a content-area professor and American students. Many of the students' comments on the questionnaires echoed these points, as the following quotations show:

- I liked it very much, because that way the best way that we become familiar with American students and the classes in the university.
- It was my first time in academic class and I had to listen, guess meanings, take notes and prepare a paper.
- It was a new experience taking part of an academic course in a foreign language. . . . We got accustomed to taking notes and taking essay quizzes also.
- I got an idea how are the academic classes and how professors teach in the American university.

The results of the questionnaires, shown in Figure 4.6, indicate that the students liked the precourse and thought that it helped prepare them for academic courses.

1. In your opinion, did your participation in Introduction to Linguistics help you prepare for academic work?
   YES 16; NO 0; NOT SURE 1

2. Please explain (sample comments):
   "I got accustomed to taking notes."
   "I found that lectures do not just cover readings."
   "It gave me confidence."
   "I got an idea about academic classes."
   "I learned to write notes faster."
   "I learned to understand an American accent."

3. Did you improve in the following activities?

   a. Understanding lectures.
      YES 11; NO 6

   (The six no votes may be partially explained by the fact that the lectures got more difficult toward the end of the unit.)

   b. Taking notes.
      YES 13; NO 4

   c. Reading and understanding articles.
      YES 15; NO 2

4. Should the English Language Institute include a similar course in future semesters?
   YES 15; NO 0; DON'T KNOW 1

5. Did you find the subject interesting and useful?
   YES 9; NO 4

   (Four students did not respond to this question, which may have been their polite way of saying no. On the other hand, this was not a good question since several students commented that the subject was useful but not interesting.)

6. What other subjects would you support?
   (The answers to this question included management, psychology, geography, chemistry, etc. The subjects seemed to reflect the students' majors.)

FIGURE 4.6   Results of the Evaluation Questionnaire.

Conclusions

The precourse appears to be an effective way to teach academic strategies in an ESL program. It fills a gap in Brinton, Snow, and Wesche's (1989) typology of ESL content courses because it is appropriate for students who would not be able to pass a regular university course, even on an adjunct basis, and might become frustrated and discouraged. These students can profit from studying college-level material for a short time on a noncredit basis if they have considerable support from the ESL program. Although in general the ESL students performed below the level of the regular students, in many ways they participated effectively in the course, writing acceptable short research papers and contributing to class discussions. The most difficult task for the ESL students was the midterm exam, but even these exams contained many acceptable answers and showed that the ESL students were following the material.

The students' biggest criticism of the precourse was that the subject of language acquisition was not interesting. It appears to be very hard to find material that is interesting to everyone. The answers to question 6 on the questionnaires suggest that the students would like to take a precourse in their majors, which ranged from computer science to zoology. In the face of this diversity, Celce-Murcia's (1987) suggestion is sensible: the selection of the content material should depend on the nature and strengths of the students and the institution.

CHAPTER 5
Academic Competence

INTRODUCTION

The case studies reveal a picture of ESL students struggling to understand difficult content material. Chapters 2 and 3 reviewed theories of the kinds of knowledge and abilities that students can call on to reach this understanding. The discussion showed that many of these theories employ similar constructs that are arranged and rearranged so as to be logically consistent and to highlight the particular findings and concerns of the researchers. Thus, in Canale and Swain's (1980) model, discourse competence was considered a special kind of sociolinguistic competence, but in Canale's (1983) model, discourse competence was given equal standing with sociolinguistic competence. Similarly, in Cummins and Swain's (1983) revised model, syntactic structures that are associated with decontextualized language were placed on a separate dimension from other syntactic structures. The various models of language proficiency are like different maps of the same territory designed to highlight particular features of interest. This chapter proposes yet another map, which highlights the types of knowledge and abilities that contribute to academic competence.

There is a temptation to model the constructs and processes associated with a theory by means of two-dimensional figures containing boxes and arrows, even though such figures inevitably oversimplify. Nevertheless, diagrams are a useful heuristic, and I shall provide one here. Figure 5.1 represents a tentative model of how ESL students accomplish academic tasks. It can be divided into two parts. The boxes at the bottom represent the knowledge and abilities that students can draw on to reach a basic understanding of content material. The rest of the model shows how they can use academic strategies to enhance their basic understanding and to complete assignments. We consider the components of basic understanding first.

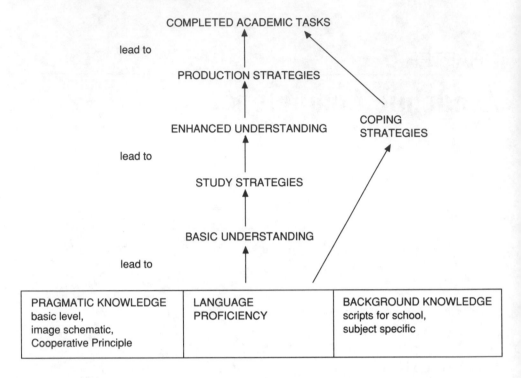

FIGURE 5.1 How ESL Students Accomplish Academic Tasks.

BASIC UNDERSTANDING

Students are able to reach a basic understanding of academic material by accessing three kinds of knowledge and abilities: universal pragmatic knowledge, knowledge and skills in the target language (that is, language proficiency in Spolsky's [1989] sense), and background knowledge. Notice that pragmatic knowledge and background knowledge are used for top-down processing, whereas language proficiency is used for both top-down and bottom-up processing.

Universal Pragmatic Knowledge

Figure 5.1 differs from other models we have discussed in that it separates universal pragmatic knowledge from language and culture-specific knowledge. Universal pragmatic knowledge includes basic-level concepts, image schemas, and the Cooperative Principle. As we have seen, Johnson (1987) claims that the first two kinds of knowledge are universal because they are directly constructed by the human concept-making capacity, and Green (1989) claims that the Cooperative Principle arises from the nature of rational behavior. Saville-Troike and Kleifgen's (1986) research shows how children can utilize these two kinds of knowledge to communicate amazingly well, even though they do not share a language.

Language Proficiency

The language proficiency box corresponds to Spolsky's preference model. This model allows for different profiles of proficient learners, who will exhibit different typical features at varying degrees of strength. Saville-Troike's (1984) research and the case studies show that there is no profile of an ideal academic ESL student, but some of the features of Spolsky's model are clearly more important than others for academic success. The following are brief comments on how some features of the preference model (see Appendix) relate to academic competence.

- *Specific variety and academic skills features.* Since learners must acquire the features of some language variety, it is obviously helpful for them to acquire the features of academic English. It seems less important for them to acquire the features of rapid, informal speech, such as "gonna" and "playin'," as has sometimes been advocated.

- *Unanalyzed/analyzed knowledge feature.* We have seen that good students copy and memorize chunks of language that they understand but cannot use productively. For example, Hiroshi, a successful student, appropriately used a phrase with elaborate syntax that he could not have produced on his own for his report on Hank Aaron. Such use of unanalyzed knowledge seems to be a profitable step on the way to acquisition. However, students can also use unanalyzed knowledge that they do not understand as a coping strategy.

- *Accuracy and explicit/implicit knowledge features.* Studies show that grammatical accuracy does not correlate with academic achievement. Nevertheless, many students in the case studies were very concerned that their English be correct. Sometimes this concern became overriding and prevented the students from speaking in class or writing original prose. Such students need to be shown how to tolerate a degree of inaccuracy, especially in spontaneously produced language, as on a test. There is an ongoing debate about whether explicit knowledge of grammar improves accuracy (compare Krashen, 1981 with Rutherford & Sharwood-Smith, 1988). In the precourse, we found that limited explicit grammar instruction, focused on the salient problems of individual students, can be helpful both for improving the student's accuracy and for helping the student understand which aspects of English he or she can control by applying explicit knowledge (monitoring).

- *Dual knowledge and integrated skills features.* Reading appears to be the most important language skill for academic achievement, followed by listening comprehension and then writing. Many content teachers seem to be happy to allow ESL students to remain mostly silent in class and to grade them entirely on their written work.

- *Integrated function and communicative goal features.* These two features include the ability to communicate appropriately and effectively, aspects of sociolinguistic competence that have been stressed in communicative teaching approaches. Savignon's (1983) tests of communicative competence for American college students studying French stressed the ability to use language functions (such as greeting and requesting), notions (such as giving directions and ordering a meal), and appropriate style, especially in a speaking context. These features of language proficiency are also stressed on the Foreign Service Institute's test of foreign language proficiency. As we have indicated, these features are not as important to academic success as was once thought; however, effective oral communication is an obvious asset in an academic setting, and lack of effective face-to-face communicative skills can be disastrous as in the case of Duc.

Background Knowledge

We have identified two types of background knowledge, and this section suggests a third. The first type is knowledge of a specific content area. As Clarke (1980) found, background knowledge can compensate for low proficiency in the target language. A lack of background knowledge sufficient to follow the American school curriculum is a major obstacle to ESL students' academic success. For example, Nopadol produced better work on assignments involving international economics and politics (areas about which he knew a great deal) than on assignments involving American politicial history. It should also be mentioned that lack of knowledge about a subject is often accompanied by a lack of interest. For example, Schepps noted that Nopadol had very little interest in U.S. history. Similarly, in discussions of U.S. customs, George (the subject of case study 5 in chapter 6) often changed the subject to a discussion of Colombian customs.

The second type of background knowledge is scripts for school. Skutnabb-Kangas and Toukomaa (1976) found that Finnish children who immigrated to Sweden after being schooled in Finnish were more successful academically than younger Finnish children who began their education in Swedish. Cummins (1979) attributed this success to the development of Cognitive Academic Language Proficiency (CALP), but Edelsky et al. (1983) claimed that it was due to the fact that the older children knew what was expected of them in school. As they put it, "coping with school nonsense transfers from first to second language" (p. 6). Saville-Troike and Kleifgen's (1986) research shows that scripts for school are important for academic success. Saville-Troike (1991) notes, "Even if . . . students do not understand the language of instruction, those who have had prior school experience enter English-medium classrooms equipped with a knowledge base for making inferences and predictions about the meaning of events that will occur there" (p. 3).

Higher-Order Cognitive Skills

The topic of inferencing and predicting brings us to another aspect of academic competence that has been mentioned only briefly. Both Bernstein (1964) and Cummins (1984a) claimed that proficiency in academic language was associated with reasoning ability. This author has argued that reasoning ability should not be considered part of proficiency in any language variety but has not yet suggested how this ability contributes to academic competence. It is clear that the ability to present and support a hypothesis clearly and logically is important for academic success. This appears to be a very difficult task for many ESL students. Recall from chapter 4 that on both papers and exams, the students in the precourse showed a tendency to argue for or against a hypothesis on the basis of personal experience rather than on the basis of research evidence. For example, in discussing the critical period hypothesis for language acquisition, Tesfaye merely speculated: "Language is acquired through interest . . . because if someone is not interested in learning a language, then he will never, and if he is interested in learning but doesn't show effort, he'll never learn." Mouna did cite research evidence in support of her argument against the critical period hypothesis (see Figure 4.5), but the research she cited did not support her claims. Turi was perhaps more aware of her limitations in academic argumentation; she simply repeated the arguments of others.

The study of what has, for convenience, been called "reasoning ability" in this text has been pursued within several different theoretical frameworks and under a variety of names, including "inductive and deductive reasoning," "higher-order cognitive skills," "problem solving," and "critical thinking skills." The best-known scholarship in this area is Bloom's taxonomy of learning objectives (Bloom, 1956), an attempt to distinguish lower- from higher-order thinking, which Cummins (1984a) cites in his discussion of CALP. Bloom identifies six increasingly complex types of learning. The first three levels of the taxonomy are: knowledge of simple facts ("George Washington was the first president"); simple comprehension (being able to use a fact in some way without understanding its implications or connection to other facts); and application (the use of abstractions in concrete situations). The higher levels are: analysis (seeing the relationship of constituent parts that make up a whole); synthesis (putting elements into a coherent whole); and evaluation (judging the adequacy of a hypothesis or argument). Cummins (1984a) suggests that the first three types of learning belong to surface proficiency in a language and that the last three types belong to a basic underlying cognitive ability that can be manifest in any language. As mentioned, these higher cognitive abilities are important components of CALP.

Bloom devised the taxonomy in the mid-1950s, the heyday of behaviorism, and the influence of behaviorism is apparent in his attempt to divide learning into component skills and in the attempt of a number of educators to teach these skills separately in a decontextualized way. One such attempt is the Mastery Learning program, which has been adopted in hundreds of school districts in the United States. Like most teaching methods, Mastery Learning divides a content subject into units. At the end of each unit the students are tested, and, if they score at the 80 percent level, they move on to the next unit. The problem, according to Smith (1986), is that there is often little logic in deciding what constitutes a unit or how units should be sequenced. An even bigger problem is the assumption that individual facts and "thinking skills" can be taught in isolation. For example, in Mastery Learning, reading is not taught by reading books but by completing exercises involving isolated linguistic patterns such as regular past tense and plurals. The Mastery Learning Program was used from 1981 to 1985 in the Chicago public schools, where it was not successful. A 1984 study of the graduating class showed that only 6,000 of the 18,500 students who graduated had reached the national twelfth grade level of reading ability, a figure that does not include the 50 percent of children who entered high school but dropped out before graduation (Smith, 1986, p. 76).

A second approach to the study of thinking ability comes from cognitive psychology (Anderson, 1980). Many cognitive psychologists accept the computer metaphor of mind/brain discussed in chapter 2, and their investigations of reasoning center on the question of how human reasoning is similar to or different from computer reasoning. It appears that human reasoning and computer reasoning are mostly different. Rather than approaching problems in a step-by-step logical fashion, human beings tend to use heuristics, rules of thumb that are better suited for inductive reasoning (i.e., probabilistic reasoning in which conclusions are likely but not guaranteed to follow from given premises) instead of deductive reasoning (i.e., categorical reasoning in which conclusions must follow from true premises) (Anderson, 1980). In fact, human beings are notoriously uncomfortable with computer-style deductive reasoning, perhaps because we are skeptical that the given premises are actually true.

Some educators have attempted to apply findings from cognitive psychology to teaching under the rubric of "critical thinking skills." In this respect, the critical thinking skills field is similar to the learning strategies field discussed on pages 70 and 71, and it has encountered similar problems of definition and classification. Beyer (1985a) reviews the critical thinking skills literature. He notes that there is no agreed upon definition or list of skills and that various writers have equated the skills with Bloom's taxonomy, logical reasoning, and problem solving, among other things. Beyer (1985a) asserts, however, that critical thinking skills are not exactly the same as any of these and that, "Specialists today appear to agree that critical thinking is the assessing of the authenticity, accuracy, and/or worth of knowledge claims and arguments" (p. 271). This definition does seem to describe very well what Tesfaye and Mouna need to learn how to do.

Like the authors of the Mastery Learning Program, authors of lessons on critical thinking attempt to divide their subject into a number of component skills. Although there is no agreed upon list of skills, some that are commonly mentioned are classifying, comparing, analyzing, deducing, solving, questioning, critiquing, being skeptical, drawing conclusions, weighing evidence, judging, and evaluating. Many critical thinking skills specialists assume that these skills can be taught separately and that they will transfer from one content area to another (McPeck [1990] critiques these assumptions).

Beyer (1985b) suggests a five-point program for directly teaching an individual critical thinking skill, such as detecting whether an author is biased. First, the teacher introduces the skill, perhaps writing "detecting bias in written documents" on the board and asking students what they understand *bias* to mean. Second, the teacher provides some clues for detecting bias, such as emotionally loaded words, overgeneralizations, and overt identification with one side of an argument. Third, the teacher reads a sample passage, pointing out any evidence of bias. Fourth, the students search similar passages for indications of bias, and fifth, the students articulate how they decided whether an author was biased or not. Beyer (1985b) notes that critical thinking skills can also be taught indirectly, without so much control by the teacher, but he recommends direct teaching "where the skill is complex, teaching time is scarce, and instructional variety is important" (p. 300).

Smith (1986, 1990) strongly objects to the entire enterprise of dividing the ability to think critically into separate skills and attempting to teach such skills directly. He objects to Bloom's taxonomy on two grounds. First, the hierarchy claims that learning individual facts isolated from context is easier than learning in situations that are comprehensible. This, says Smith (1986), is exactly backwards. "Children learn through what they do rather than doing things as a result of what they know. . . . They learn when they decide that they would like to do something for themselves—a judgment that is at the peak of the hierarchy" (p. 75).

Smith's (1990) second objection to Bloom's taxonomy is the implication that reasoning ability is the special provenance of literate, educated people. He points out that reasoning is simply thinking, the commonplace, inconspicuous, and effective way we arrange our daily affairs, the way we cope. He observes:

> The brain . . . decides and creates so efficiently that we are seldom aware of all the thinking that is going on every time we see, hear, smell, taste or touch anything that we recognize. All of this involves categorization, classification, and inferences; it is all "high-level," abstract thinking. (p. 15)

According to Smith, the "higher order thinking skills" in Bloom's taxonomy are pseudo-categories. The reality is the gestalt ability to think, which involves all of these skills. Perception itself is analytic, moving from the general (existing schemas) to the particular (what is actually seen or heard). Learning, where categories or general principles are constructed from particular instances, is synthetic. But perception never takes place without learning, nor learning without perception.

If thinking critically is as automatic and effortless as Smith claims, why do so many of us (and our students) find it so difficult? According to Smith, it is because we lack at least one of three prerequisites for thinking critically: knowledge, disposition, and authority. Clarke (1980) made the point that reading ability is not a fixed set of skills that can be applied to any text. Rather, readers employ different combinations of top-down and bottom-up processing, depending on the degree to which they understand a particular text. If understanding falls below a certain level, the entire process is short-circuited. I have made a similar claim in regard to academic strategies. Strategies do not exist in isolation; they are always practiced in relation to specific content material, and if the material is not understood, students resort to coping strategies. According to Smith (1990), a high level of understanding of a specific subject is likewise necessary for critical thinking. He observes:

> Provided we know enough, we are always capable of critical thinking. . . . But if we can make no sense of what we are trying to think about, then critical thinking becomes impossible. Critical thinking does not demand a complex array of learned skills, but competence in whatever you are thinking about. . . . If you are an experienced football fan, you can criticize a football game. If you are a particular kind of engineer, you can criticize the way a bridge or a ship has been built. If you are unable to do any of these things, it will not be because you lack essential critical thinking skills, but because you lack the essential experience. You do not know enough. (p. 193)

The second necessary condition is a disposition to think critically. According to Smith (following McPeck [1990]), critical thinkers have an attitude of "relative skepticism . . . the *judicious* suspension of assent, a readiness to consider alternative explanations, not taking anything for granted when it might be reasonable to doubt" (1990, p. 104; emphasis in original). The subjects of the case studies showed great diversity in their dispositions to doubt authority. Mouna did not hesitate to question the critical period hypothesis, whereas Lucy refused to doubt her textbook even after the professor pointed out that it contained an error. In the precourse, considerable confusion arose after my first lecture on the subject of behaviorism. A number of students did not understand that my remarks were critical of behaviorism, and that I was pointing out its flaws. These students were unaccustomed to professors' criticizing well-known authorities.

A skeptical disposition is no doubt related to a student's cultural and academic background, but it may be that such dispositions can be found even in students from the most hierarchical and authoritarian schools and societies. For example, Duc did not lack either the knowledge or the disposition to think critically, and he readily expressed his reservations about Krashen's claim that learning cannot become acquisition to his researcher. But he would not express these reservations to his professor, even though she was a paragon of supportiveness who strongly encouraged students to critically evaluate hypotheses. What Duc lacked was the third necessary condition for critical thinking: authority. Smith (1990) notes, "The right to think critically is not distributed equally, especially in hierarchical, authoritarian, and bureaucratic societies" (p. 105).

Many ESL students come from societies in which students do not have the authority to be critical. Nor do they necessarily have this authority in American academic society. Unfortunately, Duc's strategy of not disagreeing with the professor is probably the most successful strategy in most American classrooms from kindergarten to graduate school. Few American teachers are supportive of a student's skepticism of their own beliefs, and probably no professor will reward even the most lucid critical thinking that questions the socially constructed assumptions of Western scholarship and argumentation. Native English-speaking (NES) students do not have to worry much about violating such assumptions, but many ESL students do. As argued in chapter 3, what these students must learn is not just the style and nuances of an academic subculture, but an entirely different world view.

An American scholar of Islamic affairs, John Voll (1990) provides an example of how difficult it is for people who have different world views to argue critically. His example is the Ayatollah Khomeini's condemnation to death of author Salman Rushdie for slandering Islam in his novel *The Satanic Verses*. Voll notes that for an American to understand the Ayatollah's position requires more than just learning a new definition of *blasphemy*, it requires learning at least part of the underlying Islamic world view. Westerners are likely to make the secular assumption that there is a natural separation between religion, politics, and culture, but the fundamentalist Moslem sees these as inseparable parts of the same social fabric. Any discussion that assumes the Western orientation may tend to strengthen the fundamentalist Moslem's conviction that Rushdie's book is part of a continuing Western attack on Islam. Needless to say, any discussion by an ESL student that assumes the fundamentalist Moslem orientation would be penalized by an American teacher as lacking in critical analysis.

The ability to critically analyze and judge academic material, then, may be the most difficult task for many ESL students. First, they must understand a subject sufficiently to be able to make judgments. Even more difficult, they must be able to tell when they do not have a sufficient understanding. In addition, they may have to overcome a disposition to refrain from criticizing authority. And finally, they must learn exactly how far they can go in their criticism without violating the basic assumptions of Western academic culture.

In sum, critical thinking requires a large amount of subject-specific background knowledge and a high degree of acculturation into Western academic society. Since these two kinds of knowledge are included in the "background knowledge" box of Figure 5.1, critical thinking is not represented separately in this model.

ACADEMIC STRATEGIES

The upper portion of Figure 5.1 suggests how academic strategies are used to accomplish school tasks. The best students in the case studies developed effective strategies that accomplished two things. Study skills enabled them to enhance their understanding of material that they did not understand well at first. For example, a number of the subjects did not attempt to understand lectures in detail while they were taking notes, but concentrated on writing down as much information as possible. They were able to understand the material more fully when they had time to review and revise their notes. Similarly, some subjects did not aim for a high level of comprehension in their first reading of academic material, but skimmed to get the main idea and focused on a detailed understanding during the second reading. It appears that a major difference between ESL students and NES students is the relatively low degree of understanding that many ESL students have on their first encounter with new material. However, effective study skills allow them to make up much of this gap after the initial presentation. Additional study skills observed in the case studies included studying with peers, discussing content material in the native language, taking notes on lectures and readings, using dictionaries, and questioning teachers in class or in private.

An important finding of the case studies is that the same strategies were not equally effective with all types of material. The best students varied their strategies according to their degree of understanding. A common example was taking notes on difficult material in the native language but switching to English for easier material. Some subjects with less academic competence used the same strategies regardless of how much they understood. For example, Ahmad looked up the translation of virtually every word in his textbook, even when he understood the material well. Conversely, students with a large amount of basic knowledge do not have to be as adept at varying the use of academic strategies. Like native speakers, they may be able to understand and perform required tasks by using a single method of note-taking, reading, dictionary use, studying for tests, and so on.

The second function of academic strategies is to enable students to complete assignments with less than a full understanding of the material. These production strategies are necessary because even the best students were unable to understand the content material fully. For example, Manny and Mahmet relied heavily on the text when taking in-class tests. Turi stuck to information she was sure of and did not, like Mouna, attempt to provide original arguments. Some of the most effective production strategies were those taught by the ESL teachers in the precourse. These included getting reactions to drafts of papers from peers and role-playing to prepare for class discussions and tests. The role of academic strategies, then, is to enhance the student's understanding of content material and to allow the student to complete assignments as well as possible with less than a perfect understanding. However, when their level of understanding dropped below a certain point, many of the subjects resorted to coping strategies. Unfortunately, as we have seen, the use of coping strategies can result in acceptable and even highly praised academic work. Coping strategies are represented in Figure 5.1 as production strategies that bypass enhanced understanding.

To summarize, at least three abilities contribute to academic competence: (1) the ability to use a combination of linguistic, pragmatic, and background knowledge to reach a basic understanding of content material; (2) the ability to use appropriate strategies (which vary according to the degree of basic understanding) to enhance knowledge of content material; and (3) the ability to use appropriate strategies to complete academic assignments with less than a full understanding of the content material. Thus, academic competence amounts to possessing a critical mass of understanding and appropriate strategies. When understanding falls below a certain point, the process of learning fails and the only alternative is to try coping strategies.

PRINCIPLES FOR HELPING ESL STUDENTS DEVELOP ACADEMIC COMPETENCE

The theory of academic competence presented here suggests five general principles and two corollaries for preparing ESL students for mainstream courses.

1. Academic strategies should be explicitly taught on an individualized basis.
2. Students can best learn strategies in a language through content course that uses authentic text.
   a. The content material should be studied in depth.
   b. The course should provide contact with native speakers.
3. Teaching should be interactive in ways that are compatible with students' learning styles and prior scripts for school.
4. Teaching should be experiential.
5. The content subject should be one that students will need to know when they are mainstreamed.

We now consider these principles individually.

Explicit, Individualized Strategies Instruction

Without explicit teaching, students will develop their own academic strategies, usually based on the scripts for school they learned in their native countries, and these strategies are often not effective in the U.S. setting. Many of the case study subjects could have benefitted from explicit strategies instruction. Ali needed to learn not to be afraid to take notes in Arabic. Fati needed to learn how to credit original sources when writing research papers, and Nazila needed instruction in effective dictionary use so that she would not look up every word. I have emphasized that different students will find different strategies effective. Nopadol benefitted greatly from studying with Matt, a native English speaker, but Ceyong was not ready to work with an NES peer. She required the security of working with an ESL peer with whom she shared a language other than English. Ahmad, a meticulous and determined student, filled three notebooks with English words and their Arabic translations. Apparently, this strategy worked to some extent because he was doing well in his engineering course. However, an ESL teacher might suggest that Ahmad modify this strategy by omitting words that he already knows, by grouping new words into semantic fields to bring out the relationships between them, and by expanding his note-taking to include explanations of principles and hypotheses. But the teacher should not discourage an effective strategy that is compatible with a student's learning style.

Ahmad's strategy should not, of course, be required of other students. George, for example, would simply refuse to do such a tedious task. It would be better to ask him to keep a reading reaction journal (see the first section of chapter 7), in which he wrote down what he understood and did not understand about a particular reading assignment. For George, English would be the best medium for the log because his Spanish literacy skills were not well developed, but if Ahmad (who wrote beautiful classical Arabic) were to keep a log, the Arabic language would be best.

The Language through Content Course

The general principle that academic strategies should be learned in connection with authentic text implies that they should be learned in a language through content course. At present, many ESL programs offer study skills courses in which note-taking, dictionary use, outlining, speech giving, and so on are taught in connection with pseudoacademic subjects such as "making chocolate," or "how locks work." But such courses ignore important strategies like interacting with content teachers and studying with peers. A full range of strategies can be developed only in a course in which students are required to do all the tasks that they must do when they are mainstreamed.

Furthermore, *authentic text* refers not only to textbooks, but also to lectures and to the entire context of the classroom. As we have seen, ESL students need to learn how to adapt their academic strategies to the difficulty of the material. Strategies that are learned in connection with well-understood material are not necessarily effective with material that is partially understood. The only way to prepare students for the academic mainstream is to teach strategies in connection with the kind of material they will really have to study. In addition, before teachers can help students modify their preexisting academic strategies, they must find out what these strategies are. An accurate assessment can be made only in connection with authentic text.

The principle of using authentic text has two corollaries. The first is that content material should be studied in depth. As we will see in chapter 6, theme-based courses do not meet this requirement since they contain several short units on different academic disciplines such as economics, psychology, and literature. But studying content material that builds on previous material is more difficult for ESL students than studying a number of unrelated topics, because if some concepts are not understood, it is impossible to understand what follows.

The second corollary is that the language through content course should provide exposure to native speakers, whose presence is an essential element of authentic text. The precourse instructors reported that the pace and level of the content sessions with native speakers were quite different from those of the ESL sessions. In addition, we have seen that ESL students are often reluctant to speak in classes with native speakers but that they can develop strategies for doing so. The precourse students actively participated in the class discussions with native speakers because they had a good understanding of the material, having been tutored in it by their ESL teachers, and because they had practiced discussing the questions that would be asked.

The principle of exposure to native speakers has two controversial implications. The first is that sheltered courses may not be sufficient for preparing students for mainstream courses. This is not to say that sheltered courses are not valuable. On the contrary, as the discussion in chapter 6 of a sheltered introduction to psychology course at the University of Ottawa will show, these courses can be extraordinarily valuable. However, in that course (and in sheltered courses generally) the professors made a number of concessions to their students' special language needs: they lectured more slowly, taking care to make logical connections clear; they used more common vocabulary words; and they frequently asked questions and conducted discussions to make sure that their students were following the material. In addition, the students took a number of quizzes instead of writing a research paper, as was required of students in the nonsheltered sections of the course. But, as we have seen, students must develop academic strategies for understanding lectures that are delivered at full speed, using difficult vocabulary, and in which the professor does not check for comprehension. The sheltered course can be an invaluable step on the road to academic competence in a second language, but the additional step of the adjunct course may be needed as well.

The second controversial implication of the principle of exposure to native speakers is that bilingual education courses alone may not be sufficient for preparing ESL students for mainstream courses. The argument for this claim is similar to the argument just given in regard to sheltered courses. As discussed in chapter 1, bilingual education is the very best way for students to learn the background knowledge of academic subjects and scripts for school that are needed for academic success. However, they may still lack full English proficiency and so must develop academic strategies for dealing with partially understood content material.

Interactive Teaching

The language through content course should be taught interactively for two reasons. First, the teacher needs to interact with the students in order to determine how much of the content material they understand. A frequent observation in the case studies was that the content teachers thought that their ESL students were following the material better than they actually were. In most of the content courses there was little interaction between individual students and teachers. The courses consisted mainly of readings, lectures, and objective tests. As we have seen, some of the subjects effectively concealed their lack of understanding by using coping strategies in this kind of course. On the other hand, the case studies researchers interacted with their students much more often than the teachers, and therefore obtained a more accurate picture of how well the students were following the material. The cure for coping strategies, then, is to increase student–teacher interaction so that the teacher has a clear idea of what the students understand.

The second reason for interactive teaching was discussed at length in chapter 3. Recall that experiential realism claims that beyond the basic level, knowledge is socially constructed, and that gaining knowledge is like becoming acculturated into a society that shares a vocabulary and rules of discourse. Children become acculturated into their society by interacting with its members, largely by means of oral language, and students become acculturated into the society of scholars largely by interacting with its members in speech and writing. Such acculturation is particularly important for ESL students who must learn new scripts for school. To enter a new culture, one must actively participate in it, rather than passively learn facts. As Rorty (1979) says, "Coming to understand the parts of a strange culture, practice, theory, language, or whatever . . . is more like getting acquainted with a person than like following a demonstration" (p. 319). In this respect, gaining academic competence is a lot like gaining sociolinguistic competence. Through interaction with a particular speech community, one learns how to do things appropriately.

Ceyong's case study illustrates the effectiveness of interactive teaching. Remember that the naturalist at the museum did not lecture Ceyong about minerals, but rather discussed the subject with her, allowing her to ask questions as they occurred and allowing her to call him on the phone to ask more questions after she understood the material better. The role of the researcher in the learning process was particularly interesting. Koike was not an expert on mineralogy, yet she was able to help Ceyong enormously. Koike learned almost as much about mineralogy as Ceyong did, and so was not teaching her in the traditional sense. Rather, Koike and Ceyong were collaboratively constructing knowledge—doing on a small scale the same thing that a society of scholars does on a larger scale. Another form of interactive learning is peer tutoring, and some of the subjects benefitted greatly from studying with peers. Nopadol's researcher believed that the help Nopadol received from his friend Matt was the most important factor in his learning.

However, teachers who have used interactive activities with ESL students know that sometimes these activities are not as effective as they can be with native speakers. One reason for this is cultural. Students like Duc and Tri, who come from societies in which education is authoritarian, may question the value of learning with peers. Also, it is often the case that ESL students understand so little of the material that they cannot interact in a helpful way—they must get a basic understanding before they can work with others to enhance it. For this reason, ESL students need more guidance in group activities than NES students. The ESL teacher in a language through content program is in a good position to provide such guidance because to a great extent he or she is, like Koike, learning the content material along with the students.

Bruffee (1984) makes the point that joining the academic conversation does not necessarily require a partner at all times. He argues that the academic environment provides for a form of displaced conversation, namely writing. It is, of course, important to prepare students for formal, academic writing. However, there are many context-dependent forms of writing, such as lecture notes, lab notes, learning logs, and dialogue journals, that are particularly appropriate to share with peers. Such writing is part of what Rorty calls "normal discourse"—conversation among knowledgeable peers who share a vocabulary and whose work is guided by the same paradigms, values, and assumptions. In normal discourse, Rorty (1979) says, everyone agrees on the "set of conventions about what counts as a relevant contribution, what counts as a question, what counts as having a good argument for that answer or a good criticism of it" (p. 320).

Experiential Teaching

The fourth principle for teaching a language through content course is that, whenever possible, it should include experiential activities. The theory of academic competence proposed here claims that basic-level knowledge, together with the Cooperative Principle, is one of the main ways of understanding available to ESL students. As has been noted, Ceyong's case study shows how an ESL student can profit from experiential instruction. It should also be noted that Ceyong's earth science class did contain many experiential activities. The mixture of experiential and expository activities was probably about right for the native English speakers in the class, but it was not right for Ceyong. In general ESL students will need much more experiential teaching than native speakers.

The fact that experiential teaching is superior to expository teaching did not originate with the philosophy of experiential realism, although this philosophy sheds new light on why experiential teaching works. John Dewey advocated experiential teaching in the first decades of this century. Dewey's (1916) basic insight, which anticipated some of the claims of experiential realism, was that all knowledge, even the most abstract, is ultimately understood in terms of immediate, everyday experience. He said

> When education . . . fails to recognize that the primary or initial subject matter always exists as matter of an active doing, involving the use of the body and the handling of material, the subject matter of instruction is isolated from the needs and purposes of the learner, and so becomes just something to be memorized and reproduced upon demand. (p. 184)

Mohan (1986) contrasts the experiential approach with the traditional or expository approach, which he says, "will tend towards verbalism, or the mechanical memorization of sentences and undigested information" (p. 45).

Scientific subjects like mineralogy lend themselves more to teaching by means of the basic-level manipulation of objects than do subjects in the social sciences and humanities. Nevertheless, it is possible to use forms of experiential teaching in these subjects as well. For example, when introducing the research assignment in the precourse, I did not show the students how to set up a tape recorder and test to see that it was working. I simply explained this process, and the explanation was sufficient for the native speakers. However, in the ESL sections, the teachers demonstrated how to operate a tape recorder, and the students role-played tape-recording each other.

Another example of experiential teaching in a social science class comes from Schepps's (Nopadol's researcher) eleventh-grade class in U.S. history. In one unit, the class reenacted the Constitutional Convention, with student delegates representing the original thirteen colonies. George Washington, a student in costume, presided over the convention and made sure that the important points of the original agenda were covered. The delegates had to represent accurately the position of their colonies on questions such as how to elect the president, how to represent both large and small states equitably, and whether to allow slavery. The students debated these issues with some two-hundred-year-old arguments, as well as some ingenious new arguments. They held caucuses and cut deals, and when they finally voted, they did not decide the issues in exactly the same ways that their forefathers had.

Relevant Content Material

The fifth principle is that, if possible, the language through content course should cover content material that the students need to know when they are mainstreamed. This principle is automatically met in adjunct courses, but not in noncredit sheltered courses, precourses, and theme-based courses. One reason for using such material is that it provides students with relevant background knowledge, which they badly need when they are mainstreamed. A second reason is that ESL students often view the noncredit ESL courses they are required to take as ''dummy runs'' that contribute little to their academic goals, and therefore they do not exert much effort in these courses. ESL teachers whose students are simultaneously enrolled in credit content courses and noncredit ESL courses can attest that the ESL courses have the lowest priority. Therefore, the use of academic material that the students will be required to master in order to graduate is an excellent way to motivate them. A third reason for using material from the mainstream academic program is that it helps to break down the walls between the ESL program and the rest of the school, a policy that should be followed whenever possible.

In this chapter, we have considered some general principles for preparing ESL students for the academic mainstream. In the next chapter, we consider some specific programs that to varying degrees embody these principles.

CHAPTER 6

Models of Language through Content Programs

INTRODUCTION

I have suggested that the best way to teach academic competence is to expose ESL students to authentic content material while providing the necessary conceptual scaffolding and academic strategies instruction, and that the teaching approach that is most compatible with this philosophy is the language through content approach. Recall that there are four types of language through content courses: theme-based courses, sheltered courses, adjunct courses, and precourses. In theme-based courses, students study popular topics by using general audience materials, or selected academic subjects by using one of the ESL textbooks that contains chapters from college texts adapted for ESL students. Sheltered courses enroll only ESL students in special sections of a regular credit course. Adjunct courses enroll ESL students for credit in a mainstream course and an associated ESL course in which the content material is reviewed and academic strategies can be taught. Precourses combine the features of a theme-based course and an adjunct course. Students enrolled in a precourse participate in a mainstream course for less than the full term. We now consider these types of courses in detail.

THEME-BASED COURSES

Theme-based courses are most common at the college level. Students in these courses come from varied backgrounds and, as a rule, have not yet chosen their academic majors. Some plan to pursue academic careers in the United States and later return to their own countries. Others plan on eventual immigration to the United States. Still others are short-term visitors whose careers or academic advancement in their own countries can be enhanced through the knowledge of English. There are also younger students who have been sent or brought by parents. In short, the population in theme-based courses tends to be varied. This variety, however, need not be a drawback to linguistic progress. On the contrary, diversity can add interest and provide stimulus and motivation for language learning.

A theme-based course and the textbooks meant for such courses are usually organized around themes chosen for their general appeal to a wide range of students. Themes frequently encountered are the family, ecology, travel, education, money and finances, traditions, civil rights, and changing social mores. Theme-based courses feature a variety of text types. Typically a unit may consist of news articles, essays, short fiction, and poetry. Many theme-based texts feature slightly simplified versions of chapters from college texts, intended to ease students into the standard college curriculum.

The disadvantages of the theme-based course are that it does not contain truly authentic text and does not tie directly to the students' academic progress. Therefore, before they leave the ESL program, students need to participate in a language through content course in which more authentic text is used. Nevertheless, theme-based courses are a good way to prepare students for an adjunct course because they reach a wide variety of students across cultures, ages, and curricula. Theme-based units provide a coherent meeting ground for a varied student population, and well-chosen topics on relevant issues can kindle interesting language exchanges of immediacy and pertinence.

Because they reach out to such a variety of student demands, theme-based courses and textbooks cannot be rigidly constructed. Instead, such texts favor a modular approach—the kind in which one unit does not necessarily follow another, but in which units can be chosen at will by the teacher and can be lengthened, shortened, used only in part, or recycled as parts of other units. The thematic approach calls for a flexible teaching style. The teacher of a theme-based course should ideally be a person with wide general knowledge, many interests, curiosity, imagination, and a willingness to continue learning. The theme-based approach permits teachers to step back while their students assume the role of expert. Intensive as well as extensive reading fits well into the elastic framework of a theme-based course.

The key to a theme-based approach is the concept of integrating skills. Although most theme-based courses are grounded in reading, the written text serves as a basis on which lessons in study skills, grammar, speaking, and writing can be provided. For example, a class that has read, listened to, and discussed John Lennon's "Imagine" will quite naturally work on conditional constructions and *wish* clauses. They might pursue small group discussions of "life in a perfect community" and write letters to the editor about troubling social problems. All the tasks assigned are meaningful, and serve social intercourse as well as promote linguistic needs.

Theme-based units lend themselves especially well to a humanistic approach and to communicative teaching. Interesting texts discussed in class may inspire students to bring in related texts of their own. Students who are used to more traditional grammar–translation or audiolingual methods in their home countries are often delighted to actually produce coherent and meaningful language.

Three Examples of Theme-Based Courses

In the following sections, three varieties of theme-based courses are described, all taught at the Center for English as a Second Language (CESL) at the University of Arizona, a college-level, intensive ESL program that enrolls the usual heterogeneous population of preacademic students, many of whom hope to continue academic studies at the University of Arizona or at some other institution of higher learning. Some, sponsored by their employers, have come for brief stints and are learning English for professional advancement. Some come as part of an educational package arranged through their home institutions of higher learning. There is an occasional immigrant, and during the summer months a special program for teens. Occasionally, a group of ESL teachers come for inservice training. The nationalities represented are Spanish speakers, mostly from neighboring Mexico; Arabic speakers from the entire Middle East; Japanese students; and occasional French-, Italian-, or German-speaking Europeans. Eight-week courses, at seven levels from elementary to advanced, are offered by CESL. The three theme-based courses discussed here were all at the two most advanced levels.

A News Magazine Course.   This course met for a two-hour session every day. The text was *Time* magazine—a new issue once a week. *Time* features sections such as "National Affairs," "International Affairs," "Business," "Society," and "Life Styles." Each week the class scanned the magazine and decided by vote which theme would serve as core reading for the week. In addition to the class theme, each individual student picked a personal theme for extensive reading.

During the course of the week students delivered minilectures or wrote reports connected to their personal reading theme. We developed the group theme through jigsaw readings (see page 151), vocabulary expansion activities, skimming and scanning activities, and discussions on cultural perspectives on issues. We wrote letters to the editor, examined advertisements, imitated journalistic registers, and held debates on controversial issues. Whenever a structure was needed, we practiced it. Students were encouraged to read other sources on their chosen themes outside of class. When ecological issues with local interest surfaced, students interviewed local experts on the subject. Such extensive outside readings or interviews were accepted instead of final examinations. There was a vocabulary and content quiz at the end of each week before the beginning of a new issue of the magazine.

A Literature Course.   This class met once a day Monday through Friday for a one-hour session. The unit described here was studied for a period of four weeks—one-half of the length of the course. There was no textbook. The theme for these four weeks was "Decisions," a theme that seemed appropriate because all the students in the course had made an important decision in coming to the United States. This theme proved to be full of significant and emotive content highly motivating for language production.

The reading selections were from a variety of literary sources. The core texts were "The Road Not Taken," a poem by Robert Frost; "Eveline," a short story from the collection *The Dubliners* by James Joyce; "Richard Corey," a poem by Edwin Arlington Robinson; and "Stopping by Woods on a Snowy Evening," a poem by Robert Frost. An abridged version of *David Copperfield* by Charles Dickens was used for extensive reading.

We began the unit by talking about the students' own decisions to come to Tucson, Arizona, to study English. The students were asked to think about several aspects of the decision. Why was English important to them? Why had they chosen to come to the United States rather than to study the language at home or in some other English-speaking environment? Why had they chosen Tucson? Which aspects of their decision had been difficult and which had been easy? In order to organize their thoughts, the students took notes. Later, in pairs and in small groups they told each other various aspects of their particular decisions. On a chart, the students marked important decisions made during the average human life. We spoke about such decisions as whom to marry, what career to choose, where to live, whether or not to have children, and so on.

We then moved on to the reading of "A Road Not Taken" by Robert Frost. In the poem, "the road not taken" serves as an extended metaphor for reluctantly abandoned choices. The text motivated writing on topics such as "A Decision I Am Happy About" and discussions on why decisions are difficult to make. Some of the students wrote letters to advice columns, and other students answered them in mock seriousness. Pronunciation was improved through the oral reading and rereading of the poem, which is written in fluid, conversational English.

The story "Eveline" tells the fate of a young woman caught in a state of mental paralysis through her inability to make a decision. She is held back by her religious training, social constraints, and parental control. Bound by a death-bed promise made to her mother, the young woman must decide between her feelings of duty to others and her desire for self-fulfillment. This text triggered discussions and writing on topics related to self-actualization, social duty, and filial responsibility. We clearly needed the conditional structure in order to express ourselves cogently on such topics, and so it was introduced and practiced.

The poems "Richard Corey" and "Stopping by Woods" brought us to the painful issue of suicide. This was followed by discussion and writing and vocabulary clusters relating to the ethical problems connected to the value of human life and moral choices. Students brought in articles from magazines and newspapers dealing with medical and ethical decisions. Various cultural attitudes were compared. The structures necessary here were modals such as *must, ought to, should,* and so on. For a listening exercise we used the Simon and Garfunkle version of "Richard Corey."

The weekly discussions of *David Copperfield* invariably brought out all the decisions of a *bildungsroman*: Which friends does one choose? What school does one go to? What are the qualities of an ideal mate? How important is money? What is the role of women in society? Has it changed since the nineteenth century? How are personal decisions motivated by social structures? What is the role of a stepparent and why are stepparents invariably so evil in literature? What motivates a person to make the decision to remarry? Charles Dickens's colorful characters gave us ample material for speculation, talking, and writing. We found that the past perfect was a necessary structure for the telling and retelling of this lengthy narrative.

For a viewing–listening exercise, we saw the movie version of *David Copperfield.* As a previewing activity, we clearly visualized the characters and later compared our mental creations with those composed by the filmmakers.

An Academic Reading Course.   This class, as yet only in the planning stage, will use the text *Reading at the University,* by Linda Harbaught Hillman. The text is meant for students planning to enter a U.S. university and contains passages from college textbooks in several fields. The text is interactive and student centered, and, although its main focus is on reading strategies, it manages to integrate this instruction with relevant writing assignments. The book focuses on correcting frequently made reading errors such as faulty inferences, overinterpretation, and neglect of cohesion/coherence and relationship markers. There is also considerable stress on vocabulary expansion. The author also provides ESL students with some amount of background knowledge regarding U.S. culture.

Reading at the University includes a variety of genres: essays, articles, and chapters from college texts. In its suggestions for extensive reading, it sends students to other sources, thus providing research training. Useful self-tests, at the end of each three-chapter grouping, are of pedagogical as well as assessment value, since they prepare ESL students for the kind of essay or comprehension questions they will face on university tests.

Chapter 6, which focuses on human needs, might be taught as follows. As a prereading predicting activity, students begin by making individual lists of what they think is necessary for a happy human life. In small groups they compare, discuss, and expand on their lists. They then compare their lists to the hierarchy suggested by the psychologist Maslow. This hierarchy, which can be summarized into five *S*'s—survival needs, security needs, social needs, status needs, and self-fulfillment needs—is then discussed.

In small groups students consider the function and fulfillment of such needs in their own lives. In pairs, they scan the chapter to locate reading sections that fall under various need categories. Examples are

Physical needs: "Biomechanics of Sport"

Security needs: "Decline of Competition"

Self-fulfillment needs: "Rise of Counterculture"

For homework the students study articles on one of the needs and summarize its main points. They might do extended reading and class presentation on need fulfillment in their own culture.

Conclusions

As mentioned, the theme-based course does not conform to the principle that a language through content course should use authentic text. Because the theme-based courses described here are confined entirely within CESL, they are isolated from the real world of academic work. Nevertheless, this type of course is appropriate for students who are not ready to handle the intensive study of authentic material. Furthermore, academic strategies can usefully be taught in a theme-based course, as long as it is recognized that such teaching is not *all* that ESL students will need to prepare for the mainstream. In sum, the theme-based course is a valuable part of the ESL curriculum, but it should not be the final part. Before students are mainstreamed, they should encounter authentic text in the form of one of the other types of language through content courses described next.

PRECOURSES

The precourse was described in detail in case study 4. Here the precourse will be compared to the other types of courses.

As mentioned, the adjunct course seems to be best suited for preparing ESL students for mainstream content courses because it most closely duplicates those courses while providing the necessary support. Unfortunately, as Celce-Murcia (1987) observes, the adjunct course is the most difficult type to set up because it requires extensive planning and coordination with a content teacher. Another drawback of the adjunct course is that in some respects it is a submersion course because the ESL students must take it for credit, something they might not be ready to do. The case studies suggest that premature submersion can be dangerous, for if students do not understand the material adequately, they may adopt coping strategies. Thus, although the adjunct course may be well suited to a large ESL program having enough advanced students to handle a full-semester credit course, it is not well suited to a small program in which intermediate students must be included. An advantage of the precourse, then, is that it involves ESL students in authentic academic tasks but is easier to administer and is more appropriate for intermediate-level students.

Another advantage of the precourse is that it may be possible to associate it with a content course that fulfills graduation requirements, thus adhering to principle 5 in chapter 5 (see page 118). If students do go on to take the content course for credit, they will be equipped not only with academic strategies, but also with background knowledge of the content material.

A third advantage of the precourse is that ESL students seem to be more motivated when they are doing real academic work than when they are doing the "dry runs" that form the syllabus of a traditional study skills course or a theme-based course. In sum, the precourse is an effective way to help students who are not ready for an adjunct course to build academic competence.

ADJUNCT COURSES

Adjunct ESL courses are taught to students who are simultaneously enrolled in a regular content course. Perhaps the best-known adjunct course program is the Freshman Summer Program at the University of California at Los Angeles (UCLA) (Brinton, Snow, and Wesche, 1989). In this program, students who have been admitted to UCLA (but whose low Scholastic Aptitude Test scores suggest that they may have difficulty) are enrolled in a seven-week credit course, which they attend for approximately eight hours a week, and an associated ESL course, which they attend for ten to twelve hours a week. The students may choose from a variety of courses in the humanities, social sciences, and sciences that will satisfy university breadth requirements. The majority of these students are Asian Americans who have graduated from an American high school.

The adjunct course provides an excellent setting in which to develop academic strategies. First of all, the ESL component of the course is directly related to the students' academic needs. In this component, students can get help revising notes, writing papers, preparing for quizzes, and so on, as well as building the conceptual background needed to understand the content material. Second, because the course deals with real academic subject matter and because the students must earn a passing grade, they are very motivated to master both the content material and the academic strategies.

The most popular adjunct course at UCLA is Introduction to Psychology. The ESL component of this course emphasizes five areas of study: reading, writing, study skills, grammar, and discussion of the content material. During the first week of the course when the psychology instructor is covering the history and methods of psychology, the ESL reading component concentrates on previewing and predicting. The writing component covers topic sentences, paragraph unity, and writing paragraphs of definition. The study skills component emphasizes note-taking, dictionary use, and preparing for tests. The grammar component covers verb tenses, determiners, and relative clauses. These activities are not much different from those taught in a study skills course in an intensive ESL program, but the adjunct format is much more effective because the activities are not done for their own sake but rather to help students understand material in a course that they must pass in order to graduate.

It is interesting to compare the adjunct course at UCLA to a similar course at Macalester College (Guyer & Peterson, 1988). In the UCLA course, study skills instruction begins the first week. Students are given a set of sample notes from the previous day's lecture with important pieces of information missing. Working in small groups, they fill in the missing pieces using their own notes. Guyer and Peterson observe that this kind of note-taking exercise often turns into a discussion of the content material, a phenomenon that was observed in the precourse as well. In fact, students are likely to be much more interested in using class time to discuss the content material than to improve their note-taking, especially during the first few weeks of the course, when they may be overwhelmed by the great amount of reading. It is difficult for the ESL teacher to resist students' requests to spend class time explaining the content material rather than working on academic strategies. Guyer and Peterson (1988) note that "students in a fast-moving introductory course simply must understand the . . . lectures and text if they are to keep step with the class during the critical period of adjustment" (p. 98).

For this reason, study skills are not taught during the first third of the course at Macalester. Instead, the ESL section is devoted entirely to helping the students understand the lectures and the textbook. During this period, students receive study guides, reading questions, lecture outlines, and transcripts of the lectures. In the second third of the Macalester course, as in the UCLA course, the students must prepare lecture notes, outlines, and study questions themselves. During the last third of the course, the ESL section becomes somewhat independent of the content section. The ESL instructors assign library work and readings, such as current events reported in newspapers and magazines, that go beyond what is taught in the content section. Class time is devoted to oral research reports, class discussions, and peer editing of students' papers.

The Macalester adjunct course is less traditional than the UCLA course because grammar is not taught and because more effort is devoted to understanding content material than to learning academic strategies. This emphasis reflects the difference between the two student populations. The UCLA students are mostly graduates of American high schools who have had considerable experience with American teachers and textbooks. The Macalester students, on the other hand, are mostly international students who have just arrived in the United States. For them, the shock of American academic culture is probably much greater than it is for the UCLA students, and so they need immediate help with the content material just to keep their heads above water.

In sum, the adjunct course provides the most authentic setting in which ESL students can learn effective academic strategies. But care must be taken to enroll only students with the requisite combination of language proficiency and background knowledge to keep up with the course. Otherwise, the students will be overwhelmed, and the ESL section may have to be devoted entirely to enhancing understanding of the content material to the neglect of strategies instruction.

SHELTERED COURSES

Sheltered courses are content courses that enroll only ESL students, who are thus "sheltered" from competition with native speakers. We will consider a sheltered course at the college level and at the high school level.

A Sheltered Course at the College Level

At the bilingual University of Ottawa, Introduction to Psychology is taught in English and French. The syllabi for both courses are the same, and the textbook is available in English and French versions. Native French speakers can elect to take a sheltered section of the English course. One might imagine that this section and the regular sections of the English psychology course would be taught in more or less the same way, since the content material is the same. However, a comparison of the two shows that the sheltered section has been modified in a number of ways to meet the special needs of the nonnative English speakers. The nature of these modifications illustrates some of the points already made regarding what these needs are.

For the French-speaking students in the sheltered section, the most immediate need is simply to understand the material, especially during the first weeks of the course. For this reason, redundancy is built into the course in several ways. First, the lectures are more explicitly related to the readings than those in the section taught to native speakers. Second, a French language instructor from the university's intensive French program meets with the students for fifteen or twenty minutes before each lecture to go over the reading material and preview the upcoming lectures in French. Third, the lecture material is more tightly organized than it is in the native language sections, and the transitions and connections between topics are made more explicit. Wesche and Ready (1985) note that the English lectures in the sheltered section adopt the classic features of teacher talk: slower delivery, careful enunciation, the use of intonation and gestures to signal the relationship between ideas, the use of more common lexical items and syntactic patterns, and so on.

Wesche and Ready analyzed videotapes of the lectures the English professors gave to the sheltered section and to the regular English sections. The analysis showed that the professors appeared more approachable and supportive in the sheltered section. They also showed greater patience when obvious questions were asked, and they elicited more feedback in order to determine whether the students had understood. A third difference was that in the sheltered section, students took a number of short quizzes instead of writing a research paper. In the discussion of the precourse, we saw that such quizzes can be more difficult for nonnative speakers than writing a paper since they have some control over the topic of the paper and can get help from their language instructors. Therefore, numerous quizzes allow the instructor to assess more accurately whether the student is really following the material. The fact that the sheltered course was taught differently from the equivalent native language sections indicates that it was very difficult for nonnative speakers to cover the same academic material at the same speed as native speakers, even when these students were academically competent in their first language. In terms of the model in Figure 5.1, the French-speaking students in the sheltered course had the same content-specific background knowledge and scripts for school as any other students at the University of Ottawa. What they lacked was English proficiency and academic strategies adapted to dealing with material they did not fully understand.

We now consider the case of a student in a sheltered course who had high general English proficiency but a profound lack of subject-specific background knowledge, scripts for school, and effective academic strategies. This student also had great difficulty covering the same academic material at the same speed as native speakers.

Case Study 5—George: A Ninth-Grade Student in a Sheltered English Course

George is a fifteen-year-old from Colombia who arrived in the United States two and one-half years ago. He lives with his mother, a nurse at a university hospital, and sisters aged eighteen and nineteen in a Washington, D.C., suburb. George's family is a good example of a Hispanic family that is acculturating successfully to life in the United States. Both of the sisters graduated with good grades from the high school George attends and are going to a community college part-time while working. The family lives in a three-bedroom townhouse, a typical ''starter home,'' in an area that comprises immigrants from many countries as well as native-born Americans.

When George entered the United States, he enrolled in the public school district that was studied by Collier (1987). This district, which had no bilingual education program, enrolls about 10 percent nonnative English speakers from over one hundred countries. Koreans are the largest minority, followed by Vietnamese and then Hispanics. Although George had studied English in Colombia, he spoke no English when he arrived. He was placed in the seventh-grade ESL program, which consisted of three ESL courses and mainstream courses in music, art, and physical education. In the eighth grade he took two ESL courses and added a mainstream math course. This year George is taking ESL, math, social studies, physical education, study hall, and a sheltered section of ninth-grade English.

The sheltered course follows the regular English 9 syllabus, but enrolls only nonnative English speakers. The students' backgrounds reflect the demography of the area: of the twenty-five students, seven are from Korea; four from Vietnam; six from Latin American countries; and the others from Thailand, Japan, Taiwan, Iran, and the Philippines.

The teacher, Mrs. Macias, was born in the United States about fifty years ago. She speaks some Spanish, but not natively. Her teaching credential is endorsed in both English and ESL. The latter endorsement is fairly recent, earned through in-service and summer courses. She has taught in the district for about twenty years and is the coordinator of the school's ESL program. She is a friendly, outgoing teacher who gets to know her students personally and who conducts an informal yet well-disciplined class. Mrs. Macias once told me that she does not favor bilingual education because she believes that ESL is the quickest route to English mastery. She encourages her students to use only English at school and once mentioned that if she heard students speaking in Spanish she would say,

"Hey, stop speaking Korean." She said that making a joke of a potentially sensitive subject was the best way to get her point across.

Mrs. Macias suggested George as a tutee because he was doing badly in school, earning an F in English 9 and D's in social studies and math. She thought that George spent a lot of time hanging out with his friends on the community soccer team for which he played instead of studying.

When I met George for the first tutoring session, I found him to be a polite, reserved boy who was willing, though not eager, to be tutored. He spoke fluent English with a slight accent. I asked him which course he needed the most help with, expecting him to say social studies, but he said English, so we agreed to work on that. We would meet one hour a week during his study hall class, which was right before the English class.

The sheltered section of English 9 follows the syllabus of the regular course and uses the same textbook, *Adventures in Reading,* published by Harcourt (1985). The book is an anthology of modern literature in English, including short stories, essays, poetry, drama, and an abridged version of *Great Expectations*. The sections for each genre are organized according to rhetorical type; for example, the section on short stories contains stories that lend themselves to a discussion of plot, character, point of view, setting, and theme. Mrs. Macias followed this rhetorical syllabus in teaching the class. The reading passages contain footnotes explaining difficult vocabulary and are followed by study and discussion questions and suggested writing assignments. The readings Mrs. Macias assigned included "The Most Dangerous Game" by Connell, "The Cask of Amontillado" by Poe, "The Gift of the Magi" by O. Henry, and "The Necklace" by de Maupassant.

Mrs. Macias taught the sheltered course in much the same way that she would have taught a regular English 9 course. Modifications included additional vocabulary exercises in which students had to look up words and copy down definitions, shorter writing assignments, and additional study questions. Although I did not observe Mrs. Macias teaching a regular course, I suspect that in the sheltered course she lectured more than she normally would have. The classes I observed had a structure familiar to teachers of content to ESL students. Mrs. Macias's remarks on the stories were lively and full of humor. She often related her remarks to matters that interested the students. But when she asked substantive questions about the readings, they were often met with silence and averted eyes. At such times Mrs. Macias either answered the questions herself or called on one of the better students. After about thirty minutes of lecture/discussion, the class was given a writing assignment to fill out the remaining twenty minutes of class. During these classes George sat quietly copying what Mrs. Macias wrote on the board but not taking other notes. From our discussions during the tutoring sessions, I determined that he followed the general topics of the discussion, but he did not understand the details.

As I will show, the material in English 9 was too difficult for George and, I suspect, for many members of the class. Mrs. Macias let me know that she thought this might be the case, saying that she had been criticized by another ESL teacher for teaching above the students' level. But she explained that she had no choice. The students needed a certain number of English credits to graduate (regular ESL courses did not count), and the content of the sheltered course had to be substantially the same as the content of the regular course.

In order to convey the flavor, and illustrate the difficulty, of teaching content material to a nonnative speaker, this text quotes extensively from the transcript of one of the tutoring sessions. Notes written after the session appear in brackets. The goal of the session was to prepare George to discuss the first half of "The Most Dangerous Game." This session occurred about halfway through the semester, after we had worked our way through several other short stories. Mrs. Macias had not introduced this story, nor had George read it before the session. In this story, a common fixture of ninth-grade literature books, Rainsford, a hunter, is shipwrecked on an island where he is captured by Zaroff, an exiled Russian count who hunts human beings for sport. The part of the text covered in the transcript of the tutoring session is provided in Figure 6.1.

George's assignment, due in two weeks, was to answer the study questions in the text. These questions, and George's answers, are shown in Figure 6.2. My goal in this session, and in most of the sessions, was to help George understand literally what happens in the story. Whenever possible, I also tried to point out aspects of character development, plot, and so on (G—George; A—Adamson).

A: (reading) "The place has a bad reputation."
   "Cannibals?"
   (to George) Do you know what cannibals are?

G: People that eat another people.

A: That's right. (continues reading) "Cannibals?" suggested Rainsford.
   "Hardly. Even cannibals wouldn't live in such a Godforsaken place. But it's gotten into sailor lore, somehow. Didn't you notice that the crew's nerves seemed a bit jumpy today?" "They were a bit strange, now you mention it. Even Captain Nielsen—"
   "Yes, even that tough-minded old Swede, who'd go up to the devil himself and ask him for a light. Those fishy blue eyes held a look I never saw there before. All I could get out of him was: 'This place has an evil name among seafaring men, sir.' Then he said to me, very gravely: 'Don't you feel anything?'—as if the air about us was actually poisonous. Now, you mustn't laugh when I tell you this—I did feel something like a sudden chill."
   "There was no breeze. The sea was as flat as a plate-glass window. We were drawing near the island then. What I felt was a—a mental chill; a sort of sudden dread."
   (to George) What's *dread*? [ten seconds of silence] Well, you know, you can figure it out from here. When he was passing by this island, how did he feel?

G: Scary.

A: That's right. *Dread* means "scared, fear." (continues reading) "Pure imagination, said Rainsford. . . . Good night Whitney."
   (to George) All right, so these two men are talking about this island on the deck of their yacht. Do you have any questions so far?

G: No.

A: Now which one is the good hunter?

G: Whit . . . Whitney?

A: Whitney. Let's see if that's right. Let's look at this moose thing. . . . "You've got good eyes," said Whitney. I've seen you pick off a moose moving in the brown full bush at four hundred yards."
   O.K. Whitney *said* that, so who did he *see* shooting the moose?

G: Rainsford.

A: Rainsford, yeah. So Rainsford must be the good hunter.

G: Mmmm.

FIGURE 6.1 Part of the Text Covered in the Tutoring Session with George.[1]

"Off there to the right—somewhere—is a large island," said Whitney. "It's rather a mystery—"

"What island is it?" Rainsford asked.

"The old charts call it 'Ship-Trap Island,' " Whitney replied. "A suggestive name, isn't it? Sailors have a curious dread of the place. I don't know why. Some superstition—"

"Can't see it," remarked Rainsford, trying to peer through the dank tropical night that was palpable as it pressed its thick warm blackness in upon the yacht.

"You've good eyes," said Whitney, with a laugh, "and I've seen you pick off a moose moving in the brown fall bush at four hundred yards, but even you can't see four miles or so through a moonless Caribbean night."

"Not four yards," admitted Rainsford. "Ugh! It's like moist black velvet."

"It will be light in Rio," promised Whitney. "We should make it in a few days. I hope the jaguar guns have come from Purdey's.[2] We should have some good hunting up the Amazon. Great sport, hunting."

"The best sport in the world," agreed Rainsford.

"For the hunter," amended Whitney. "Not for the jaguar."

"Don't talk rot, Whitney," said Rainsford. "You're a big-game hunter, not a philosopher. Who cares how a jaguar feels?"

"Perhaps the jaguar does," observed Whitney.

"Bah! They've no understanding."

"Even so, I rather think they understand one thing—fear. The fear of pain and the fear of death."

"Nonsense," laughed Rainsford. "This hot weather is making you soft, Whitney. Be a realist. The world is made up of two classes—the hunters and the huntees. Luckily, you and I are hunters. Do you think we've passed that island yet?"

"I can't tell in the dark. I hope so."

"Why?" asked Rainsford.

"The place has a reputation—a bad one."

"Cannibals?" suggested Rainsford.

"Hardly. Even cannibals wouldn't live in such a Godforsaken place. But it's gotten into sailor lore, somehow. Didn't you notice that the crew's nerves seemed a bit jumpy today?"

"They were a bit strange, now you mention it. Even Captain Nielsen—"

"Yes, even that tough-minded old Swede, who'd go up to the devil himself and ask him for a light. Those fishy blue eyes held a look I never saw there before. All I could get out of him was: 'This place has an evil name among seafaring men, sir.' Then he said to me, very gravely: 'Don't you feel anything?'—as if the air about us was actually poisonous. Now, you mustn't laugh when I tell you this—I did feel something like a sudden chill."

"There was no breeze. The sea was as flat as a plate-glass window. We were drawing near the island then. What I felt was a—a mental chill; a sort of sudden dread."

"Pure imagination," said Rainsford. "One superstitious sailor can taint the whole ship's company with his fear."

"Maybe. But sometimes I think sailors have an extra sense that tells them when they are in danger. Sometimes I think evil is a tangible thing—with wavelengths, just as sound and light have. An evil place can, so to speak, broadcast vibrations of evil. Anyhow, I'm glad we're getting out of this zone. Well, I think I'll turn in now, Rainsford."

"I'm not sleepy," said Rainsford. "I'm going to smoke another pipe up on the afterdeck."

"Good night, then, Rainsford. See you at breakfast."

"Right. Good night, Whitney."

[1]From Richard Connell, "The Most Dangerous Game," in *Adventures in Reading,* Heritage Edition, revised (Orlando: Harcourt, 1985), p. 2.

[2]*Purdey:* a famous English manufacturer of hunting rifles and shotguns.

Question 1

"The Most Dangerous Game" tells of a struggle between Sanger Rainsford and General Zaroff. Who are these two men, and what have they in common? Why would their struggle be less interesting if Rainsford were a doctor, for example, rather than a hunter?

George's Answer

General Zaroff and Rainsford were hunters. Rainsford was a hunter so he got away from Zarroff but if he wasn't a hunter he could not get away.

Question 2

Two parts of the story provide clues for the struggle that is to come: the discussion on ship between Rainsford and Whitney; and Rainsford observations—what he sees and hears— as he swims to the island and as he walks to Zaroff's chateau. How do these episodes hint at the coming struggle?

George's Answer

This episodes provide clues for the coming struggle that Rainsford and Whitney knew that there was a hunter in the island. Rainsford first find out when he heard shots and screams.

FIGURE 6.2 George's Answers to the Study Questions.

A: Um. Now, Rainsford and Whitney have different ideas about hunting. One of them kind of feels sorry for the animals and thinks the animals are afraid. Which one thinks that?

G: Rainsford.

A: O.K., let's check that out. Can you . . . can you find out? . . . Why do you think Rainsford thinks that? [forty seconds of silence while George examines the passage]

G: I don't . . . [ten seconds of silence]

A: Look through here (points to a portion of the text). One of them cares about how the jaguar feels. See if you can decide which one cares about the jaguar.

G: Whitney.

A: That's right. O.K. So, what does Rainsford say when Whitney says, "Maybe the jaguar feels fear"?

G: Uh huh. He says, "They've no understanding."

A: What does he mean by that?

G: They don't feel fear.

A: O.K., Um . . . Does this . . . does this island have cannibals on it?

G: [ten seconds silence] Um humm.

A: Where does it say that? How do you know it has cannibals?

G: Rainsford said that the place has a reputation . . . a bad one.

A: O.K. Well, does that mean cannibals necessarily? Could be other things. Yeah, we don't know just from that. It has a bad reputation. But maybe it's not cannibals. (reading) "Cannibals, suggested Rainsford, *hardly*." Does that mean there are cannibals?

G: Maybe.

A: [I now realize that George doesn't know the meaning of *hardly*.] No, it means no cannibals. Why not? Well, next he tells you. "Even cannibals wouldn't live in such a Godforsaken place."

The transcript covers a discussion of about the first full page of text, and as George's answers show, he is already having problems understanding what is going on. The transcript gives a clue to the nature of some of his problems. Whitney says that the island has a bad reputation. Rainsford asks if that is because the island has cannibals. Whitney answers directly: "Hardly." Then he elaborates with an indirect answer: "Even cannibals wouldn't live there." George is able to follow some of this. He understands that the island is a bad place, and he understands that a possible reason for this is that there could be cannibals on it. But he does not know the word *hardly,* so he does not comprehend Whitney's direct negative reply. I believe that George is capable of understanding the indirect reply and thus figuring out the meaning of *hardly* from the context, but he is not accustomed to doing this. Instead, he is accustomed to following only the basic action and plot development. It is certainly logical that the reason the island is dangerous is that it has cannibals, and a cannibal-infested island would fit with the scary mood of the story and the hunting theme. In other words, George uses the strategy of top-down processing based on the words he understands and the general logic of the story, without checking on the correctness of his guesses.

George's answers to study questions 1 and 2 suggest that his top-down processing strategy is fairly effective. (It should be noted that I did not help George with these questions.) George answers the first part of question 1, which requires a factual answer, minimally but adequately: Zaroff and Rainsford are both hunters. The second part of the question asks for interpretation: Why does the fact that Rainsford is a hunter make the struggle more interesting? This question invites some discussion of a principal theme of the story: the ethical aspects of hunting. However, I do not believe that George understands that such issues are involved in the story. His answer is based only on his understanding of the plot and action: Rainsford makes an interesting prey because he is difficult to kill. Similarly, in question 2, the student is invited to discuss two struggles between Rainsford and Zaroff: their debate about the morality of hunting men (which is foreshadowed by Rainsford and Whitney's debate about the morality of hunting animals) and their physical struggle (which is foreshadowed by Rainsford's hearing shots and the death cry of "a large animal"). George answers only the second part of the question, which again is based only on his understanding of the action.

It is clear why George needs to rely on top-down processing in the literature class. In a one-hour tutoring session, George and I were able to read closely (as in the transcript) only about four pages of the story, but the story is sixteen pages long, and without a tutor George reads even more slowly. Furthermore, English was only one of four classes for which George had to do homework. Therefore, if he wanted to gain more than a superficial understanding of the material, George would have to spend virtually all of his time studying. In the case studies we found students like Ceyong who were willing to do this (with considerable pressure and support from their parents), but George was not.

Comments on the Case Study of George.   I believe that George profited from the sheltered course, although students who had more academic competence and better motivation undoubtedly profited more. As his answers to the study questions show, George learned strategies for completing assignments in an adequate way based on material that he understood only partially. As we have seen, ESL students must have such strategies to survive in the mainstream. It is not unreasonable for an ESL program to teach such strategies to its students, and I believe that this might have been Mrs. Macias's goal in the course. But George's answers also make it clear that the sheltered course was not the optimal course for him. In particular, what George needed was close reading and discussion of literature so that he could fully understand and thereby construct a script for what understanding literature involves. I think that George was ready for literature but not for Poe, de Maupassant, and Dickens. Connell would have been a good text for near the end of the course, but George needed more time to read it, and he needed more opportunity for close reading, which could be done only with shorter, more accessible texts, perhaps something like Shirley Jackson's "The Lottery."

The important point to emerge from George's case study is that in sheltered courses ESL students should not be expected to cover the same material in the same amount of time as native English-speaking (NES) students, at least not without extensive backup support. The ideal solution in George's case would have been to change the syllabus of the sheltered section of English 9 so that it would cover more appropriate material (perhaps including some of the selections in *Adventures in Reading* only during the last part of the course) and so that the course would teach academic strategies as well. But such curricular change is often very difficult. It can be opposed by content teachers and administrators who believe it has the effect of weakening the curriculum and the value of the diploma. A more practical suggestion, then, would be to provide backup support for the course, and I believe that this could have been done at George's school. Every day George attended an ESL class in which he had to learn grammar and vocabulary, complete workbook exercises, and write essays that were not connected to any of his content courses. I suggest that this course could have helped him more effectively if it had been related to the material of the literature course. A second suggestion would be to provide peer tutoring for George. The tutoring sessions helped George a great deal, not only because I was able to explain the content material to him, but also because I was able to help him organize, keep track of assignments, plan when to study for tests, and in other ways acculturate him to academic life. I believe that a good twelfth-grade student tutor could have been equally helpful. It is important to note, though, that the tutor would have to be someone whom George respected and liked. Part of George's lack of motivation in school had to do with the fact that he felt some hostility toward Anglo boys, especially popular athletic types. However, he did have many Anglo friends, both boys and girls, and I believe that the right person, Hispanic or Anglo, could help George greatly.

Having completed a sheltered course that covered more appropriate material, George would, I believe, be ready to tackle English 9 on an adjunct basis. He would still, however, need considerable backup support from ESL teachers and tutors, spending at least as much time in support activities as in regular class activities. In short, the ESL program at George's high school needs to make full use of the resources available in the mainstream to build a bridge for ESL students.

CHAPTER 7

Activities for Developing
Academic Competence[1]

INTRODUCTION

This chapter presents examples of activities that the language through content teacher can use to help students understand content material and develop academic strategies. The chapter is divided into three parts. The first part takes the reader through a typical week in a content-based course in introductory linguistics, describing the schedule and the nature of the activities. The second part describes additional activities that could be used at other times during the course or in other kinds of language through content courses. The final part presents sixty-one short suggestions for more activities, most of which are best suited to theme-based or lower-level courses. The described activities are intended to improve strategies for reading, listening/note-taking, preparing for tests, speaking in class, writing, and using sources of information.

Most of the activities can be roughly divided into three types: those that help students understand the literal meaning of content material, those that teach academic strategies, and those that invite students to have fun with the concepts being taught. These latter activities are called "humanistic activities," and we believe that they are important in a language through content course. For one thing, as noted throughout the book, there is usually a wide gulf between the nature and style of a typical ESL class and a typical content class, and since humanistic activities are more like traditional ESL activities, they provide familiar ground for students struggling in an unfamiliar environment. In addition, humanistic activities can help to build class morale. A frequent problem in language through content courses is that students can become frustrated and discouraged. Therefore, it is important to deviate occasionally from the traditional regimen and have some fun.

A SAMPLE UNIT FROM AN ADJUNCT COURSE

Figure 7.1 shows a schedule for the third week of the ESL section of an adjunct course on introductory linguistics for undergraduate college students. The content section of the course meets for an hour a day three days a week, when the instructor lectures, conducts discussions, gives quizzes, and makes reading assignments from the textbook, *An Introduction to Language,* by Fromkin and Rodman. The ESL section of the course meets for an hour every day. For the week represented in the schedule, the ESL instructor's goals are to review and explain the readings and lectures, to prepare for a quiz that will be given the following week, and to help the students choose a topic for a short research paper, which will involve collecting and analyzing spoken or written language data. The following describes how to conduct the activities mentioned on the schedule.

Monday—Prereading Questions (a Reading Activity)

When the content instructor makes a reading assignment, for example, a chapter in the textbook, ask the students to write for five minutes explaining what they usually do to preview a new book or chapter, and to note whether their previewing activities depend on whether they are reading in their first or second language. Then briefly discuss the various prereading strategies that the students have mentioned.

Next, demonstrate how you would preview the assigned chapter, while the students follow along in their books. You might "think aloud" as you thumb through the chapter, noting the various headings and explaining your reactions. One ESL teacher had the following reactions to some of the headings in the chapter on language acquisition in *An Introduction to Language*.

FIGURE 7.1 An ESL Unit for One Week.

Day	Reading	Listening/ Note-Taking	Speaking/ Discussing	Preparing for Tests	Writing
Monday	Prereading questions	Video note-taking			
Tuesday	Prove your answer			Make your own, part 1	
Wednesday		Attentively yours	Attentively yours	Make your own, part 2	Keeping a reading reaction journal
Thursday		Divided-page note-taking		Headache and aspirin	
Friday		Demo lesson How a tape recorder works			Selecting a research topic

From telegraph to infinity: "Cute. I wonder what that's about."

Sign languages: Evidence for the biology of languages: "Great, sign language is really interesting. I wonder if I can learn any signs by reading this. Yes! Here's a chart of finger spelling."

Summary: "This looks like an interesting chapter, a lot better than the one on syntax. It covers a lot of subjects in a short space, so it probably doesn't go into much detail, and it probably isn't very hard."

Be sure to make clear to the students that your method of previewing works for you, but some of the other methods that have been discussed may work better for them.

Next, hand out a worksheet on which the students, in groups, write the definitions of key terms and short answers to questions, as in the following example from chapter 10 of *An Introduction to Language:*

1. What are the four major headings in chapter 10?
2. The first four paragraphs of the chapter do not have a heading; they just appear under the chapter title. What heading would you give this section?
3. How many subheadings are there under the major heading *Stages in language acquisition*?
4. Write short definitions of the following terms. The terms appear in boldface in the text.
    babbling
    mean length of utterance (MLU)
    inflectional errors
    reinforcement
    primes
    holophrastic stage
5. Answer the following questions in a few sentences. The section in which the answer appears is indicated before the question.
    a. *The two word stage.* At about what age do children begin to produce two word utterances?
    b. *Do children learn by reinforcement?* Do children learn by reinforcement?
    c. *American sign language.* Does sign language have a syntactic system?
    d. *Can chimps learn human langauge?* Can chimps learn human language?
    e. On the basis of what you have read so far, do you think Fromkin and Rodman's account of first language acquisition fits better with behaviorism or with cognitive psychology? Why do you think so?

Monday—Video Note-Taking
(a Listening/Note-Taking Activity)

Record the content instructor's lecture on videotape. Tell the students not to take notes while they listen, but to concentrate on understanding because you are going to play the tape during the ESL class. They should, however, write down any questions or note any parts of the lecture that they don't understand. In the ESL section, play the videotape while you and several other students take notes on the board. Be sure to use abbreviations and to mark the organization of the lecture by means of indenting. The other students should use whatever combination of English and their native language is comfortable. After several minutes, stop the tape and compare the various note-taking systems, especially the main points and the organizational schemes. The note-takers should explain why they wrote down what they did and why they used English or their native language when they did.

After this demonstration, tell everyone to return to their seats and resume the lecture, stopping from time to time to check for comprehension and to answer any questions the students might have.

Tuesday—**Prove Your Answer (a Reading Activity)**

Pass out a list of true–false questions made up from a chapter in the textbook that the students have already read. The students are to skim the chapter and find the answers to the questions. Then they must quote the sentence or sentences from the book that prove their answers. Students will often not understand how a quotation can prove a statement false, and this should be demonstrated for them.

This exercise is a good way to teach how to quote from scholarly works, because the students should employ ellipses and paraphrase when appropriate, as in the following examples.

> *Comprehension Exercise, Chapter 10*
> Answer the following questions *true* or *false*. Then quote the sentence or sentences from the chapter that prove your answer, and write the number of the page where the sentence appears.
>
> 1. Tok Pisin was once called "Melanesion Pidgin English."
>   TRUE "A notable pidgin . . . is called Tok Pisin. It was once called Melanesion Pidgin English" (p. 261).
> 2. Pidgin languages have no syntactic rules.
>   FALSE "In Tok Pisin, verbs that take a direct object must have the suffix -*m* . . ." (p. 262).
> 3. Creoles are more complex lexically and syntactically than pidgins.
>   TRUE "Creoles . . . [have] more lexical items and a broader array of grammatical distinctions than pidgins" (p. 263).

Tuesday—**Make Your Own (a Testing Activity)**

Tests are the most difficult part of a content course for many ESL students, so they should take practice tests before the real tests are administered. To prepare for a test, tell the class that you would like to give the content instructor some ideas about what kinds of questions your students prefer, and, if possible, secure the content instructor's consent to use some of the questions suggested by your students on the real test (or at least to use them as input). Ask the students what kinds of questions they would prefer and encourage them to talk about their test-taking experiences both in the United States and in their home countries.

In the first part of this activity, the students brainstorm about various test formats while someone makes a list on the board. The list will probably include such items as essay questions, multiple-choice questions, true–false questions, short-answer questions, matching-answer questions, and so on. Now divide the class into groups of three or four and have each group appoint a secretary. Assign each group a portion of the content material—for example, a chapter from the textbook—and ask them to make up five questions in the format they prefer. It is usually best to let the groups get started in class with your help and then to finish the assignment as homework.

In a subsequent class, each group passes their questions on to another group, who must jointly write answers. In the case of questions that require a longer answer, the authors should pass on only their favorite question. After the time limit is up, ask for volunteers to read their answers. The class can then discuss the correctness of the answers as well as the appropriateness of the questions. Finally, deliver all the questions and answers to the content instructor.

Wednesday—Attentively Yours (a Speaking/Listening Activity)

In this activity, the students get to talk to someone who is really listening. Assign each student a conversation partner, trying to match people who will work well together but who are not best friends. In other words, try to find congenial partners who will provide a new audience for each other. Have the students move their chairs around so that each pair has some privacy. Tell them that they will be given a topic that they are to talk to one another about for two minutes, and that both conversation partners are to speak on the same topic.

The listener is to give the speaker complete and undivided attention, without asking questions or interrupting, but showing through body language and facial expression that he or she is truly listening to what the speaker is saying. When finished, the speaker tells the listener what it felt like to be completely attended to.

When you are sure that all the students have understood your instructions, announce the topic. It can be one related to the content material, as long as the material is well understood and the topic is interesting, for example, "Can chimps learn to sign?" Allow a moment of thinking time and then signal the speakers to begin.

When two minutes is up, signal the speakers to stop. Remind the students that this is the time for the speakers to tell the listeners whether they have done their job adequately. Allow about a minute for this and then signal the second speaker to begin. Repeat the procedure. This exercise is a good way to give the students practice for discussions in the content sections. If possible, find out from the content instructor what questions will be asked in an upcoming class and base the topics on those.

Topics need not be based on the academic material, in which case the exercise becomes simply a chance to practice speaking English before an attentive audience. General topics that we have found to be successful are

Games I played as a child

A person who has influenced me

An object that is important to me

Something I'll never forget

Something I learned from my parents

The house I lived in as a child

A place I love to visit

My favorite foods

A time when I was in danger of death (use discretion with this one).

This exercise can be repeated many times during a term, using different topics and different partners, as it facilitates communication and helps to create a supportive class environment.

Wednesday—A Reading Reaction Journal (a Reading Activity)

In the reading reaction journal (sometimes called a "learning log"), students record their personal reactions to the reading material. These may be questions, comments regarding the relevance or importance of the material, or emotional reactions to it. The journal is not a summary but rather a kind of "talk with or to the text."

The students may wish to make some entries in their native language, and they should be encouraged to do this if it feels more comfortable. These comments, of course, can be shared only with other speakers of that language. The students must make at least one entry, which should be dated, each week. Some authors suggest that the journal can be housed in whatever form the student prefers: spiral notebook, loose-leaf notebook, even computer disks and printouts. We have found, however, that the spiral notebook is best because loose pages are easily lost. The disadvantage of spiral notebooks is that the teacher must carry home a heavy stack of journals to comment on. The teacher's comments can be very brief, as their main purpose is to assure the students that they have an audience. The comments should always be nonjudgmental, in both the moral and the grammatical sense. However, if incorrect grammar gets in the way of meaning, it is a good idea to ask for a clarification.

On the day the journals are handed back with comments, volunteers, in small groups, tell each other about one item from their journals. If it is a question about the content material, the other members of the group try to answer it. If the item expresses frustration about not being able to read everything assigned, or disagreement with the author's claims, the other members offer opinions and advice. If the author wishes, these comments can be entered into the journal.

At the end of the term, each student's journal will document his or her journey through the course.

Thursday—Divided-Page Note-Taking (a Note-Taking Activity)

This method of note-taking is good for less proficient students. Before a content lecture, tell the students to draw a line down the middle of each page they take notes on and to write only on the right side of the line. After the lecture, the students discuss what was said and augment their notes by writing on the left side of the page. A student might add points he or she missed during the lecture or explanatory comments, such as translations or explanations of new terms, as shown in Figure 7.2. The discussion of the lecture might be done in small groups, with the class as a whole, or using a videotape of the lecture. Less proficient students can be assigned note-taking partners with whom they always review the lecture.

FIGURE 7.2 An Example of Divided-Page Note-Taking.

Feb. 24

behavior is observed no reference to conscious behaviorism - 1930-1960.	Behaviorism- a school of psychology that takes the objective evidence of behavior as the only concern of its research. Behaviorism is old. Replaced by cognitive psychology
Pavlov - Russian psychologist This is *classical* <u>conditioning</u> Salivation is natural, not learned response.	Dog experiment stimulus - food salivation - response learned response when door opens associate something natural will always produce response
	bell - new stimulus door or bell → situation
	Operant Conditioning
Skinner box →	rats — lever / food tray
B.F. Skinner American behaviorist There is no exact stimulus.	stimulus - whole box response - pressing the bar, not natural behavior. reward - food
the whole environment. Response is most important.	

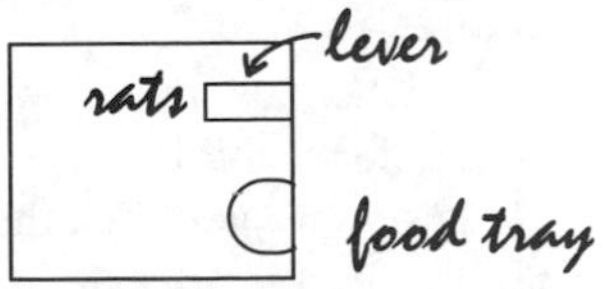

Thursday—Headache and Aspirin (a Speaking/Test-Taking Activity)

This exercise is a variation of Attentively Yours, described earlier. It should be done only after students are familiar with the conversation partners format. The purpose of the exercise is to let students give vent to their frustrations and anxieties about tests. It can also lead to some good practical suggestions for alleviating those frustrations and anxieties. Ask the students to pair up with a friend and tell them that they are going to ask for advice about test-taking. Give them several minutes to write down some of the problems they have with tests. These should be very specific. "I get nervous before tests" is too general; "Before tests, I can't remember anything I have studied" is better. Then have the partners sit facing each other and give their undivided attention.

The speaker explains his or her worries about tests, and the listener listens. After the speaker has finished, the listener gives advice, and then the roles are reversed.

If there are students who would be uncomfortable talking about this fairly personal topic, they may substitute focused freewriting (see "Selecting a Research Topic") on the subject, "What I don't like about tests." After five to ten minutes, the writers should read each other's papers and offer suggestions.

Finally, in a group discussion, the class reviews the problems and solutions that have been mentioned.

Friday—How a Tape Recorder Works (a Listening/Note-Taking Activity)

This activity embodies principle 4 in chapter 5, "Teaching should be experiential." Before the activity, the content instructor gave a lecture and a brief demonstration on how a tape recorder works and how to conduct a tape-recorded interview. He mentioned what kinds of machines and cassettes are best, how to clean the heads, where to place the microphone for recording, and how to label and store tapes. This demonstration lesson expands on some of these topics.

Lesson Plan for "How a Tape Recorder Works"
1. The students bring tape recorders and cassettes to class. Since they must do a short research project involving an analysis of language, most of them will be using a tape recorder.
2. Open an old cassette and show what it looks like inside. Point out the tape spools, the guide pillars, and the pressure pad. Pull out some of the tape and show how one side is smooth and the other side is covered with iron oxide dust that will rub off on your fingers. Pass the cassette around and let the students examine it.
3. On the board, make a rough drawing of how the recording mechanism works, as in Figure 7.3, describing and labeling the various parts. As you talk, the students should take notes and locate the various parts on their own tape recorders. Mention the following components: guide pillar, pressure pad, tape spools, erase head, recording/playback head, cores, and coils. During the lecture, review some of the points that the content teacher made during his lecture: forty-five-minute cassettes should not be used because the tape is so thin that it easily becomes

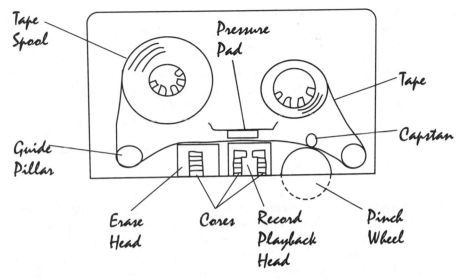

FIGURE 7.3   A Rough Drawing of How a Tape Recorder Works.

tangled; most tape recorders have good electronics—differences in quality usually have to do with the mechanical parts; and so forth.

4. Tell the students to push the various function keys: play, rewind, record, and so on, with the cassette in and out of the machine, and observe what happens.

5. Erase the diagram from the board and ask the students, working in pairs, to recreate it, using their notes and their own tape recorders. Ask them to describe briefly in writing the function of the parts you mentioned. With the help of the class, write the first description on the board. For example, "Erase head: While the machine is recording, an electrical current passes through the erase head coil, turning the core into an electromagnet and creating a magnetic field. The magnetic field scrambles the iron oxide particles on the tape, destroying their previous pattern and thus erasing the recording."

Friday—Selecting a Research Topic (a Writing Activity)

This activity involves a form of freewriting, which is explained at greater length on pages 164–165. As noted there, ESL students must usually be shown how to freewrite, so this exercise should be undertaken only after the students are comfortable with this form of writing.

Focused freewriting is like true freewriting, except that the students are given a subject to write about. True freewriting is useful for finding topics when the writing assignment is completely unrestricted, as is often the case in a freshman composition course. In a content course, however, the students must write about a topic related to some aspect of the content material, so focused freewriting is more appropriate.

In the following example of focused freewriting, a student from Mexico wrote on the question, "What part of the Introduction to Linguistics course is the most interesting?" (The freewriting was done directly after the ESL instructor had done some freewriting on the board in his own second language, which is Spanish.)

> The subject of second language acquisition is for me the most interesting part of this course. Right now it occurs to me that the idea of free-writing could be very useful to detect the "errors" a student of a second language might have when writing a short essay in the target language. This seems to be useful to prove, or at least, to help proving the theory (well, it is a theory already) of the natural order of acquisition.
>
> For example, and according to the demonstration we just saw, Dr. Sanford has acquired most of the basic skills pertaining Spanish, on the other hand, he still has to accomplish some more rules, the ones are or come after acquisition.

Is there a research topic in these paragraphs? Well, a couple of possibilities come to mind. First, note that the student appears to be engaged in the class. He has obviously been thinking about a research project involving the analysis of language, and it occurs to him that freewriting might be a good way of collecting data. Also note that the student is somewhat confused about Krashen's (1981) theory of a "natural order" of structures in language acquisition, and that he may need to review it. However, it seems likely that this student's research project should involve second language (L2) acquisition and that he should use freewriting to collect data.

The next step in helping this student select a topic would be to find an area within these parameters to focus on. Because the student is a Spanish speaker, he might look for Spanish influence in the English of native Spanish speakers or English influence in the Spanish of native English speakers. The student seems interested in Krashen's theories, so he might ask his subjects to freewrite and then to edit their freewriting. The errors and nonerrors that the subjects change could shed light on how they use their "monitors," especially if they are asked to explain why they made the changes.

The example of focused freewriting was more useful for selecting a research topic than some of the others produced by this group of students. But in all of the freewritings, some areas of the students' interests emerged. These included first language (L1) acquisition, the effectiveness of grammar teaching in learning a second language, the differences between British and American English, and teenage slang.

MORE ACTIVITIES FOR STUDYING CONTENT MATERIAL AND DEVELOPING ACADEMIC STRATEGIES

Introduction

This section suggests additional activities for helping ESL students develop academic competence. Other activities have been described elsewhere in the book, especially in the discussion of the precourse on page 95. Here we will focus on the areas of

1. Reading
2. Note-taking

3. Preparing for tests
4. Speaking in class
5. Writing research papers.

Not all of the suggested activities will be appropriate for all content-based courses. Some are intended for theme-based courses, in which the content material is usually presented by the ESL instructor. Within each of the five sections, the activities intended mainly for adjunct courses (and thus for fairly advanced students) are presented first and those intended for theme-based courses (and less advanced students) are presented last, although there is considerable overlap among them. The decision about whether a particular activity is appropriate or not is, of course, up to the ESL teacher.

Reading Activities

Academic reading means previewing and rereading. However, as the case studies show, students frequently waste time and emotional energy with inefficient reading strategies. They are in need of a process that helps them to focus, organize, analyze, and review. The SQ3R method offers such direction. As Eskey and Grabe (1988) note, "For the second language reader, who is often . . . an insecure reader . . . strategies like the ancient and venerable SQ3R are even more important than they are for the native reader, and the teacher must therefore coach students in their use" (p. 229). The version of SQ3R described here is extensive and will take several days to complete. It can and should be abridged when less time is available and when students have become more familiar with the process.

Survey.   Before you assign any reading material, ask your students to preview the text, looking over the title and any introductory summary (such as a blurb preceding a newspaper article), any pictures that might accompany the text, and the opening sentences of each paragraph. The students might do this work individually at first and then, in small groups, share their results.

In small groups, the students make an outline of what they predict the content of the text will be. This need not be a formal outline—they might simply make a list of what they foresee as the major points of the text. Their outline may be as brief or as detailed as they wish to make it.

Next, have each group join with another group and compare their outlines, making changes until they arrive at an outline that contains the best features of both of the previous versions.

Question.   In small groups, the students make lists of what they have learned from surveying the article. Then representatives from each group contribute facts while the teacher or a student makes a master list on the blackboard of "What We Think We Already Know." Then, in pairs the students consider the idea of "What We Still Don't Know." They write as many questions as possible about the content of the article. Give a time limit for this activity, no more than five minutes.

If you have enough blackboard space, let all the pairs of students go to the board to write their questions. One partner should dictate while the other writes. Then everyone looks over the questions written on the board. Many will be duplicates; some will have grammatical errors, which might be corrected. Some students will want to try to answer some of the questions. There will be suggestions for other questions. Leave everything on the board. If this activity will continue during the next class period and the board is likely to be erased, assign a student to copy everything so that you can reproduce the questions on a handout.

Read.   The students read the text individually. Before they start, assign a reading task such as finding the answer to one of the questions on the board, defining a specific vocabulary word, or writing a title for each paragraph. Remember that academic reading is never done without a purpose. A good rule of thumb is never to assign silent reading without some sort of reading task.

Instead of silent reading, you might read some of the text aloud or ask the students to do this, perhaps in small reading groups. Reading out loud is a good way to focus everyone's attention on a difficult passage, and a good reader (especially the teacher) can help to make the meaning clear by using intonation and emphasis. Don't be afraid to read aloud to the class often.

Recite.   Individually the students write short answers to the questions on the board (or a handout), not worrying about grammar. In small groups, they compare and discuss their answers and prepare an oral summary of the text.

Review.   In small groups, or perhaps as homework, students write summaries of the text. The summaries are exchanged and commented on. Students should look for similarities and differences in summaries.

In a group discussion, a summary is composed on the board. Students take turns writing on the board while everyone writes in their notebooks. For homework, students make out a test on the text. Assign different parts of the test to different groups of students. Let some make up essay questions, others true–false questions, and still others matching or multiple choice.

A Study Guide for Reading.   When ESL students first encounter academic reading, they sometimes feel that the material before them is insurmountably difficult. A study guide helps to alleviate such feelings of helplessness. As the course progresses, students will take over some of the responsibility for writing the study guide and thus become exposed to the material twice. Study guides not only provide a sense of direction but also expand the students' active use of content vocabulary. Don't worry about not being an expert in the content subject. Your students are not experts either, and your lack of expertise will help you experience their problems, as you collaboratively construct the meaning of the text.

To write a study guide, go through the text and make a list of all the words related to key concepts. Provide more words from the first paragraph than from sections later in the text. Tell the students to read the key words before each section of the text and to concentrate on these concepts as they read. When they finish reading a section, they should be able to review it mentally by checking the list of concepts. If they do not remember anything connected with a certain concept, they should go back and check the text.

Do a dry run with the first paragraph. Write the key concepts on the board and ask the students to read through the first paragraph, checking the key concepts as they go. When they have finished, ask them to retell the text by looking at the key concepts. Then assign the reading for homework. The following is a list of key concepts used as a study guide for a reading in biology:

1. Mendelian inheritance
2. Homologous chromosomes
3. Alleles
4. Meiosis
   Parent cell
   Daughter cells
   Gametes
5. Fertilization
6. True breeding
7. Parent generation
   F1 generation
   F2 generation
8. Homozygous state
   Heterozygous state
9. Genotypic ratio
   Phenotypic ratio
10. Particular inheritance hypothesis
    Blending hypothesis
11. Dominant gene
    Recessive gene

The following day, the students in small groups review their reading, following the key concepts.

As the year progresses, ask students to read sections of texts to be assigned and, in pairs or small groups, create study guides for their small section. Each group then writes its own guide on the board, and the class has a student-constructed study guide for the entire reading.

Split Possibilities (a Predicting Activity).   As we saw in the first section of chapter 3, Clarke (1980) found that students are reluctant to use top-down processing when reading in their second language, even though they may be adept at this strategy in their first language. Predicting activities such as Split Possibilities and Picture the Future (which follows) encourage students to make intelligent guesses about what they are likely to find in a reading passage and thus to develop an interactive reading style.

From the text you are about to study with your class, pull out two significant words or phrases. These should not be related to each other but should be of importance to the text. For example, in an article that was critical of the policies of apartheid, Natalie spoke about her own private boycott of South African apples. The two key words she chose from this article were

    a. Apples
    b. South Africa.

Divide the class into two even groups (four groups if you have a large class), give each group one of the words you have chosen, and ask them to brainstorm for associations. A secretary in each group should write all the associations, on the blackboard if possible. Then, the secretaries explain the lists of associations to the whole class.

Next, ask the students to pair up so that each sits with a partner from a different group. Together the pairs try to find as many connections as possible between the two words: What are all the possible connections between apples and South Africa? After a few minutes, ask several of the pairs (all if your class is small) to report their projected connections to the whole class.

Tell the class that you are going to read a text in which both of the ideas are mentioned, and that they are to find out whether any of the suggested connections are correct.

Picture the Future (a Prereading Activity).   Find a large, colorful picture of any interesting subject—it need not be relevant to the content material of the course. Art books are good sources, and they can be obtained cheaply in stores that sell used books. Show the picture to the class, letting them have only a brief look at it before you put it away. Then ask the students to write down what they think they saw in the picture.

In pairs, the students compare their notes. Then show the picture again, this time letting everyone get a more careful look to add information to their lists. Have several lists read aloud to the class.

Teli the class that you are going to read a story, article, poem, book chapter, or anything pertinent and ask them to find possible connections between the picture and the text. Students invariably do make connections. For example, Natalie once showed a picture of an old man in a coffin. Then she announced that they were going to read a magazine article about identical twins. Suggestions for possible connections were

This man has been killed by his jealous twin brother.

Someone killed this man, but he meant to kill his twin.

His long-lost twin sister killed him—she was in love with him and didn't know that he was her brother.

Twins live long lives.

Twins live short lives because they fight so much.

This man wanted to die at the same time as his twin brother.

Finally, read the text, noting whether the associations fit or contradict the information in the article.

What's the Purpose? (a Skimming Activity).   We *skim* a text to get the gist of it. We may, for example, skim a text to see whether it has any information of use to us when we plan a journey or a research project. We *scan* a text to search rapidly for a specific piece of information. We may scan a Dickens biography to find facts about the author's relationship to his daughters or the year in which one of his books was published. The activity Prereading Questions contained both skimming and scanning tasks. Skimming and scanning are necessary skills for ESL students, who, as we have seen, read much more slowly than native speakers and therefore may not have time to read all the material that is assigned. These students must make intelligent choices about what to read in depth, what to read superficially, and what not to read at all. This and the following activities will help to improve skimming and scanning abilities.

To begin What's the Purpose, divide the class into groups of four or five students and have each group appoint a secretary. Ask the groups to think about all the reasons writers write. They will come up with reasons like to earn money, to have fun, to become famous, to spread propaganda, to teach, to entertain, to share important information, to advertise, to make a record for history, and so on. The secretary should note all of the ideas. In a class discussion, each group reports its ideas. As the groups report, make a master list on the blackboard.

Then, ask the students to skim the text you have chosen and try to determine for what purpose it was written. Set a time limit. In pairs, the students talk about the purpose they have decided on and explain why they have made that decision. Next, several pairs report to the class on their decisions, and a discussion may develop when there are points of agreement or disagreement. Finally, the class reads the text more carefully and judges which of the predictions appear to be right.

Treasure Hunt (a Scanning Activity).   Prepare a list of questions on a text. These should be questions that are fairly easily located in the text, and the answers should be quite specific. If the text were "Little Red Riding Hood," the questions might include How did Little R. R. get her name? What is in her basket? Who does she meet in the woods? Why must she go to see her grandmother? Divide the class into small groups and have each group appoint a secretary, then pass out a different list of questions to each group.

Give the class a time limit in which to scan the text quickly, trying to locate answers to all the questions. The secretary writes down all answers. The group that finishes first is declared the provisional winner. This group reads its answers and, if they are correct, is declared the final winner. If one or more of the answers are wrong, these can be corrected by the members of another group, which then becomes the winner. Some groups will realize very quickly that they can assign different questions to each member. These are, of course, the groups that will win. Other groups will simply have all the members search for all the answers. Either way, they practice scanning.

Finding Voices (an Interpretation Activity).   Each written passage has been composed from the point of view of a narrating voice. When we read in our own language, we fairly quickly spot the "voice" behind the printed word. For example, most of us can detect the opinion of a journalist, even if the journalist's article does not appear on the opinion pages of the newspaper. The sooner ESL students learn to read voices, the better they will be able to comprehend and interpret. The following activity is particularly suitable for controversial articles or essays.

First, ask the students to read through an article, underlining all the facts. Stress to them that you want facts only and ask for several definitions of the word *fact*. (*Contra* Rorty, the dictionary defines *fact* as a thing that has actually happened or is undisputably true; reality; actuality; truth). Next, in small groups the students compare their lists of facts and eliminate the items on which everyone does not agree. Then, several groups read their lists to the entire class, and the whole group considers the "factuality" of the items. At this stage students often change their minds about what they had previously considered hard facts. For example, when an authority is quoted ("President Bush said that . . ."), the students may not immediately understand that the actual content of what was said might well be an opinion. Furthermore, some students may raise paradigm-negating objections, as discussed in chapter 3. For example, in connection with an article on socio-linguistics, one student objected to the fact that the speech of middle-class New Yorkers can differ from the speech of working-class New Yorkers on the ground that in America there are no social classes.

Write the list of items that the whole class considers factual on the board. This list will be amazingly short. Now, ask the students to reread the article, this time searching for opinions. Several students should read aloud their lists of opinions. They will be much longer than the list of facts.

Finally, ask the students to define the voice of the narrator. Where are the sympathies expressed by the voice? Point out that the voice need not necessarily be that of the writer. Ask: Can we trust the voice? Does the voice mean what it says? How do we know what the voice means? (Very frequently, so-called objective newspaper articles place sympathetic causes at the beginning or at the end, while the opposing side is squashed into an insignificant middle position.)

Fifty Does It (a Reviewing Activity).   The students in the precourse (see page 95) were eager to review lectures and articles in order to prepare for tests. This exercise and the two that follow are good ways to review.

Pass out three-by-five-inch index cards and ask the students to summarize the reading or lecture on one side of the card. The summary must not exceed fifty words and so must include only the most important points. Collect all the cards and arrange them like a fan in a card game. Walk around the class and ask the students to pick a card. If a student chooses his or her own card, try again.

The students read the cards and note whether they agree with the writer regarding the most important points. Then, in small groups, the students tell each other about the card they picked and compare it to the card they had written. Finally, the whole class discusses the most important aspects of the article.

The Acrostic (a Reviewing Activity).   An acrostic is a verse or an arrangement of words in which certain letters in each line such as the first or the last, when taken in order, spell out a word or message. First, divide the class into small groups and have each group appoint a secretary. Then, write the topic you have been reading about vertically in large letters on the board (the names of individuals work best in this exercise). For example, if you have been reading about Albert Einstein, write

E

I

N

S

T

E

I

N

Each group of students then composes an acrostic, using the letters of *Einstein* to start sentences, phrases, or words that summarize the content of the text they have just read. An *Einstein* acrostic might look like this:

Entered the world in Ulm, Germany, 1879.

Interested in mathematics and physics.

Not appreciated by his teachers or professors.

Started work at the Geneva Patent Office in 1902.

Then wrote his article on the special theory of relativity, published in 1906.

Eventually received recognition and fame, after being ignored by leading physicists.

Interested in finding a unified theory that would explain gravity, electromagnetism, and nuclear force.

Noted for humanity and sense of humor, in addition to genius.

Each group should write its acrostic on the board and explain how it summarizes the text.

The Jigsaw (a Reviewing Activity).   This activity is good for motivating less able students in the class, who will have their chance to be "experts." The technique also shows students that they can understand a lot of a text without knowing the meaning of every word.

Before class, divide a passage that can be legally photocopied into four sections. Label each section with a letter: A, B, C, or D. Make enough copies so that each member of the class can have one of the four sections to read; that is, each student now has one-fourth of the article. It does not matter which fourth. Now ask the students to read their sections and make notes on the important ideas. Next, the students consult with the others who have read *the same* section. Together they decide on what the important ideas in their own section are.

Then, the students form new groups, so that everyone in a group has read a *different* section. Thus, each group contains an expert on a different part of the text. Each expert must explain his or her section to the others. If there are two experts in a group, they share the responsibility. The entire group now pieces together the content of the article.

Finally, the whole class discusses the article, and a rereading of the article is assigned as homework.

Gut Reactions (a Humanistic Activity).   Humanistic activities, based on the psychological principles of Abraham Maslow (1954) and Carl Rogers (1983), have been used with
great success in the foreign language classroom, as, for example, in Moskowitz (1979).
Humanistic activities add a level of emotional involvement to any cognitive content. In
addition, they provide an opportunity for communication based on the students' personal
feelings and experiences, areas in which they are truly expert. As noted in chapter 4,
because of their educational backgrounds, some students do not consider these kinds of
activities appropriate for an academic course and may not wish to deviate too far from the
content instruction. Nevertheless, properly used, humanistic activities can help students
and teachers create a supportive learning environment in which students can value their
own accomplishments and create a climate of acceptance and self-actualization.

This and the following activity are aimed at rereading. In both, students are encouraged to become personally and emotionally involved with a text and to share their
involvement with one another.

In Gut Reactions, the students are asked to reread a text that has been read and
discussed in class, this time looking for one sentence—and only one—that in some way
speaks to them. Perhaps they think that this is the most important sentence in the text.
Perhaps they think that it is the most beautiful. Perhaps it is a sentence with which they
agree or disagree. Perhaps it is a sentence that reminds them of something, upsets them,
or makes them angry. Whatever it is, they should underline this sentence.

Next, in small groups, each student tells the others which sentence he or she underlined and why. The teacher circulates among the groups, listening to the choices and
explanations.

Finally, all the students who have chosen the same sentence (there are usually three
or four) sit as a panel in front of the whole group. They read their sentences and explain
the reasons for their choice. The class may ask questions or offer comments.

Everybody's a Critic.   Divide the class into small groups and ask each group to appoint
a secretary. Ask the students to write a group letter recommending or not recommending
a text they have recently read to a publisher for immediate publication. The text can be a
chapter from the textbook, an assigned article, a story, a poem, and so on. The critics
should consider the prospective audience for the text, the purpose for which the text was
written, the influence the text might have, and any other aspects. The secretary of the
group writes the letter, while other students provide ideas. Each group then reads its letter
to the class while students from other groups play the role of the prospective publishers,
asking questions and arguing the merits of the submission.

Listening/Note-Taking Activities

The following activities are intended to improve strategies for listening and note-taking,
and to suggest ways of making content material more comprehensible to ESL students.

A Note-Taking Study Guide.   This exercise allows students to focus on finding the
answers to questions they themselves have written. Before a lecture, informally discuss
with the class the general content of the lecture or give them some relevant background
material (perhaps from the textbook) to be read in groups. Then, in small groups students

make up any questions they think may be answered in the upcoming lecture. Collect these questions and take them home. Before the lecture, go over the questions and, with the help of the content instructor, if possible, consolidate them into a set of questions that reflect some of the material to be covered in the lecture. Hand out the questions and ask the students to use them as a listening guide during the lecture. After the lecture, students in small groups compare their answers.

Example
Below is a set of questions that served as a study guide for a biology lecture:

1. What are genes?
2. Draw a diagram for *replication* and explain the process.
3. Draw a double helix DNA. Show how it unwinds. What is ''semi-conservative'' replication? Illustrate this in your diagram. Include the base pairs.
4. Enzymes play a part in DNA replication. Explain their function. What is a ''repair enzyme''? What does it eliminate?
5. What are two causes of mutations in our environment?
6. After DNA replication, what are the two other processes of transferring genetic information to the cell?
7. Which processes involve the ''genotype''? the ''phenotype''?
8. What is RNA? What are the three types of RNA? Which is most important for transcription?

Follow the Plan.   With the help of the content instructor, prepare a set of notes to cover the first ten to fifteen minutes of an upcoming lecture. (For a theme-based course, prepare the lecture yourself, or invite a guest speaker.) Then, make another set of notes in which sections of the first set are eliminated, keeping only the main headings. Duplicate one copy of both sets of notes for each student. Tell the students that they don't have to take notes during the first part of the lecture; they can just follow along with the notes they have been given (of course, when those notes run out, they must start their own note-taking).

Before the lecture, the students study the set of complete notes to make sure they understand everything. Then they listen to the lecture. After the lecture, the class discusses the material, answering any questions that have come up. Now collect the set of completed notes and give out the set of incomplete notes. In small groups, students complete this set from memory. Finally, hand out the set of complete notes again and let the students compare the notes they reconstructed.

For more advanced students, the following variation of this exercise can be used. Attend the content course lecture with your students and tell them to take notes in whatever combination of English and their native language is comfortable. Eliminate sections from your own notes, perhaps keeping just the main headings, and hand out this version to the students. Working in groups and consulting their notes, the students fill in the missing sections on the handout. Then, pass out your complete notes and ask the groups to compare them to the notes they have just produced.

Your Share.   Tell the students that you would like everyone to investigate some aspect of the content material in greater depth than it has been covered in class and to give an oral presentation based on their research. Let the students decide what subject they would like to investigate, perhaps using brainstorming or freewriting techniques. For example, in a literature class someone might report on the life of one of the authors. In a psychology class, someone might report in more detail on the theory of physiognomy, which is often mentioned in the introductory chapters of psychology books.

This exercise could require some fairly serious research, and, if so, it could be used as a follow-up to the library use activities described later in the chapter. Or the research could require no more than consulting a good encyclopedia. If a student has personal knowledge that is relevant to the content material (for example, a student from Mexico might know a great deal that is relevant to U.S. history), that is even better. In theme-based courses the oral reports can be summaries of texts studied in class or of articles from newspapers or magazines; in fact, they can be based on any topic of interest.

Talk to each student before he or she delivers the lecture in order to learn the gist of the content. Then help the student choose several main topics of interest. Together with the student, write each of these topics on index cards or slips of paper, one card for each member of the class (if a lecture has five main topics and you have twenty students in the class, each card will be duplicated four times). Then ask everyone in the audience to draw a card.

The speaker delivers the lecture while the others listen and take notes only on their own specific interest areas. Then, in small groups, the students meet with others who have taken notes on the same interest area, and they compare their notes. Some of the students should expand their notes with new information gleaned from their peers. Finally, in a class discussion, representatives from each group talk about their interest areas and encourage a general discussion on each topic.

An alternative version of this exercise is to ask the content instructor for a list of general topics to be covered in an upcoming lecture, and use that lecture as the basis for selective note-taking and subsequent discussion. Each student should, of course, later construct notes covering the whole lecture.

Which Elements Make Up Water? (a Demonstration Activity).[2]   Principle 4 in chapter 5 says that teaching should be experiential. It is easier to find experiential activities, especially those that involve the observation and manipulation of basic-level objects, for science classes than for social sciences or humanities classes. Nevertheless, the ESL teacher should be on the lookout for realia relevant to these subjects. Recall that when Elizabeth missed a lecture in her geography class, she went to the library in search of maps, and by studying them she was able to get an A on the test. Similarly, ESL teachers in a U.S. history course might bring in pictures or movies to supplement the text. For recent historical periods, class members might be able to bring in period clothing, dishes, tools, knick-knacks, and so forth. Or the class could visit a museum to observe the material culture of the period.

This activity and the two that follow illustrate how the ESL teacher can provide experiential, hands-on activities that enrich the content material. Most science textbooks and lab manuals contain more demonstrations and experiments than the content teacher can fit into the course, so the ESL section of an adjunct course provides a good place for additional basic-level experiences. Of course, the ESL teacher will have to work closely with the content teacher to find suitable experiments and the necessary equipment.

To demonstrate which elements make up water, you will need a beaker, test-tube holder, water, wood splint, two test tubes, insulated copper wire, a six-volt dry cell, dilute sulfuric acid, and matches. First review the background concepts relevant to the experiment: elements, molecules, and the periodic table. Remind the class that a water molecule consists of two atoms of hydrogen and one atom of oxygen (H_2O). Review the content instructor's lecture on electrolysis and how passing an electric current through water will separate out these elements.

Fill the beaker half full of water. Fill both test tubes with water and place them upside down inside the beaker. Place an exposed end of a piece of wire inside each of the test tubes (see Figure 7.4). Now pour about fifteen milliliters of dilute sulfuric acid into the water in the beaker. CAUTION: Wear safety goggles. Never pour water into acid.

Complete the electrical circuit by hooking the other ends of the wires to the dry cell. Tell your students, working in groups, to sketch and label this apparatus as in Figure 7.4. Answer any questions they have about vocabulary and spelling.

The students should observe and make notes on what happens to the exposed ends of the wires under the test tubes and also on what happens at the top of each test tube. After five minutes, disconnect the dry cell. Both test tubes will contain columns of gas, one about twice as long as the other. Ask the students which one they think contains hydrogen and which one oxygen. Ask how they think you could be sure. If necessary, ask what effect hydrogen and oxygen have on a flame.

Light a wood splint and, using a test-tube holder, pick up the test tube containing the largest amount of gas (the hydrogen), keeping the open end pointing down. Hold the splint near the test tube and turn the opening toward the flame. Blow out the flame and test the other tube in the same way, using the glowing end of the splint.

Hand out sheets with the following questions, which the students answer in groups:

1. What appeared along the bare end of the wire when the wires were connected to the dry cell?
2. What gas do you think was in the first test tube? Why do you think so?
3. What gas do you think was in the second test tube? Why do you think so?
4. Since you held the test tubes upside down, what does this tell you about the gasses inside?

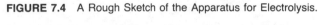

FIGURE 7.4 A Rough Sketch of the Apparatus for Electrolysis.

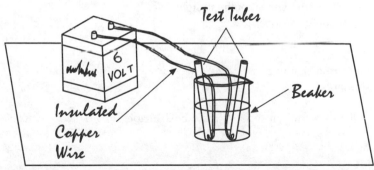

How Does the Third Law of Motion Work? (a Group Demonstration Activity).[3]   This
activity is intended for students who are at a lower level than the audience for the previous
activity. It would be appropriate for a sheltered course in science that includes students at
an intermediate level. This demonstration is more complete than the previous one. It
contains a *dictocomp* exercise—a useful technique for reviewing any content material—
and a practice test.

Review of Background Material.   First, review the laws of motion the class has been
studying, as in the following brief lecture, which should be accompanied with appropriate
gestures and demonstrations of objects hitting each other.

> Sir Isaac Newton proposed his three laws of motion in 1665. The First Law of Motion
> says that if an object is at rest, or not moving, it will stay at rest unless some force makes
> it move. If an object is moving, it will keep moving unless some force stops it. Also, it
> will keep moving in a straight line and at the same speed. This is called *inertia*. All
> matter has inertia.
>   The Second Law of Motion says that if one object pushes against another, it will make
> the second object move or, if it is already moving, change its direction. How far the
> second object moves or how much it changes direction depends on how much force the
> first object has. If a small object hits a large object, the large object won't move very
> much, but if a large object hits a small object, the small object will move a lot.
>   The Third Law of Motion says that action equals reaction. This means that if one
> object pushes against another, both of them will be affected. For example, if two people
> who weigh the same are on skates, and one pushes the other, both of them will move
> backwards. The pushing is an action that causes the other person to move, but it also
> creates an equal reaction (that means a force in the opposite direction) that causes the
> pusher to move. The force of the action equals the force of the reaction, so both of the
> skaters will move an equal distance.

We are going to demonstrate the third law by using baking soda and vinegar in a
closed bottle. When baking soda and vinegar mix, they make the gas carbon dioxide.
When enough gas forms, it will blow the cork out of the bottle. That is the action. There
will also be an equal reaction, as we will see.

Demonstration.   Divide your class into small groups. Each group will need the following
equipment:

1. Soda pop bottle with smooth, straight sides
2. Cork or rubber stopper
3. Tissue paper
4. Four pencils
5. Cup from which to pour
6. Tablespoon.

In addition, the following materials should be available on a table to which everyone has
access:

7. Bottle of vinegar
8. Box of baking soda
9. Jar of petroleum jelly.

First, demonstrate the procedure for the class. As you demonstrate, clearly state what you are doing and ask a spokesperson in each group to repeat the instructions. Then ask a representative from a group to write the instructions on the board. Choose a different representative for each step.

Next, smear some petroleum jelly around the outside of the cork or stopper. Then pour half a cup of vinegar into the bottle. Place two tablespoons of baking soda on a piece of tissue. Roll the paper and twist the ends closed. Put the wrapped tissue in the bottle and quickly fit the cork into the mouth of the bottle. Do not force the cork in tightly. Lay four pencils side by side on your desk, set the bottle on the pencils, and observe what happens.

Now have each group perform its own demonstration, following the set of instructions they have written on the board. Supervise the corking of the bottles to be sure that the corks are well lubricated and not in too tightly; otherwise, the flying corks and bottles could injure someone.

Creating a Practice Test.   After an experiment like the preceding one, it is important that students consolidate their knowledge by rethinking what they have observed. Asking and answering questions about the experiment permit such a consolidation, while also giving students an opportunity to become familiar with tests of content material.

To make up a practice test, ask each group to write at least four questions related to the experiment. Ask them to begin at least two questions with the word *did* and at least one question with the word *how*. Circulate among the groups helping out with question formation. Some examples of questions include: Did the cork fly out of the bottle? Where did it go? Did the bottle move? How could the third law of motion explain what happened? Why did the cork fly out?

When the groups have finished formulating their questions, each group passes its questions to the next group, which attempts to answer them. Finally, with the whole class, discuss the questions that have come up and clarify problems.

A Dictocomp for Review.   A dictocomp is a reconstruction or reformulation activity. You may also think of it as a delayed dictation. Students listen to material twice. The first time they listen without taking notes. The second time they take brief notes on the main points of the dictation, or they write down verbal clues that they feel will trigger their memory. After the second reading, students are given a set time (ten minutes is about right for the following passage) to recreate the passage as accurately as possible. Once the passage has been recreated, students can, in pairs, compare their results. As they will usually have forgotten slightly different things, the exercise serves as an excellent review. Before you attempt a longer dictocomp, it is a good idea to practice one composed only of three to four sentences.

The following is a passage that could be used as a dictocomp to review Newton's third law of motion:

Imagine you and a friend are on skates. You stand facing each other and push each other away. Would just one person move, or would both of you move? Each of you makes a force act on the other person. The forces are in opposite directions. So each of you will move backward, away from the other person.

Now suppose you and your friend face each other again. This time you do not push your friend. Instead, you just stand there, and your friend pushes you. Will you move backward while your friend stays in the same place? Will your friend move backward while you stay in the same place? Or will you both move backward?

Field Studies (Observing, Note-Taking, and Writing Activities). Roger K. Brown (1979) reports that as a high school biology teacher, he noticed that his students seemed to learn a lot more from their science club activities than they did from their traditional science classes (and, of course, the science club was a lot more fun). So he decided to turn the class into a club and study biology by using class time to perform field studies and related experiments.

First, he used traditional reading and discussion techniques to make the class familiar with the basic ecology of their community. Then, the students divided themselves up into teams according to their areas of interest, and they were turned loose to observe the local fields, forests, ponds, and streams. Brown notes that they might just as well have studied parks, vacant lots, and window wells.

The students collected living specimens and housed them in terraria, tanks, aquaria, and cages, in conditions as natural as possible. The teams wrote field reports describing the creatures' natural habitats, food, and behavior. Throughout these activities, the teacher acted as a guide and facilitator rather than as an all-knowing authority, suggesting that this role could easily be taken by an ESL teacher without special training in biology.

The field reports produced questions that suggested experiments. How do ants communicate the location of food? Hang a piece of suet by a string from a tree branch and place a single local ant on the suet. After the ant has eaten its fill, it will make its way up the string and down the tree. The next day, there will be a line of ants tracing the original ant's path up the tree, down the string, and back. Place a bunch of crushed eucalyptus leaves (or spray some poison) across the path, and the ants will fan out, going around the obstacle and searching until they pick up the scent of the ant trail.

All observations and experiments should be written up, reported to the class, and discussed.

Empathetic Note-Taking (a Humanistic Activity). Empathetic note-taking is designed to add variety to the class and should not replace normal note-taking. Empathetic note-taking could be used in connection with a lecture given by the ESL teacher to provide background for the regular lecture, or in connection with a videotape of the content instructor's lecture. For this exercise to be successful, students should understand the material very well.

In this exercise, students take notes not as themselves but as famous people. For a lecture on the American Revolution, they might choose identities from a list that included George and Martha Washington, Thomas Jefferson, and Benjamin Franklin. Students might also choose the identities of present-day politicians or well-known personalities such as Madonna or Milli Vanilli. Three or four students should take the same identity.

After the note-taking session, the students meet with others who have chosen the same personality and compare and discuss their notes. Finally, a spokesperson for each group explains the point of view of that personality.

Pyramid Introductions (a Humanistic Activity).   This exercise is a good way to help the students of any class get to know each other. In small groups, students make out questions that they would want to use when interviewing a new member of the class. They should compose five to seven questions. Each group reads its questions before the whole class, and the teacher or a student makes a composite list of the most interesting questions on the board. Next, the students sit in pairs facing each other. They interview one another, using the questions on the board. Each interviewer takes notes on the information he or she obtains. Then, the pairs of students combine to create groups of four. Using their notes, each interviewer introduces his partner to the foursome. Finally, members of each four-some introduce other members to the whole class. Anyone can jump in to contribute information about other students. Students may also correct or add to any information about themselves.

Preparing for Tests

Everyone hates tests. Teachers dislike preparing them and despise marking them. Students fear and dread them. Tests make us tense and uncomfortable because they are often artificial and unfair. Through years of habit, students have grown accustomed to giving far too much credit to isolated test results. A good grade on a test gives students an exaggerated sense of feeling qualified and capable, while a poor grade may leave them despondent. Such feelings are unjustified. Doing well on a test often means merely that one was lucky enough to have been asked about familiar topics.

For better or for worse, tests are an integral part of the academic world. Teachers need them as reviewing mechanisms, measures of students' progress, and a yardstick by which to measure the adequacy of their own teaching methods. Many educators feel that tests are required in order to keep up a certain level of stress for adequate learning.

ESL students who, in addition to the usual academic pressures, also endure culture shock and linguistic uprooting, certainly need all the help they can get in preparing for tests. Probably the most useful way to prepare for tests is to take practice tests, like the one described in How Does the Third Law of Motion Work? The following are several additional possibilities.

Branching.   *Branching,* sometimes called "mind-mapping," is a brainstorming activity. Students are given a seed word on an appropriate topic and are asked to produce four (or so) branches of thought associated with the seed word. Each branch will then produce more branches, and these, in turn, will make still more branches. The procedure works well as a preparatory activity for essay tests.

Choose a topic that is likely to be questioned, or better yet, that you *know* will be questioned, on an upcoming test. Write the topic in a circle in the middle of the board, as shown in Figure 7.5. Then ask the students to call out associated ideas, and connect them logically to the circle. Next, provide a seed word and ask the students individually to branch out this idea until you stop them. Working in small groups, the students should

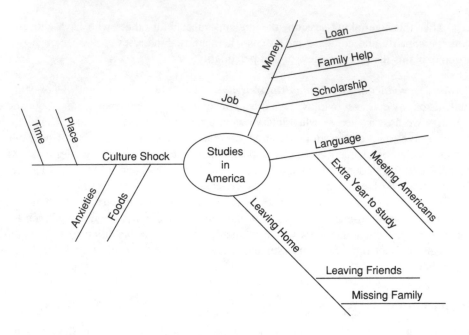

FIGURE 7.5 A Branching Diagram.

explain their branching to each other. This is a very interesting stage because, although the entire class has been provided with the same seed word, each student will have branched it differently. Then ask each group to select its most interesting branching and invite the students who produced them to explain them to the class.

Next, divide the class into small groups and assign sections of the studied material as seed words to the different groups. Ask each group to branch its word and then to turn the branching into a mini-essay on the topic. Finally, invite representatives from groups to read their mini-essays to the class. Encourage questions and comments on the material.

Which One Are You? (a Humanistic Activity).   Provide each student with the following list:

> I always put things off to the last minute.
>
> I am very organized.
>
> I always lose things.
>
> I feel frightened before a test.
>
> I have a hard time sleeping the night before a test.
>
> My best bet is to pretend I am sick on the day of the test.
>
> I find taking tests a challenge.
>
> How do I get started?
>
> Sometimes I feel like giving up.
>
> If it were not for tests, I would actually enjoy my studies.

Ask the students to mark one or two statements with which they can identify. Then, in pairs, the students tell each other which statements they have chosen and the reasons behind their choices. Next, read each statement to the whole class and ask all the students who identified with it to explain. This step is very interesting because students who have chosen the same statement provide different reasons, and a great deal of tension is released.

Speaking in Class

As we have seen, speaking in a class with native speakers is often a major problem for ESL students. Participating in class discussions is something that needs to be worked on throughout the semester in a variety of ways. We have found that ESL students are less reluctant to speak up in class if they get to know the content professor and feel more comfortable talking with him or her on an individual basis. Therefore, we suggest a series of role-playing activities designed to prepare the students for an office visit, during which they can talk to the professor one-on-one. Following the role-play activities, we will suggest exercises for preparing the students to participate in class discussions and to give individual oral presentations.

The Office Visit (a Role-Playing Activity).   Most students hesitate to visit a professor during office hours, and this can be especially difficult for international students. We have seen how Duc was unable to communicate with his writing professor because culturally based inhibitions prevented him from questioning her or telling her that he did not understand her assignment. This exercise is intended to prepare students to pay a visit to their content instructor during office hours.

Before beginning, explain to the students that a requirement of your course is that they visit the content professor or a teaching assistant once during the semester and report on the visit to the class. This requirement should, of course, be cleared with the content instructors. So far, we have found them to be cooperative. Tell the students that many books on how to survive college advise visiting every professor at least once a semester, even if the student doesn't have any particular questions or problems, just to get acquainted and establish a personal relationship. To prepare the students for the dreaded visit, do the following two activities.

Impromptus.   The purpose of impromptus is not to practice for the actual office visit, but to lessen the students' anxiety by having fun and thereby making the point that the office visit is no big deal.

Divide the students into pairs and assign one the role of the student and the other the role of the professor. It is usually best to assign particular identities as well, so that the students do not play themselves: "You're a fraternity boy—Joe Cool"; "You're the best student in the class, you have always gotten straight As"; "You're really fed up with school, you're here because your parents made you come." Similarly: "You're a very sympathetic professor who loves students"; "You're an absent-minded professor who can't remember anyone's name or what assignments you have made"; "You're very strict and formal." After the identities have been assigned, the pairs are given a slip of paper with each student's problem written on it. Several pairs can be given the same problem; it's interesting to see how the various actors handle the same situation.

The actors have one minute to think about what they are going to say, and perhaps to ask for some vocabulary words. Then they must perform their impromptus for the class. Usually an impromptu will come to a natural conclusion after several minutes, but if it drags on, step in and say that time is up. Examples of problems include (1) you want to miss the final exam because you have tickets to a rock concert; (2) you didn't do well on the test, but it wasn't fair because . . . (the student thinks of a reason); (3) you have to drop the course because . . . (the student thinks of a reason); (4) you're doing all right in the course, but you're bored—could the professor please make the material more interesting? (5) you're failing the course, but you will pay the professor $100 to pass; (6) you have to pass the course or you'll lose your scholarship; (7) you want the professor to change your grade on a problem—your answer was wrong, but you *knew* the right answer. After several impromptus have been performed, ask the students to think up some more problems. These are likely to reflect the students' points of view.

After each impromptu, discuss how it went. Do professors really talk like that? What would a professor be more likely to say? How could the student have made the point more effectively? What reasons would a professor really accept for excusing a student from a final exam? For accepting a late assignment? Suppose the professor refused to let you drop the course—what recourse do you have? How much money would it take to buy a passing grade?

Mock Interviews.   This role-play is a dress rehearsal for the office visit. Brainstorm with the students about what topics they might bring up and what questions they might discuss. Encourage the students to ask real questions that have puzzled the class, possibly ''I don't completely understand why brain lateralization implies that there is a critical period for language acquisition,'' or ''Please explain the difference between an error and a mistake.'' After writing these topics on the board, each student makes up an outline for the upcoming interview that includes questions and topics relevant to his or her personal situation; for example, ''What's my grade so far?'' or ''Can I analyze the writing of Korean students for my project?''

In a later class, do the role-plays in small groups, with a student playing the role of the professor. After each role-play, the observers make comments, which must begin with several positive comments. In response, the students might revise their outlines for the interview.

Finally, as the students complete their visits with the professor, they report on how it went, noting whether they were able to cover the topics and questions they had prepared and making suggestions for future interviewees.

Speech Making.   Before the course begins, go through your calendar and make a list of all the dates on which your class will meet. During one of the early sessions, announce to the students that they will have to make two oral presentations to the class (in larger classes make it only one presentation). Neither presentation is to be longer than ten minutes. In the first presentation the students will speak about themselves. They may talk about any aspect of themselves they wish—their families, their countries, their interests. In the second presentation the students will talk about some aspect of the content material, explaining some difficult point or adding some new information (this can be the speech for Your Share, on page 153).

Pass around the list of dates and ask the students to write their names in two places.

These are the dates on which their presentations are to be made. Remind the students to write these dates down in their personal calendars. Each day after the speaker's presentation, remind the next day's speaker that his or her turn is on the following day.

Talk with the class about what makes a good speech and about ways to prepare and organize a speech. Talk about eye contact and demonstrate how difficult or disconcerting it is to pay attention to speakers who look at the floor, bury themselves in their notes, or talk to the board. Talk about the fact that while a speech can be written, it cannot be read aloud, but must be spoken. Discuss attention-getting openings with the use of pictures or anecdotes. Encourage the students to practice with a friend or at least before a mirror, and to time their speeches. Invite them to practice once in your office before they speak in front of the group. Invite suggestions from the class on how best to prepare and organize a speech.

Prepare an evaluation paper to be marked by each student while a fellow student presents. The most simple evaluation is the most effective. Here is one possibility:

Speech evaluation:

Name of speaker:

Your name:

Did the speaker speak clearly?

Did the speaker look at the class?

Was the speech interesting?

Did the speaker speak naturally?

Was the English correct?

One thing I liked about this speech was . . .

The students should mark their papers during the speech and later provide instant feedback. The last item on the sheet is particularly important, as it teaches students to look for something positive in each presentation. At the end of each speech, all the students should read their positive reactions. Such a shower of praise is most encouraging for reluctant ESL speakers.

Class Discussion.   This activity was used often in the precourse, where it was successful in preparing students to participate in discussions in the content course. With the help of the content instructor, make up a list of the questions that will be asked in an upcoming class discussion. Ask the students to write short answers to these questions as homework. Then, in the ESL section, perform a role-play with you or a student standing at the front of the class in the role of the content instructor, who asks the questions and conducts a discussion. The students may refer to their written answers if they like. Finally, attend the session of the content course that covers the material you have rehearsed. Tell your students (and the content instructor) that they are expected to participate in the discussion.

Equal Attention.   This humanistic activity, like Attentively Yours (described on page 139), works particularly well for very reluctant class participants. Ask the students to form groups of three. Each student will talk to an "audience" of two. The speakers will have

have to divide their attention evenly between the two persons in their audience. Point out that we tend to favor people on our right side.

Assign a topic and set a time limit (two to three minutes). The topics may be the same as those suggested in Attentively Yours (games I played as a child, a person who has influenced me, an object that is important to me, something I'll never forget, something I learned from my parents, the house I lived in as a child, a place I love to visit, my favorite foods, a time I was in danger of death [use discretion]).

The first student speaks while one of the listeners acts as timekeeper, signaling how much time the speaker has left. After the speech, both members of the audience say whether they felt properly attended to or whether they felt neglected.

The procedure is then repeated until all members of the groups have given their talks. Finally, discuss with the whole class the importance of paying attention. Ask them how they felt both as listeners and as speakers.

Writing Research Papers

Being able to write a research paper is an important part of academic competence. The research paper requires students to do a great deal of independent reading on a subject of interest to them. It encourages them to analyze, synthesize, interpret, and summarize. It teaches them how to credit sources and how to make use of the ideas of others without plagiarizing. Unfortunately, students often view the research paper as a monstrosity they must produce in order to pass a course. Yet if properly approached, the paper need not be burdensome.

In our opinion, the best way to prepare students to write a full-blown research paper is to first have them write an "I-search" paper. Described by Macrorie (1988), the I-search paper is a research paper on a topic of personal interest, such as "What is required for state teacher certification in Arizona?" or "How can I buy a good used car?" or "Should I get a pot-bellied pig for a pet?" The value of the I-search paper is that it involves students in an investigation that is of personal interest and immediate benefit. Furthermore, the processes by which one chooses a topic, collects and analyzes information, and writes the paper are essentially the same as those required for a research paper. Here we briefly describe how to write an I-search paper, noting the ways in which writing a research paper might differ.

Choosing a Topic.   The first step is deciding what to investigate. Macrorie says that you should not choose a topic, but rather let a topic choose you. His point is that investigation is a natural activity that everyone is involved in every day. Is the new Mexican restaurant any good? Read the review in the paper and ask some friends. Does my car really need a new timing chain? What is a timing chain? Better get a second opinion from a mechanic. To find a topic, we need only pause to ask ourselves what we need to know and what we would enjoy finding out about. Here are three ways to do that.

Freewriting.   The use of focused freewriting to find a subject for a research paper was discussed on page 143. In that exercise, the student had to investigate some aspect of language use, but in the I-search paper the student has complete freedom in regard to topic. Therefore, true freewriting rather than focused freewriting is a better vehicle for discovering where one's interests lie. True freewriting is a way of tapping into the subconscious. As in focused freewriting, the rules are that you write quickly without stopping and without worrying about grammar and punctuation. Because there is no assigned topic, the mind wanders freely and, amazingly, often produces more lucid and better-organized prose than traditional writing.

As mentioned earlier, international students usually need to learn how to freewrite. Their first efforts may seem contrived, as though they are trying to please the teacher (which you might already have noticed in the freewriting sample reproduced earlier). But after a few sessions of freewriting and sharing freewritings with classmates, most students will recognize that this is a powerful tool, not only for focusing on areas of interest, but also for becoming more comfortable and relaxed in a second language.

Macrorie says that freewriting should tell the truth, and encourages writers to bare their souls and to write with passion. It is often difficult for American students to do this because it requires them to lower their defenses—to be "uncool." When students do succeed in lowering their guards and writing with honesty and passion, it can be a liberating experience and can lead to genuine engagement in a search for knowledge. It is especially difficult for many international students to bare their souls in the writing class, and they should not be expected or asked to do so. Let them do what is comfortable when freewriting. They may find it enjoyable and useful. Or they may prefer to let a research topic find them by using one of the other techniques described here.

Branching.   Have the students write down several possible topics as seeds to a branching diagram, and branch them out as discussed earlier and illustrated in Figure 7.5. After doing this, they should have a better idea of what they really want to write about.

Pick a Card.   The content instructor provides a list of suggested topics, or the students generate a list by brainstorming. From this list each student writes down five topics of greatest interest, each on an index card. Then (perhaps the next day) each student discards three cards, keeping the topics of greatest interest. In pairs, students tell each other about the two topics, and with the help of their partners, eliminate one. Finally, in groups of three, students help each other to narrow their topics. Examples: "Amharic speakers' pronunciation of English" is too broad; "Amharic speakers' pronunciation of English /r/" is better. "My city" is too broad; "The tourist attractions of Athens" is better.

The Search.   The main source of information for an I-search paper is other people, and a good place to start is in the class. If a student has chosen the topic, "What graduate programs in electrical engineering should I apply to?" ask the class if anyone knows any electrical engineers on or off campus. The following activity can also help students find sources of information.

The Source.   Ask the students to write a list of topics they need or want information about. This may be any kind of information—"What is it like to be a tourist in Japan?" "Can I work in the United States after I get my degree?" "Where can I find a good inexpensive apartment to rent?" Have the students read their information requests to one another in small groups and ask each group to choose the three most interesting requests. Then, in a class discussion, each group contributes its requests and the teacher or a student makes a list on the blackboard.

Returning to their groups, the students brainstorm for sources of information. Where does one get information?—from people, from books, from computers, from magazines, and so on. One student from each group writes the possible sources on the blackboard.

For homework, the students choose a topic that they would like to research and report on what they found. Several students might take the same topic but use different sources of information. For example, if the topic is ''How to find an apartment,'' one student might ask his American roommate, another might look in the paper, and another might ask at the housing office. The information is shared with the whole class the next day, and the student who originally requested the information expresses satisfaction or lack of satisfaction with the information given.

Having decided where information might be found, the researcher must then seek it out. If the source is a person, the researcher must undertake to contact that person and interview him or her. Macrorie advises students not to be intimidated by authority figures. Teachers have office hours for the purpose of sharing their expertise with students, and even deans and regional sales managers have secretaries who will sometimes make appointments with strangers. Teachers are a good source of information about academic topics. They are authorities on the literature of their field, and it is part of their job to direct students to books and journals that are appropriate for various levels of expertise. If possible, the student should visit with an authority on the research subject before visiting the library.

The Brain of the Library.   Tell the students that the class is going to visit the library and give them a question sheet asking for specific information related to the content material, as in Figure 7.6. In a theme-based course, the questions on the information sheet might be of more personal interest, such as

1. How can you find a book if you don't know the name of the author?
2. Are there any books in your native language?
3. Are there any dictionaries for your native language? Where are they located? Would any of them be useful for academic purposes?
4. Find two translations into English of books by your favorite national author. Check out one of these books.

Show the students how to find the required information by using the computer catalogue, card catalogue, abstracts, indexes, and so forth. In the class following the library visit, students in small groups compare their findings and discuss what can and cannot be found using the various resources.

Writing the Paper.   An I-search paper differs from a traditional research paper in that it is the story of a search, not just the presentation of findings. The I-search writer should describe each interview and tell what was learned from it. The writer might even describe how written sources were located, including visits to the card catalogue and stacks.

The writing process will not be described in detail here. It is explained by Macrorie

FIGURE 7.6 A Library Worksheet: Finding Information in Psycholinguistics.

ARIZONA
University of Arizona Library

Your name _____

What is your topic? _____

I. FINDING DEFINITIONS OF UNFAMILIAR WORDS AND CONCEPTS (reference books)

As you learn anything new, you usually need to expand your vocabulary. The specialized dictionaries, encyclopedias, and handbooks for a subject are tools that can help you do this. In psycholinguistics, check:

Concise Handbook of Linguistics (Ref P 29 .S8 C6)
Dictionary of Language and Linguistics (Ref P 29 .H3 D5)
Dictionary of Linguistics (Ref P 29 .P4 D5)
Encyclopiedic Dictionary of the Sciences of Languages (Ref P 29 .D813)
Glossary of Linguistic Terminology (Ref P 29 .P4 G6)

As an exercise, choose ONE of the books listed above, and look up a word that begins with the first letter of your own first name.

What word did you choose? _____

What does it mean? _____

_____

II. FINDING BOOKS (the subject card catalog)

The subject card catalog lists books by topic. However, to use the subject catalog effectively, you need to look up your subject using the same terminology that the catalog uses. The books *Library of Congress List of Subject Headings* (big red books that sit next to the subject catalog) explain correct subject headings. Consult the *List* to find the catalog's terminology for your topic.

Remember, subject headings that the catalog uses will be:

    A. printed in darker type *OR*
    B. preceded by the symbol "sa" ("sa" = "see also") *OR*
    C. preceded by the symbol "xx" ("xx" = "see this related heading")

List three headings that *Library of Congress List of Subject Headings* gives for your topic:

_____

_____

_____

Look these headings up in our subject card catalog. Find one book; list:

Subject heading used: _____

Author of book: _____

Title of book: _____

(continued)

FIGURE 7.6   (continued)

Call number: _____   Is the book in the main library?

_____   If so, what floor? _____

III. FINDING ARTICLES IN JOURNALS (periodical indexes, found in reference room)

Since psycholinguistics is an interdisciplinary subject, there are many places to check for information in journals. The following five indexes to journal articles may prove useful:

> *Humanities Index* (Index AI 3 .H85)
> *Social Sciences Index* (Index AI 3 .s62)
> *MLA Bibliography* (Index P 1 .M24)
> *Language and Language Behavior Abstracts* (Index P .L2)
> *Psychological Abstracts* (Index BF 1 .P8)

1. Choose either the *Humanities Index* or the *Social Sciences Index,* and find an article.

Subject heading used: _____

Author of article: _____

Title of article: _____

Journal: _____ Volume: _____ Pages: _____ Date: _____

Is this article available at the University of Arizona? _____ At which Library? _____

2. Find an article in the *MLA Bibliography*:

Broad heading you used: _____

Author of article: _____

Title of article: _____

Journal: _____ Volume: _____ Pages: _____ Date: _____

3. Choose either *Language and Language Behavior Abstracts* or *Psychological Abstracts,* and find an article.

Subject heading used: _____

Abstract number chosen: _____

Author of article: _____

Title of article: _____

Journal: _____ Volume: _____ Pages: _____ Date: _____

Is this article in a language you can read? _____

(1988), Murray (1968), Graves (1982), and others. The process of drafting and revising that these authors describe is the same for native and nonnative speakers. Both groups of writers should focus on logic and organization on the first drafts, without worrying about mechanics. Only in the final editing stages should questions about grammar and punctuation enter in. It may be difficult to get ESL students to commit words to paper without concern for grammar because most of them have been told that this is the most important aspect of writing. It is helpful to remind the students that many scholars publish in a second or third language and that the great majority of them have their manuscripts read by native speakers before they are submitted for publication. Assure the students that before turning in a paper you and other members of the class will help them edit for surface problems, and that their first and most important task is to write up their research in a logical and convincing way. Freewriting is a good technique for getting students to relax about grammar and concentrate on substance.

Getting It Down.   Taking notes on reading material is different from taking notes on lectures and should be practiced in connection with the I-search paper. One way to practice is to ask the students to read a page of a text and choose a paragraph of interest to them. Then, they re-read this paragraph. Next, they pair up with someone who has read a different paragraph, and each partner tells the other about his or her paragraph. The students may in the course of telling refer back to the paragraphs. The partners read the paragraphs they have been told about and comment on the accuracy of what they have been told. Then the students write down everything they remember from the paragraph on cards without referring back to the original source. Next, they check the source for accuracy and give credit in the accepted way. Finally, the partners check the cards and comment on them.

Citations.   The I-search paper should include references to written and/or live sources of information. To show students how to construct a working bibliography, bring to class a set of $3'' \times 5''$ index cards and enough books and magazines to have one for each student. On the blackboard write two examples of a working bibliography card. Make one sample for a book and one for a journal article. Explain the purpose of a working bibliography in a research project: it is a flexible list of sources that can be used for locating material for a project. It is better to keep these sources on cards, since a card can always be added or thrown away. The students then create mock working bibliography entries using the books, magazines, and cards you have brought. Finally, in pairs, students check each other's cards.

SIXTY-ONE ADDITIONAL ACTIVITIES

In the first two sections of this chapter, we described in some detail activities that can help ESL students understand academic subjects taught in English and complete academic assignments. In this final section, we offer sixty-one additional short suggestions. We hope that having read this far in the book, the ESL teacher will have a good idea of how the suggestions offered here apply to his or her own teaching situation and will be able to expand and adapt these activities to fit the needs of the students.

Reading

1. Give students the first and last lines of a text and ask them to predict the content of text to be read.

2. In a text that contains several numbers, list them on the board and ask students to scan the article, finding what each number refers to.

3. Give students the title of a text to be read and ask them to predict the content of the text.

4. On the board list key words and phrases from a text recently read. Write the words in the same order as they appear in the text. Ask students to retell the content of the text using the words on the board as clues.

5. On the board list several key lines from the text. Ask students to scan the text, finding these lines.

6. Ask students to make up interesting test questions on a text recently read. Use some of the questions on your next test.

7. Ask students to compose brief crossword puzzles with key vocabulary from the text. As each group finishes a puzzle, they can pass it on to the next group for solution.

8. Give timed readings lasting two minutes. Let students keep self-monitoring charts on which they mark how much they read each time.

9. On each student's back pin a piece of paper with the name of an important person or place that has appeared in a recent reading. Students mingle about, asking one another questions until they discover what is written on their backs.

10. Give students the central idea of the text they are about to read and ask them to brainstorm for content. Example: "Our next article is about crocodiles. What kind of issues do you think it might bring up?"

11. As a prereading activity, ask the class to brainstorm vocabulary they think might appear in a text on a certain topic. Example: "We are going to read an article about air pollution. What words do you think might appear in such an article?"

12. Give the class sentences from a text to be read. Tell them that these sentences are answers and ask them to make up the questions that could prompt such answers.

13. On the board, list the relative pronouns that appear in a text to be read, together with the line-number in which these pronouns appear. Ask students to scan the text and find the reference for each relative pronoun.

Listening/Note-Taking

1. Ask students to make notes in the margins of a text and share them with other students. (Make sure you legally photocopy a text with large margins.)

2. Ask students to jot down their thoughts on any topic before they share these thoughts in pairs.

3. Ask students to formulate and write questions on a topic as they listen to a text read or a lecture delivered on this topic.

4. Ask students to speak for three minutes about a topic without having prepared notes. Then let them have another topic with a three-minute period of note-taking preparation. After the second three-minute monologue, let them compare experiences.

5. Ask students to take notes planning a weekend or a shopping trip.

6. Ask students to take notes that summarize a movie they have seen recently. Have them read their summaries to the class.

7. Give students a two-sentence summary of a well-known story and ask them, in small groups, to expand it.
8. Ask students in groups to contract a well-known story into three sentences. Each group passes its contraction on to another group, which expands on it.
9. Together with your students, work out a shorthand system for annotations to be used in their own note-taking. Examples: Imp.—important; *—read up more on this; ?—not clear, ask instructor about this.
10. Ask students to evaluate one another's note-taking.
11. Ask students to listen to a song and note its central ideas. It can be listened to several times for checking.
12. Show students a picture and ask them to note any questions about what *is not* made clear or explicit in the picture.
13. Start the reading of a dialogue, perhaps an opening scene from a play; plays by Arthur Miller are very suitable. Ask students to take notes on how they might finish the dialogue. For homework they could actually finish the job. Later it could be compared to the real scene.
14. Together with your students, make out a list of common speech markers used by lecturers. Examples include transitional expressions such as numbers (first, second, and third) and adverbs (moreover, nevertheless, however, although), as well as expressions of emphasis (I want to stress, it is significant).

Preparing for Tests

1. Students keep an alphabetized vocabulary notebook to go through before each test.
2. Students quiz each other daily on material covered during the previous lesson.
3. Each Friday, students in small groups review material covered during the week.
4. Before each test, students make out test questions and do a practice test.
5. Students mark and evaluate each other's tests.
6. Students correct their own tests, evaluate them, and explain the reasons behind the evaluation.
7. Declare a week-long "free zone" in which there is to be absolutely no testing.
8. Students make rules regarding test-taking—open or closed book? essay or short answers? and so forth.
9. Students write lists of positive and negative aspects of testing.
10. Students relate stories about their most or least successful test experiences.
11. Students make acrostics with the word *test*.
    Example:
    Tell
    Every
    Silly
    Thing
12. Students do two practice tests, one take-home test and one in-class test, and compare the experiences.
13. Students do one open-book/open-note test and one closed-book/closed-note test and compare the experiences.
14. Students find their most frequently made mistakes and create a poster that will

teach them not to make those mistakes. Example: a student who habitually left out the letter *s* in the third person drew a hand with a hammer nailing the letter *s* to a third-person verb inflection. The posters are displayed and explained.

15. Together with the class, make out a list of ten to thirty often repeated mistakes. Declare these the "terrible tens," "terrible twenties," and "terrible thirties." Students are allowed to keep the list in front of them during all exams.

Speaking

1. Ask students to react to controversial statements by first marking their reactions with "Agree," "Disagree," or "Not sure" and then explaining and amplifying their original reactions. Example of controversial statement: "Capital punishment is immoral."

2. Follow the procedure of item 1, but use content material for review.

3. Ask students to rate choices and then explain why they rated them as they did. Example: "You are preparing yourself for a job interview. Someone has given you the following items to think about. Rate them in order of importance, and later in pairs explain to each other why you ordered them as you did."

4. Use a rating list as in item 3, but this time use content material as a review. If rating is not appropriate, ask students to choose the most important item on the list and explain their reasons for doing so. They could possibly also choose the most important item and the least important item.

5. After a weekend, ask students in pairs or small groups to tell each other about a movie, book, or outing they experienced during the weekend.

6. Ask students to complete, in writing, any evocative sentence, such as "My life will be a success if _____," and then in pairs explain their completions to each other.

7. Ask students to bring a snapshot from their family album and, in pairs, tell each other where and why the picture was taken.

8. Ask students to role-play situations encountered in their campus life, in readings, or in current events. Example: "In pairs, you are a student and a professor. The student has come to complain about his grade. The professor feels that she has already been too generous, but each is trying hard to be polite."

9. Do a double role-play. One pair of students acts out a scenario such as the preceding one, and two other students act as the egos of the role-players, standing behind them and saying what the role-players really think.

10. Ask students to think of a controversial statement or question related to course material such as "The South had a right to secede from the Union," or "If we could have either the Declaration of Independence or the Constitution, which would you choose?" and write it on a slip of paper. Then ask everyone to draw a slip. The students form small groups, and each group chooses its topic from among the slips of its members. Students discuss their chosen topic and report their conclusions to the group as a whole.

11. Ask students to provide both positive and negative arguments for controversial topics.

12. In small groups, assign the most vocal speaker the job of seeing to it that everyone participates.
13. Ask each group to assign as its spokesperson the best "quiet thinker."
14. Instead of asking comprehension questions on a text, play dumb. Say, "There is something here in chapter 2 that I don't really understand. Could someone explain it to me?" Play devil's advocate. Say, "The examples this writer gives are really unclear. They just confuse me. Did they do that to you, too?" Such behavior puts you in a normal speaker's place in a social interaction rather than in the role of the teacher, who already knows the answer and is just testing. Remember that the classroom is the only place where those who know the answers ask the questions and those who don't know bravely try to answer.

Information-Gathering Activities

1. Ask students to guess information about each other's countries—size of population, name of capital city, national food, and so on. Students verify information about their own countries.
2. Students guess personal information about one another—family, hobbies, and so on—which is then verified.
3. Students ask each other real questions about information in the city where they now live—good stores and restaurants, movies worth seeing, laundromats, courses worth auditing or taking, trips and outings to make, for example.
4. Students present information, and the rest of the class guesses where and how it was obtained.
5. Students interview locals about professions, marriage customs, life and job opportunities. This can be part of an I-search paper or report.

NOTES

1. This chapter was written by Natalie Hess and H. D. Adamson.
2. This activity is adapted from *Experiences in Physical Science* by M. A. Magnoli, J. A. Shymansky, J. A. Blecha, and M. K. Holly.

Spolsky's (1989) Preference Model of Language Proficiency[1]

1. Features of the Learner's Interlanguage

a. Language as system (necessary): A second language learner's knowledge of a second language forms a systematic whole.

b. Specific variety (necessary): When one learns a second language, one learns one or more varieties of that language. As a corollary, goals for a formal course of instruction need to specify the variety or varieties of language being taught.

c. Variability (necessary): Like first language knowledge, second language knowledge is marked by variability.

d. Academic skills (typical, weighted): Learning a second language may be associated to varying degrees with the development of academic language skills.

2. Features of the Learner's Psycholinguistic System

a. Unanalyzed knowledge (necessary, graded): Unanalyzed knowledge (memorized chunks of the second language) may be used by second language learners, but unanalyzed knowledge by itself provides for very restricted, language-like behavior.

b. Analyzed knowledge (necessary, graded): As linguistic knowledge is analyzed into its constituent parts, it becomes available for recombination; this creative language use may be enriched with unanalyzed knowledge.

c. Implicit knowledge (typical, graded): Language knowledge, analyzed and so available for recombination, may be intuitive and so not be consciously available to the learner.

d. Explicit knowledge (typical, graded): Analyzed language knowledge may be consciously available to the speaker who is able to state a rule or explain the reason for a decision to use a certain form.

e. Dual knowledge (necessary): When one learns a second language, one develops both knowledge and skills in using that knowledge. As a corollary, goals for a formal course of instruction or tests of proficiency need to distinguish between knowledge and use, as well as between various levels of automaticity and accuracy in use.

f. Discrete item (necessary): Knowing a language involves knowing a number of the discrete structural items (sounds, words, structures, etc.) that make it up.

3. *Features of the Learner's Abilities and Skills*

a. Automaticity (necessary, graded): Ability to use language knowledge varies in automaticity; this is shown by the fluency with which a person speaks.

b. Accuracy (necessary, graded): Ability to use language varies in accuracy.

c. Productive/receptive skills (necessary, graded): Individual language learners vary in their productive and receptive skills.

d. Receptive skills stronger than productive (typical, graded): Receptive language skills (understanding speech or written text) usually develop before productive skills (speaking, writing) and usually develop to a higher level.

e. Integrated skills weighting/ordering condition (typical, graded): The weighting (relative importance) and ordering of integrated skills are dependent on individually or socially determined goals for learning the language.

f. Native speaker target (typical, graded): Second language learner language aims to approximate native speaker language.

g. Communicative goal (typical, graded): Language learners may aim to achieve various degrees of control of a language for communicative purposes.

h. Integrated function (necessary): Knowledge of a language involves control of one or more integrated functional skills.

i. Overall proficiency (necessary): As a result of its systematicity, the existence of redundancy, and the overlap in the usefulness of structural items, knowledge of a language may be characterized as a general proficiency and measured.

NOTE

1. Adapted from *Conditions for Second Language Learning* by Bernard Spolsky (Oxford: Oxford University Press, 1989), pp. 16–18.

References

Adamson, H. D. (1987). *Variation theory and second language acquisition*. Washington, DC: Georgetown University Press.

Adamson, H. D. (1990). ESL students' use of academic skills in content courses. *English for Specific Purposes, 9,* 67–87.

Adamson, H. D., Duryee, P., & Allen, M. (1990). Creating a precourse to develop academic competence. *WATESOL Journal, 1,* 1–6.

Adventures in reading, Heritage revised edition (1985). Orlando: Harcourt, Brace, Jovanovich.

Anderson, J. R. (1980). *Cognitive psychology and its implications* (2nd ed.). New York: Freeman.

Anderson, J. R. (1983). *The architecture of cognition*. Cambridge, MA: Harvard University Press.

Arlington Public Schools. (1983). *Culture capsules*. Arlington, VA: Author.

Asher, J. J. (1969). The total physical response approach to second language learning. *The Modern Language Journal, 53,* 1–17.

Austin, J. L. (1962). *How to do things with words* (J. O. Urmson, Ed.). New York: Oxford University Press.

Bailey, N., Madden, C., & Krashen, S. (1974). Is there a ''natural sequence'' in adult second language learning? *Language Learning, 21,* 235–243.

Bakhtin, M. M. (1981). *The dialogic imagination* (C. Emerson & M. Holquist, Eds.). Austin: University of Texas Press.

Barnes, B., & Bloor, D. (1982). Relativism, rationalism and the sociology of knowledge. In M. Hollis & S. Lukes (Eds.), *Rationality and relativism* (pp. 21–47). Oxford: Blackwell.

Bartlett, F. C. (1932). *Remembering: A study in experimental and social psychology*. Cambridge: Cambridge University Press.

Bensen, M. (1989). The academic listening task: A case study. *TESOL Quarterly, 23,* 421–445.

Berlin, B., Breedlove, D. E., & Raven, P. H. (1974). *Principles of Tzeltal plant classification*. New York: Academic.

Berlin, B., & Kay, P. (1969). *Basic color terms: Their universality and evolution*. Berkeley: University of California Press.

Bernstein, B. (1964). Elaborated and restricted codes: Their social origins and some consequences. *American Anthropologist, 66*(6), 55–69.

Bernstein, B. (1972). A sociolinguistic approach to socialization: With some reference to educability. In J. J. Gumperz & D. Hymes (Eds.), *Directions in sociolinguistics* (pp. 465–497). New York: Holt.

Beyer, B. K. (1985a). Critical thinking: What is it? *Social Education*, pp. 270–276.

Beyer, B. K. (1985b). Teaching critical thinking: A direct approach. *Social Education, 49*, 297–303.

Bialystok, E. (1988). Psycholinguistic dimensions of second language proficiency. In W. Rutherford & M. Sharwood-Smith (Eds.), *Grammar and second language teaching* (pp. 31–50). New York: Harper/Newbury.

Biber, D. (1986). Spoken and written textual dimensions in English: Resolving the contradictory findings. *Language, 62*, 384–414.

Biber, D. (1988). *Variation across speech and writing.* Cambridge: Cambridge University Press.

Bickerton, D. (1981). *The roots of language.* Ann Arbor, MI: Karoma.

Birdsong, D. (1990). Universal grammar and second language acquisition theory: A review of a research framework and two exemplary books. *Studies in Second Language Acquisition, 12*, 331–340.

Bley-Vroman, R. (1988). The fundamental character of foreign language learning. In W. Rutherford & M. Sharwood-Smith (Eds.), *Grammar and second language teaching* (pp. 19–30). New York: Newbury House.

Bley-Vroman, R., Felix, S., & Ioup, G. (1988). The accessibility of universal grammar in adult language learning. *Second Language Research, 4*, 55–62.

Bloom, B. (1956). *Taxonomy of educational objectives, the classification of educational goals: Handbook I. Cognitive domain.* New York: Longmans, Green.

Bloomfield, L. (1933). *Language.* New York: Holt.

Bower, T. G. R. (1974). *Development in infancy.* San Francisco: Freeman.

Brinton, D. M., Snow, M. A., & Wesche, M. B. (1989). *Content-based second language instruction.* New York: Harper/Newbury.

Brown, R. (1965). *Social psychology.* New York: Free Press.

Brown, R. K. (1979). Science teaching in the bilingual classroom. In H. Trueba & C. Barnett-Mizrahi (Eds.), *Bilingual/multicultural education and the professional* (pp. 228–236). Rowley, MA: Newbury.

Bruffee, K. A. (1980). *A short course in writing* (2nd ed.). Cambridge, MA: Winthrop.

Bruffee, K. A. (1984). Collaborative learning and the "conversation of mankind." *College English, 46*(7), 635–652.

Bruffee, K. A. (1986). Social construction, language, and the authority of knowledge: A bibliographical essay. *College English, 48*(8), 773–790.

Canale, M. (1983). From communicative competence to communicative language pedagogy. In J. Richards & R. Schmidt (Eds.), *Language and communication* (pp. 2–25). London: Longman.

Canale, M., & Swain, M. (1980). Theoretical bases of communicative approaches to second language teaching and testing. *Applied Linguistics, 1*, 1–47.

Carrell, P. (1988). Some causes of text-boundedness and schema inferencing in ESL reading. In P. Carrell, J. Devine, & D. Eskey (Eds.), *Interactive approaches to second language reading* (pp. 101–113). Cambridge: Cambridge University Press.

Carrell, P., Devine, J., & Eskey, D. (Eds.). (1988). *Interactive approaches to second language reading.* Cambridge: Cambridge University Press.

Carroll, J. (1965). The contributions of psychological theory and educational research to the teaching of foreign languages. *Modern Language Journal, 49*, 273–281.

Celce-Murcia, M. (1987, May). *New concerns in English as a foreign language.* Paper presented at the National Association of Foreign Student Affairs Annual Conference, Long Beach, CA.

Chamot, A. U., & O'Malley, M. (1984). Using learning strategies to develop skills in English as a second language. *Focus.* Arlington, VA: National Clearinghouse for Bilingual Education.

Chomsky, N. (1957). *Syntactic structures*. The Hague: Mouton.

Chomsky, N. (1959). A review of B. F. Skinner's Verbal Behavior. *Language, 35*(1), 26–58.

Chomsky, N. (1965). *Aspects of the theory of syntax*. Cambridge, MA: MIT Press.

Chomsky, N. (1981). *Lectures of government and binding*. Dordrecht: Foris.

Chomsky, N. (1984). *Modular approaches to the study of mind*. San Diego: San Diego State University Press.

Chomsky, N. (1986). *Knowledge of language: Its nature, origin and use*. New York: Praeger.

Clahsen, H., & Muyskin, P. (1989). The UG paradox in L2 acquisition. *Second Language Research, 5*, 1–29.

Clarke, M. (1980). The short circuit hypothesis of ESL reading—or when language competence interferes with reading performance. *Modern Language Journal, 64*(2), 203–209.

Coleman, J. S., Campbell, E. Q., Hobson, C. J., McPartlang, J., Mood, A. M., Winfeld, F. D., & York, R. L. (1966). *Equality of educational opportunity*. Washington, DC: Department of Health, Education and Welfare, Office of Education.

Collier, V. P. (1987, March). *Age and rate of acquisition of cognitive-academic second language proficiency*. Paper presented at the American Educational Research Association Annual Convention, Washington, DC.

Collier, V. P. (1989). How long? A synthesis of research on academic achievement in a second language. *TESOL Quarterly, 23*(3), 509–531.

Cook, V. (1988). *Chomsky's universal grammar*. Oxford: Basil Blackwell.

Cummins, J. (1979). Linguistic interdependence and the educational development of bilingual children. *Review of Educational Research, 49*, 222–251.

Cummins, J. (1980). Entry and exit fallacy in bilingual education. *NABE Journal, 4*(3), 25–59.

Cummins, J. (1984a). *Bilingualism and special education*. San Diego: College-Hill.

Cummins, J. (1984b). Wanted: A theoretical framework for relating language proficiency to academic achievement among bilingual students. In C. Rivera (Ed.), *Language proficiency and academic achievement* (pp. 2–19). Clevedon, England: Multilingual Matters.

Cummins, J. (1989). *Empowering minority students*. Sacramento: California Association for Bilingual Education.

Cummins, J., & Swain, M. (1983). Analysis-by-rhetoric: Reading the text or the reader's own projections? A reply to Edelsky et al. *Applied Linguistics, 4*(1), 23–39.

Cummins, J., & Swain, M. (1986). *Bilingualism in education: Aspects of theory, research and practice*. London: Longman.

DeSaussure, F. (1966). *Course in general linguistics* (C. Bally & A. Sechehaye, Eds.). New York: McGraw-Hill.

Dewey, J. (1916). *Democracy and education*. New York: Macmillan.

Diller, K. C. (1978). *The Language teaching controversy*. Rowley, MA: Newbury.

Dorian, N. (1980). *Language death: The life cycle of a Scottish Gaelic dialect*. Philadelphia: University of Pennsylvania Press.

Dowty, D., Wall, R., & Peters, S. (1981). *Introduction to Montague semantics*. Dordrecht: D. Reidel.

Dulay, H., & Burt, M. K. (1974). Natural sequences in child second language acquisition. *Language Learning, 24*, 37–53.

Dulay, H., Burt, M. K., & Krashen, S. (1982). *Language two*. New York: Oxford University Press.

Durkheim, E. Translated by Steven Lukes. (1982). *The rules of sociological method* (English ed.). New York: Free Press (Original work published 1885)

Edelsky, C., Hudleston, S., Flores, B., Barkin, F., Altwerger, B., & Jilbert, K. (1983). Semilingualism and language deficit. *Applied Linguistics, 4*(1), 1–22.

Emig, J. (1971). *The composing processes of twelfth graders*. Urbana, IL: National Council of Teachers of English.

Eskey, D. E. (1986). Theoretical foundations. In *Teaching and second language reading for academic purposes* (pp. 2–23). F. D. Dubin, D. E. Eskey, & W. Gabe (Eds.), Reading, MA: Addison-Wesley.

Eskey, D. E., & Grabe, W. (1988). Interactive models for second language reading: Perspectives on instruction. In P. Carrell, J. Devine, & D. Eskey (Eds.), *Interactive approaches to second language reading* (pp. 223–238). Cambridge: Cambridge University Press.

Fathman, A. (1975). Language background, age and the order of acquisition of English structures. In M. K. Burt & H. Dulay (Eds.), *New directions in second language learning, teaching, and bilingual education* (pp. 33–43). Washington, DC: TESOL.

Feyerabend, P. (1978). The spectre of relativism. In P. Feyerabend (Ed.), *Science in a free society* (pp. 197–230). London: NLB.

Fillmore, C. (1982). Frame semantics. In *Linguistics in the morning calm* (pp. 111–138). Hanshin: Linguistic Society of Korea.

Fillmore, L. W. (1982). Language minority students and school participation: What kind of English is needed? *Journal of Education, 164*(2), 143–156.

Fodor, J. (1975). *The language of thought*. New York: Crowell.

Fries, C. C. (1945). *Teaching and learning English as a second language*. Ann Arbor: University of Michigan Press.

Fromkin, V., & Rodman, R. (1983). *An introduction to language, third edition*. New York: Holt, Rinehart and Winston.

Gattengno, C. (1972). *Teaching foreign languages in schools: The silent way*. New York: Educational Solutions.

Genesee, F. (1976). The role of intelligence in second language learning. *Language Learning, 26,* 267–280.

Genesee, F. (1987). *Learning through two languages: Studies of immersion and bilingual education*. New York: Newbury.

Goodman, K. (1967). Reading: A psycholinguistic guessing game. *Journal of the Reading Specialist, 4,* 126–135.

Goodman, N. (1978). *Ways of worldmaking*. Indianapolis: Hackett.

Gould, S. J. (1981). *The mismeasurement of man*. Hammondsworth, England: Penguin Books.

Grabe, W. (1988). Reassessing the term "interactive." In P. Carrell, J. Devine, & D. E. Eskey (Eds.), *Interactive approaches to second language reading* (pp. 56–70). Cambridge: Cambridge University Press.

Graves, D. (1982). *Writing: Teachers and children at work*. Exeter, NH: Heinemann.

Green, G. M. (1989). *Pragmatics and natural language understanding*. Hillsdale, NJ: Erlbaum.

Grice, H. P. (1975). Logic and conversation. In P. Cole & J. Morgan (Eds.), *Syntax and semantics: Vol. 9. Pragmatics* (pp. 113–127). New York: Academic.

Guba, E. G., & Lincoln, Y. S. (1989). *Fourth generation evaluation*. Newbury Park, CA: Sage.

Gumperz, J. J., & Hymes, D. (1972). *Directions in sociolinguistics: The ethnography of communication*. New York: Holt.

Guyer, E., & Peterson, P. W. (1988). Language and/or content: Principles and procedures for materials and development in an adjunct course. In *Ending remediation: Linking ESL and content in higher education* (pp. 91–111). Washington, DC: TESOL.

Hairston, M. (1982). The winds of change: Thomas Kuhn and the revolution in the teaching of writing. *College Composition and Communication, 33,* 76–88.

Halliday, M. A. K., & Hassan, R. (1976). *Cohesion in English*. London: Longman.

Harley, B., Cummins, J., Swain, M., & Allen, P. (1990). The nature of language proficiency. In B. Harley, P. Allen, J. Cummins & M. Swain (Eds.), *The development of second language proficiency* (pp. 7–25). Cambridge: Cambridge University Press.

Harris, D. P. (1969). *Testing English as a second language*. New York: McGraw-Hill.

Hillman, L. H. (1990). *Reading at the university*. Boston: Heinle & Heinle.

Hirsch, E. (1987). *Cultural literacy: What every American needs to know*. Boston: Houghton Mifflin.

Holtzman, P. (1967). English language testing and the individual. In *Selected conference papers of the Association of Teachers of English as a second language*. Washington, DC: NAFSA.

Hymes, D. (1971). Competence and performance in linguistic theory. In R. Huxley & E. Ingram (Eds.), *Language acquisition models and reality* (pp. 3–28). London: Academic.

Illich, I. D. (1971). *Deschooling society*. New York: Harper & Row.

Jackendoff, R. (1983). *Semantics and cognition*. Cambridge, MA: MIT Press.

Johnson, M. (1987). *The body in the mind*. Chicago: University of Chicago Press.

Justenias, C., & Duarte, L. L. (1982). *Hispanics and jobs: Barriers to progress*. Washington, DC: National Commission for Employment Policy.

Katz, J. J., & Postal, P. M. (1964). *An integrated theory of linguistic description*. Cambridge, MA: MIT Press.

Kay, P., & McDaniel, C. K. (1978). The linguistic significance of the meanings of basic color terms. *Language, 54*, 610–645.

Keenan, E. (1976). The universality of conversational implicature. *Language in Society, 5*, 67–80.

Koda, K. (1982). *English language acquisition by four Japanese girls: Case studies and influencing factors*. Unpublished manuscript, University of Illinois, Urbana-Champaign.

Kozol, J. (1972). *Free schools*. Boston: Houghton Mifflin.

Krashen, S. (1981). *Second language acquisition and second language learning*. Oxford: Pergamon.

Krashen, S. (1982). *Principles and practices in second language acquisition*. Oxford: Pergamon.

Krashen, S. D., & Terrell, T. D. (1983). *The natural approach*. Hayward, CA: Alemany.

Kuhn, T. S. (1959). *The Copernican revolution: Planetary astronomy in the development of Western thought*. New York: Vintage.

Kuhn, T. S. (1970). *The structure of scientific revolutions*. Chicago: University of Chicago Press.

Kuhn, T. S. (1977). *The essential tension*. Chicago: University of Chicago Press.

Labov, W. (1972). *Language in the inner city: Studies in the black English vernacular*. Philadelphia: University of Pennsylvania Press.

Labov, W. (1973). The boundaries of words and their meanings. In C.-J. N. Bailey & R. Shuy (Eds.), *New ways of analyzing variation in English* (pp. 340–373). Washington, DC: Georgetown University Press.

Lakoff, G. (1987). *Women, fire, and dangerous things*. Chicago: University of Chicago Press.

Larsen-Freeman, D., & Long, M. (1991). *An introduction to second language research*. London: Longman.

Lenneberg, E. (1967). *Biological foundations of language*. New York: Wiley.

Lyons, J. (1977). *Semantics* (Vol. 2). Cambridge: Cambridge University Press.

McLaughlin, B. (1987). *Theories of second language learning*. London: Edward Arnold.

McPeck, J. E. (1990). *Teaching critical thinking: Dialogue and dialectic*. New York: Routledge.

Macrorie, K. (1988). *The I-search paper: Revised edition of searching writing*. Portsmouth, NH: Heineman/Boynton/Cook.

Magnoli, M. et al. (1987). *Experiences in physical science*. River Forest, IL: Laidlaw.

Maslow, A. H. (1954). *Motivation and personality*. New York: Harper Brothers.

Mason, M. K. (1942). Learning to speak after six and one-half years. *Journal of Speech Disorders, 7*, 295-304.

Medina, M., & Valenzuela de la Garza, J. (1987, March). *Bilingual instruction and academic gains of Spanish-dominant Mexican-American students*. Paper presented at the annual meeting of the American Educational Research Association, Washington, DC.

Mohan, B. (1986). *Language and content*. Reading, MA: Addison-Wesley.

Moskowitz, G. (1979). *Caring and sharing in the language classroom: A sourcebook in humanistic techniques.* Rowley, MA: Newbury.

Murray, D. (1968). *A writer teaches writing.* Boston: Houghton Mifflin.

Naiman, N., Frohlick, M., Stern, H. H., & Todesco, A. (1978). *The good language learner.* Toronto: Modern Language Center, Ontario Institute for Studies in Education.

National Assessment of Educational Progress. (1977). *Hispanic student achievement in five learning areas: 1971–75.* Washington, DC: U.S. Government Printing Office.

Neisser, U. (1976). *Cognition and reality.* San Francisco: Freeman.

Oakshott, M. (1962). *Rationalism in politics.* New York: Basic Books.

Oehrle, R. T., Bach, E., & Wheeler, D. (Eds.). (1988). *Categorial grammars and natural language structures.* Dordrecht: D. Reidel.

Oller, J. W., Jr. (1976). Language testing. In R. Wardhaugh & H. D. Brown (Eds.), *A survey of applied linguistics* (pp. 275–300). Ann Arbor: University of Michigan Press.

Oller, J. W., Jr. (1979). *Language tests at school.* London: Longman.

Oller, J. W., Jr. (1983). *Issues in language testing research.* Rowley, MA: Newbury.

O'Malley, M., & Chamot, A. U. (1990). Learning strategies in second language acquisition. Cambridge: Cambridge University Press.

O'Malley, M., Chamot, A. U., Strewner-Manzanares, G., Russo, R. P., & Kupper, L. (1985). Learning strategy applications with students of English as a second language. *TESOL Quarterly, 19*(3), 557–586.

Osherson, D., & Smith, E. (1981). On the adequacy of prototype theory as a theory of concepts. *Cognition, 9*(1), 35–58.

Oxford, R. (1990). *Language learning strategies: What every teacher should know.* New York: Newbury.

Peyton, J. K., & Reed, L. (1990). *Dialogue journal writing with nonnative English speakers: A handbook for teachers.* Alexandria, VA: Teachers of English to Speakers of Other Languages.

Politzer, R., & McGroarty, M. (1985). An exploratory study of learning behaviors and their relationships to gains in linguistic and communicative competence. *TESOL Quarterly, 19,* 103–123.

Popper, C. (1970). Normal science and its dangers. In I. Lakotos & A. Musgrave (Eds.), *Criticism and the growth of knowledge* (pp. 51–58). London: Cambridge University Press.

Rogers, C. (1983). *Freedom to learn for the 80's.* Columbus, OH: Merrill.

Rorty, R. (1979). *Philosophy and the mirror of nature.* Princeton: Princeton University Press.

Rorty, R. (1989). *Contingency, irony, and solidarity.* Cambridge: Cambridge University Press.

Rosch, E. (1973). Natural categories. *Cognitive Psychology, 4,* 328–350.

Rosch, E., & Mervis, C. B. (1975). Family resemblances: Studies in the internal structure of categories. *Cognitive Psychology, 7,* 573–605.

Rubin, J. (1975). What the "good language learner" can teach us. *TESOL Quarterly, 9*(1), 41–51.

Rubin, J. (1987). Learner strategies: Theoretical assumptions, research history, and typology. In A. Wenden & J. Rubin (Eds.), *Learner strategies in language learning* (pp. 15–30). Englewood Cliffs, NJ: Prentice-Hall.

Rubin, J., & Thompson, I. (1982). *How to be a more successful language learner.* Boston: Heinle & Heinle.

Rummelhart, D. E. (1980). Schemata: The building blocks of cognition. In R. J. Spiro, B. C. Bruce, & W. F. Brewer (Eds.), *Theoretical issues in reading comprehension* (pp. 33–58). Hillsdale, NJ: Erlbaum.

Russman, T. A. (1987). *A prospectus for the triumph of realism.* Macon, GA: Mercer University Press.

Rutherford, W. (1968). *Modern English.* New York: Harcourt, Brace, Jovanovich.

Rutherford, W., & Sharwood-Smith, M. (Eds.). (1988). *Grammar and second language teaching: A book of readings.* New York: Newbury.

Sampson, G. (1980). *Schools of linguistics.* Stanford, CA: Stanford University Press.

Savignon, S. (1983). *Communicative competence: Theory and classroom practice*. Reading, MA: Addison-Wesley.

Saville-Troike, M. (1984). What really matters in second language learning for academic purposes? *TESOL Quarterly, 18*(2), 199–219.

Saville-Troike, M. (1987). Dilingual discourse: Communication without a common language. *Linguistics, 25*, 81–106.

Saville-Troike, M. (1991). Teaching and testing for academic achievement: The role of language development. *Focus, 4*.

Saville-Troike, M., & Kleifgen, J. (1986). Scripts for school: Cross-cultural communication in the elementary classroom. *Text, 6*(2), 207–221.

Savin, H., & Perchonock, E. (1965). Grammatical structure and the immediate recall of English sentences. *Journal of Verbal Learning and Verbal Behavior, 4*, 348–353.

Schacter, J. (1989). Testing a proposed universal. In S. M. Gass & J. Schachter (Eds.), *Linguistic perspectives on second language acquisition* (pp. 73–88). New York: Cambridge University Press.

Schieffelin, B. B. (1985). The acquisition of Kaluli. In D. I. Slobin (Ed.), *The crosslinguistic study of language acquisition, Vol. 1: The Data* (pp. 525–594). Hillsdale, NJ: Erlbaum.

Schneider, W., & Shiffrin, R. M. (1977). Controlled and automatic processing: I. Detection, search, and attention. *Psychological Review, 84*, 1–64.

Shuy, R. W. (1978). Problems in assessing language ability in bilingual education programs. In H. LaFontaine, H. Persky, & L. Golubchick (Eds.), *Bilingual education* Wayne, NJ: Avery.

Shuy, R. W. (1981). Conditions affecting language learning and maintenance among Hispanics in the United States. *NABE Journal, 6*, 1–18.

Skutnabb-Kangas, T., & Toukomaa, P. (1976). Teaching migrant children's mother tongue and learning the language of the host country in context of the socio-cultural situation of the migrant family. Helsinki: Finnish National Commission for UNESCO.

Slobin, D. I. (1973). Cognitive prerequisites for the development of grammar. In C. A. Ferguson & D. I. Slobin (Eds.), *Studies of child language development* (pp. 175–208). New York: Holt.

Slobin, D. I. (1985). Crosslinguistic evidence for the language-making capacity. In D. I. Slobin (Ed.), *The crosslinguistic study of language acquisition: Vol. 2. Theoretical issues* (pp. 1157–1256). Hillsdale, NJ: Erlbaum.

Smith, B. H. (1988). *Contingencies of value*. Cambridge, MA: Harvard University Press.

Smith, E. E., & Medin, D. L. (1981). *Categories and concepts*. Cambridge, MA: Harvard University Press.

Smith, F. (1986). *Insult to intelligence: The bureaucratic invasion of our classrooms*. New York: Arbor.

Smith, F. (1990). *To think*. New York: Teachers College Press.

Spolsky, B. (1968). Language testing: The problem of validation. *TESOL Quarterly, 2*, 88–94.

Spolsky, B. (1973). What does it mean to know a language, or how do you get someone to perform his competence? In J. W. Oller, Jr., & J. C. Richards (Eds.), *Focus on the learner: Pragmatic perspectives for the language teacher* (pp. 164–176). Rowley, MA: Newbury.

Spolsky, B. (1989). *Conditions for second language learning*. Oxford: Oxford University Press.

Staton, J. (1984). Thinking together: Interaction in children's reasoning. In C. Thaiss & C. Suhor (Eds.), *Speaking and writing K–12* (pp. 144–187). Urbana, IL: National Council of Teachers of English.

Steffensen, M., Joag-dev, S. C., & Anderson, R. C. (1979). A cross-cultural perspective on reading comprehension. *Reading Research Quarterly, 15*, 10–29.

Stevick, E. W. (1980). *Teaching languages: A way and ways*. Rowley, MA: Newbury.

Talmy, L. (1985a). Lexicalization patterns: Semantic structure in lexical forms. In T. Shopen (Ed.), *Language typology and syntactic description*, Vol. 3. Cambridge: Cambridge University Press.

Talmy, L. (1985b). Force dynamics in language and thought. In W. H. Eilfort, P. D. Kroeber, &

K. L. Peterson (Eds.), *CLS 21: Part 2. Papers from the Parasession on Causatives and Agentivity* (pp. 293–337). Chicago: Chicago Linguistics Society.

Tannen, D. (1982). Oral and literate strategies in spoken and written narrative. *Language, 58,* 1–21.

Test of English language proficiency. Ann Arbor: University of Michigan English Language Institute.

Voll, J. (1990). Scholars must combat facile generalizations about the Middle East. *The Chronicle of Higher Education, 37* A48.

Vollmer, H. J. (1983). The structure of foreign language competence. In A. Hughes & D. Porter (Eds.), *Current developments in language testing* (pp. 3–30). New York: Academic.

Wenden, A., & Rubin, J. (1987). *Learner strategies in language learning.* Englewood Cliffs, NJ: Prentice-Hall.

Wesche, M. B. (1985). Immersion and the universities. *Canadian Modern Language Review, 41,* 931–940.

Wesche, M., & Ready, D. (1985). Foreigner talk in the university classroom. In S. Gass & C. Madden (Eds.), *Input in second language acquisition* (pp. 89–114). New York: Newbury.

White, L. (1988). Markedness and second language acquisition: The question of transfer. *Studies in Second Language Acquisition, 9*(3), 261–280.

White, L. (1990). Second language acquisition and universal grammar. *Studies in Second Language Acquisition, 12*(2), 121–134.

Whorf, B. L. (1956). *Language, thought and reality: The selected writings of Benjamin Lee Whorf.* Cambridge, MA: M.I.T. Press.

Widdowson, H. (1978). *Teaching language as communication.* London: Oxford University Press.

Widdowson, H. G. (1978). *Teaching language as communication.* London: Oxford University Press.

Wittgenstein, L. (1953). *Philosophical investigations.* New York: MacMillin.

Wong Fillmore, L. (1979). Individual differences in second language acquisition. In C. Fillmore, D. Kempler, & W. S. Y. Wang (Eds.), *Individual differences in language ability and language behavior* (pp. 203–228). New York: Academic Press.

Wong Fillmore, L., Ammon, P., McLaughlin, B., & Ammon, M. S. (1985). *Final report for learning English through bilingual instruction.* National Institute of Education.

Wundt, W. (1911, 1912). *Volkerspsychologie, Vols. 1 and 2.* Die Sprache.

Yin, R. K. (1984). *Case study research: Design and methods.* Beverly Hills, CA: Sage Publications.

Index